Contents

Cause and Cure

Second Edition

PATRICK MINFORD

With

Paul Ashton, Michael Peel, David Davies and Alison Sprague

Basil Blackwell

First published 1983
Second edition 1985

Basil Blackwell Ltd
108 Cowley Road, Oxford OX4 1JF, UK

Basil Blackwell Inc.
432 Park Avenue South, Suite 1505,
New York, NY 10016, USA

British Library Cataloguing in Publication Data

Minford, Patrick
Unemployment: cause and cure.
1. Unemployment – Great Britain 2. Manpower policy – Great Britain 3. Great Britain – Full employment policies
I. Title
331.13'77'0941 HD5765.A6

ISBN 0-631-14506-0
ISBN 0-631-14611-3 Pbk

Library of Congress Cataloging in Publication Data

Minford, Patrick
Unemployment: cause and cure.
Bibliography: p.
Includes index.
1. Unemployment – Great Britain. 2. Insurance, Unemployment – Great Britain. 3. Industrial relations – Great Britain. 4. Unemployment – European Economic Community countries. I. Ashton, Paul. II. Title.
HD5765.A6M55 1985 331.13'7941 85-13511

ISBN 0-631-14506-0
ISBN 0-631-14611-3 (pbk.)

Phototypeset by Dobbie Typesetting Service, Plymouth, Devon
Printed in Great Britain by The Bath Press, Avon

This book is dedicated to
Mrs Margaret Thatcher
who has had the courage to begin
tackling the deepseated problems
discussed in these pages

Preface to the Second Edition

The first edition was prepared in 1982. Much has happened since that time – only two and half years ago. Labour laws have been passed, taxes and benefits changed, the Rent Acts have been somewhat modified, Wages Councils are being reviewed, and so on. These developments alone make it desirable to update this book and its recommendations.

But there have been intellectual developments also. Thinking has changed among both academics and practical men. Many have now begun to warm to the analysis set out in (though by no means unique to) this book, where first reactions were dismissive of an unfamiliar way of thinking. This too makes it desirable to restate the arguments and, if possible, make them more widely available.

Then there have been comments, criticisms and second thoughts which require response, rebuttal, or incorporation. The first edition was prepared at a furious speed to meet the urgency of the problem. Though the essential structure of the argument has not changed, there is much in the detail which could be, and to some extent has been, improved.

Finally, the policy canvas has been broadened in the last two years as some business has been concluded successfully and new areas of action have consequently opened up. Privatization – still controversial in 1982 – has now acquired unstoppable momentum. The principle is now seen to be extendable far beyond the obviously saleable nationalized industries into many areas of public sector activity that have been unquestioningly accepted as such in the post-war period. With the success too of union law reforms, the confidence has grown to tackle other legal minefields such as the Employment Protection (and related) Acts and the Rent Acts. These and other policy issues are highly germane to the topic of this book, and it seems right to include them in this edition.

Having said this, I have not altered the original text except where necessary to update, correct or add material. I have aimed to keep the book's original crusading spirit (together with its provocatively succinct title, suggested by Michael Hay). That spirit offended some, but it was an integral part of the book; it is not a dry-as-dust treatise but an attempt to communicate to as wide a public as possible the principles for understanding the problem of unemployment and to persuade them of its necessary cure. Those principles have been overlaid and obscured by fashionable economic and popular thinking for too long; their perception was painful and difficult for me, brought up as I was too with these fashions. My aim is to bring that same perception home to others, if possible with less pain and difficulty than I experienced.

One failing of the book is that, much as I would like it to communicate directly to the widest possible audience – so important is the problem – it does assume a certain basic knowledge of economic forces. Notably, it assumes an understanding of supply and demand. That may not seem an unduly harsh requirement, but experience has taught me that it is restrictive, though it ought not to be in a capitalist society with a properly functioning secondary education system. Be that as it may, I cannot escape from this restriction for there is an irreducible minimum of technical explanation required in what is, after all, a major area of social science.

In this second edition, Paul Ashton has joined my previous co-authors. He and Michael Peel have assisted me in rewriting this edition, respectively on the economic and the legal aspects. Longman's kindly gave permission to reproduce the material from *Economic Affairs* (Supplement to Vol. 4, No. 3, April–June 1984) which appears in chapter 3. The Economic and Social Research Council Consortium for Modelling and Forecasting the UK Economy has provided continuing financial support (under ESRC Grant No. B HG 2/64/3/5) for our research programme since the first edition was prepared. The Wincott Foundation also gave us support for research on housing, the results of which are briefly reported in chapter 6.

As ever, I have a debt to those who have argued with or commented on the practical and theoretical aspects of the previous edition. In particular, I would like to thank Michael Beenstock, David Peel, Arthur Seldon, Adrian Smith and Alan Walters. Finally, I am most grateful to Maureen Kay for preparing the ever-changing manuscript with her usual unflappable efficiency.

Preface to the First Edition

This book was written in response to demands from various quarters sympathetic to our previously published work, for a comprehensive account of the unemployment problem in Britain and a properly worked out programme of measures to combat it. It embodies the results of the research programme of the Liverpool Research Group in Macroeconomics over the past six years, as well as practical insights gained from periodic policy commentary and forecasts published in the group's *Economic Bulletin*. It has been published with all possible speed in order to promote public debate of the wide issues involved. Decisions on these require wide public understanding of the side-effects of measures whose obvious impact is socially popular and desirable; at the same time, people must take into account the social dimension of measures which would have substantial effects on the country's purely economic performance.

During the past decade increased understanding of the mechanism of inflation, due largely to the work of Professor Milton Friedman and those who have followed his pioneering research programme, has led to the political acceptability of apparently harsh measures to reduce and, it is hoped, eliminate inflation from many Western economies, and in particular, Britain. In Europe, and again particularly in Britain, unemployment has risen first steadily, then sharply. It has, however, been greeted with intellectual bewilderment on the part of the public and on the part of politicians, with a plethora of minor, cosmetic measures, as well as a refusal (correct in the authors' view) to abandon their anti-inflation programme. In our view, expounded in the following pages, there does exist a coherent anti-unemployment programme which could be embraced, though with a variety of different forms depending on the social preferences of the people in each given country. We hope that over the next decade there will be an increased understanding of the unemployment mechanism, which in its turn will lead to the embracing of such a programme, politically unacceptable as it may seem at present to many observers conditioned by the post-war period. We hope too that this book will be a contribution to that process.

We gratefully acknowledge crucial assistance and support from a number of sources. First, that of our colleagues in the Liverpool Research Group, who have been involved over a number of years in the development of the Liverpool model used in this book: Chris Ioannidis, Satwant Marwaha, Kent Matthews and David Peel. Secondly, that of the Social Science Research Council, which has financed our research programme since 1977. Third, that of officials in this country and overseas who have patiently answered our requests for often detailed information and analysis of tax/benefit systems, and other institutions. Finally, we thank Paula Banks, assisted by Jackie Fawcett, Chris Nash and Vivienne Oakes, for typing this manuscript expertly within our exacting deadlines.

Summary

INTRODUCTION

Unemployment in the United Kingdom fluctuated moderately within the range of 1–2 per cent of the labour force throughout the 1950s and early 1960s. From the middle of the 1960s it began a more or less steady rise, by 1970 to 3 per cent, by 1976 to 6 per cent, and by 1984 to 13.5 per cent. Part of the current higher unemployment rate is to be attributed to the extremely severe world recession, associated with US policies to reduce inflation, while insufficiently curbing public sector deficits. Another part is the effect associated with the Conservative Government's policies to reduce inflation in the UK. Both these effects are temporary in nature. In response to the Government's policies at home, and as a better balance in US fiscal and monetary policies allows world real interest rates to fall, recovery from the recession will continue to occur, though at a rate and with a timing that is inherently hard to predict as world events over the past four years have repeatedly demonstrated.

However, these elements account for a limited part of the unemployment total. Precise calculations are difficult, but, assuming none of the proposals made here were to be carried out, unemployment at the next peak of the economic cycle, whenever that comes, would seem unlikely to fall below 2–2½ million (8–10 per cent of the labour force). Some would regard even the upper end of that range as optimistic, a view that would leave even more of the rise in unemployment to be explained by factors other than the recession at home and abroad.

In this book, we focus on these 'underlying' factors and remedies for them, rather than on cyclical or 'demand-management' factors and policies. We fully accept the present framework of Government demand management and anti-inflation policy; and within that framework, discussion of details for the money supply and Public Sector Borrowing Requirement targets lies outside the scope of the book.

THE CAUSES OF UNEMPLOYMENT

It is a widespread opinion among economists – and one which we fully endorse – that the proximate cause of unemployment is excessively high wage costs, produced either by high wages or by low productivity. We have identified this as a strong mechanism in the UK.

However, one cannot stop at this point in the analysis and proclaim, as has from time to time been done, that government can, by direct intervention in the wage-setting process, reduce real wages or increase productivity. Such direct intervention (or incomes policy) has repeatedly failed to achieve anything of the sort in the UK, besides being inconsistent with the economic freedom that is this Conservative Government's aim. The reason for this failure is that there are market forces and distortions of considerable power driving real wages and productivity to the levels we observe. In order to modify these levels and so the level of unemployment, we have to understand these forces and modify the market distortions.

This book identifies two major distortions in the UK labour market which prevent real wages and productivity from adjusting naturally to shifts in technology, demand, and industrial structure, and relocating those freed from one sector into other sectors.

1 The first, and the fundamental cause of unemployment, is the operation of the unemployment benefit system. The minimum flat rate benefit including any supplementary benefit 'top-up' is paid indefinitely to an unemployed man for as long as he remains unemployed. Such a man will very naturally expect to be re-employed at a wage after tax and work expenses which is at least as high as this benefit, and probably somewhat higher because he may not wish to 'work for nothing', whatever his personal attitude towards work. His work even at this wage may well be poorly motivated because of his lack of reward, so that productivity also suffers. Hence wages cannot effectively fall below this level for even the most unskilled worker. This level then acts as a floor under the whole wage structure, and working practices accepted at this unskilled level may similarly affect higher levels of the occupational structure. It follows that shifts in economic conditions which would

warrant a fall in real wage costs, will have only a limited effect on them and unemployment will result instead. This mechanism, in other words, substantially limits the wage flexibility of the UK economic system.

The second major distortion is the power of unions to raise wages relative to non-union wages. Given the way the benefit rate sets a floor below the non-union wage, as unions raise wages for their members, the workers who then lose their jobs cannot all find alternative work in the non-union sector because wages there do not fall sufficiently; the overall effect is increased unemployment.

Though union power is a major contributory cause of unemployment, it is not fundamental, in the sense that were benefits *not* to set a floor beneath non-union wages, it would not add to unemployment. There are other factors which play a similar contributory role. They include changes in taxation, shifts in technology, adverse movements in the terms of trade and in world demand for UK products, and changes in population size and structure. Many of these are frequently cited in press and other commentary on unemployment as 'reasons' for unemployment. They are so only in the limited sense we have defined. To repeat, if wages and productivity adjusted without constraint, these factors would not alter unemployment, but would instead have their effect on real wages. Nevertheless, *given* our benefit system, such alterations in these factors as lie within our power *can* help reduce unemployment, and we give some attention to them in what follows.

The explanation of the labour market we have just given is not to be tested by any very simple relationship such as, for example, one between unemployment and the ratio of benefits to work-income. There are a number of complex interactions which need to be disentangled. The book details some work of this nature that we have undertaken; some 1300 observations of post-war UK behaviour have been used in this work and the analysis given emerges unrefuted from these tests. These were supplemented by analysis of the post-war experience in four Continental countries, West Germany, France, Italy and Belgium. These provided economic support for the approach and useful institutional comparisons. In particular we found that the behaviour of Belgian wages and unemployment closely mirrored that of the UK, even in the size of its unemployment problem, because of its similar flat rate benefit system and powerful unions. In the other three countries with ratio systems, however, behaviour – as the approach predicts – was quite different. We also obtained estimates of the relevant relationships for the UK. These, approximate as they must be, form the basis of the estimated effects of policy changes shown below.

POLICY PROPOSALS

Our proposals fall into three parts:

(1) suggested changes in the benefit system;
(2) supporting changes in tax and income supplements for those in work;
(3) changes in the law and institutions regulating the labour and the closely related housing market.

Colloquially, (1) may be said to deal with the 'unemployment trap', (2) with the 'poverty trap', and (3) with union monopoly power and government regulation of wages, employment conditions, and rents. Taken as a whole, our proposals are capable of reducing unemployment very substantially over a five-year period. Politically we believe them to be well capable of implementation with public acceptance as a programme for reducing unemployment, though they will be strongly resisted by particular vested interests. They will increase incentives and get the labour market operating effectively once again.

The Benefit System

Wage flexibility is substantially reduced by the fixed ('flat rate') benefit level. This is because benefits do not vary with wage levels. Hence as wages fall, benefits do not fall in like proportion and act as a floor below wages, reducing their flexibility.

Our first proposal is therefore to introduce a maximum statutory ratio ('benefit capping') of 70 per cent for total unemployment benefits to net income in work. This is similar to the ratio used on the Continent, for example Germany where it is 68 per cent for family men. This cap would be widely seen as fair, in view of the need to maintain minimum work incentives. It would be simple to work (Continental practice shows it to be quite feasible), and it would, according to our estimates, bring about a sizeable reduction in unemployment – about ¾ million over four years. It would also of course greatly increase the flexibility of wages, since for many workers (around 40 per cent) benefits would vary proportionally with wages.

We also propose the introduction of a jobs pool, consisting of all available vacancies and other community work specially organized, in each area (as in the US 'workfare' scheme), together with tighter procedures for denying benefit. Benefits should be conditional on acceptance of a job from the pool – after three months for workers under 25, after six months for other workers. In essence, this is an extension of the existing Community and Youth Training Schemes, but modified to increase substantially the pressure on people to take a job at lower wages, recognizing that there is help *in* work for the low-paid.

Tax and the Support of Work Income

The introduction of the above measures will increase work incentives substantially for those in low-paid occupations. But a further contribution to reducing unemployment can be obtained by raising tax thresholds. This will increase incentives for those a little further up the pay scale, whose benefits will not be affected by the cap. Furthermore it will also increase the social acceptability of the cap by raising the in-work incomes of those affected by it, so both mitigating the fall in their living standards when unemployed, and implying an absolute rise in living standards if they now choose to work even at a lower wage.

Our proposals here are for substantial falls in taxation, paid for by wide-ranging reduction in the responsibilities of the state through the privatization of virtually all state production, of state consumption of goods that are not 'public', and of some transfers (notably pensions). To protect the poor in work, we propose a negative income tax (health insurance, education and pension contributions would be compulsory). By 1990, the aim would be to double income tax thresholds and to abolish the national insurance scheme and its contributions, to raise child benefits to offset the cost of children's education and health insurance, to lower the standard rate to 25p and to eliminate the higher rates. The cost of this programme (net of tax revenue generated by higher activity) would be some £43 billion.

Laws and Regulations

Union power. With labour legislation currently in place, though rights to restrain union actions through the courts have been substantially strengthened, enforcement of these rights is still patchy. In many cases, the public sector is involved and the Government should ensure that public sector bodies enforce their rights fully. Nevertheless, private sector bodies may for various reasons, including intimidation and legal costs, be unwilling to pursue actions that it would be in the public interest to have pursued.

Furthermore, the law is by now extraordinarily complex and still fails in its original objective of eliminating labour market monopoly power. Closed shop practices are still permitted and unions still have immunity in respect of 'primary' actions. A bolder approach which goes all out to eliminate labour monopoly power is required. This should be seen to be even handed between workers and employers, for as such, charges of discrimination against workers – or 'union bashing' – would be turned aside.

Our proposals here are simple and threefold:

(1) *to restore jurisdiction of the common law to all union actions* (i.e. withdrawal of all immunities);
(2) *to legislate a 'status' provision* such that any contract contingent on the union status of the employee would be invalidated; this would render closed shop agreements, explicit or implicit, null and void;
(3) *to institute a Labour Monopolies Commission* under the existing competition laws with independent power to investigate any apparent breaches of the public interest in labour market competition, and to bring actions under common law to obtain enforcement of the investigation's proposed remedies.

Proposal (1) would make all union strikes actionable unless expressly covered by a negotiated strike clause in a collective contract; this would give a stimulus to collective agreements, provided these were permitted by the Labour Monopolies Commission. Proposal (2) would give freedom for any person to enter into a contract with any employer; evidence of employment or dismissal because of union membership or lack of it would be actionable. Proposal (3) supplies an active agent to ensure that monopoly positions are broken up, regardless of whether the parties wish it or not, and regardless of whether the offence is by employers or unions. The activities of the Commission would build up a body of case law that should, over time, have the same effect in the labour market as the Restrictive Trade Practices Court and the Monopolies and Mergers Commission have had in the goods market under existing laws.

Minimum wages and employment protection. Wage Councils and laws to set minimum 'conditions' of work (such as restrictions on dismissal, on the work environment, and on discrimination) are extensions of union power largely brought about by the actions of unions in the political domain. Their effects are similar to union actions in raising wages in that they reduce employment. We propose here a series of steps that generally fall short of total abolition:

(1) *Wage Councils and wage regulations should be suspended as their terms run out.*

(2) *Small businesses should be effectively exempted from all employment protection laws* (where this does not violate treaties such as the Treaty of Rome).

(3) *The qualifying period for workers to enjoy their rights under the Employment Protection Act should be raised to five years; and workers should be allowed to contract out of these rights.*

(4) *Health and safety rules should be advisory, and industries should be self-regulatory on these.*

(5) *Benign neglect should be shown by the executive arm of the state towards other laws in this general area.*

Housing and the Rent Acts. Mobility between regions, which would reduce unemployment, is impeded by the Rent Acts interacting with subsidies to council house rents and 100 per cent rent rebates to the unemployed receiving supplementary benefit. It is usually prohibitively expensive for a worker to move from a high unemployment area where he has a council house to a low unemployment area where he would need to rent on the restricted private market. *The solution to this problem lies in simultaneously liberalizing the private rental market and eliminating council house rent subsidies*, while limiting (via benefit capping) the amount paid to the unemployed as set out earlier. Steps to deregulate private rentals are: include 'scarcity' as a factor in setting fair rents; allow landlords to designate *new* tenancies as being 'assured' or 'shorthold' or 'licences', effectively outside the Rent Acts; allow new tenants to contract out of their rights to go to a rent tribunal for a rent assessment; and finally allow as a new ground for eviction that 'comparable' accommodation be offered. Ultimately the Rent Acts should wither away under these alterations.

ECONOMIC EFFECTS

Insofar as the effects of these proposals can be quantified with the estimated relationships available to us, they should be sufficient to eliminate unemployment. This is one objective. But in the process, they will also substantially increase the general efficiency and wealth-creating capacity of the UK economy, which must be our ultimate objective. They should do so while maintaining protection at their current levels for the poor in work and the disadvantaged, and so achieving what we take to be the major distributional aim of society. They will finally increase people's economic freedom, which has also been a traditional objective of the British people.

1

The Causes of Unemployment in the UK

ANALYSIS OF UK UNEMPLOYMENT

The theory of unemployment that is currently most popular among labour economists is 'search' theory. Suppose that a man has been made redundant or otherwise is out of work. He then searches for a new job for his particular skill. Extra time spent searching costs him extra. This cost includes the outlays on search, net of any utility derived from leisure (which of course could be negative). He gets job offers at intervals with a wage attached to it, which is taken randomly from a distribution (which he knows) of potential wages for the job type. He accepts an offer when it is equal to or greater than the expected wage from the next offer minus the extra cost of search involved in waiting for another period.

This theory is undoubtedly suitable for individuals in certain labour markets, notably where the individual has a clearly defined job preference, and jobs of that type become available periodically, and have a wage distribution attached to them. For example, professional people, such as an economics lecturer, may be well described by it. However, the vast mass of jobs are manual or semi-skilled non-manual. Within these jobs, some are restricted by union entry conditions, others are in industries with little union intervention. There would seem to be for such jobs a 'going rate', one in the union sector where jobs are rationed, and one in the non-union sector (if there is one for that job type) where jobs are freely available at the rate. Take taxi-drivers, for example: there are areas such as Newcastle where there is close regulation of rates and attempted control of entry, and areas such as Liverpool which are effectively deregulated. An unskilled man could become a taxi-driver in Liverpool at will, or he could try to get a more profitable regulated job in Newcastle. But it is by no means clear that he will 'search' and remain unemployed. Rather, he may well decide whether it is worth his while to do either. If he concludes that the deregulated one is good enough, but the regulated one would be better if it came up, he may take the deregulated one and be ready to drop it and shift if and when the other comes up. It seems unlikely that he would remain unemployed, 'searching' the union or regulated sectors, unless he decided that the non-union rates were just not attractive at all. If he did so, he would lose income without necessarily enhancing his chances of a union job.

Such a person will furthermore be content to choose from a wide menu of jobs. Take, for example, the recent case of a Liverpool taxi-driver who had been made redundant from an engineering firm. He decided that, given the scarcity of union jobs, the taxi rate was acceptable; no doubt he is keeping engineering places under review as they come up.

These considerations suggest an alternative model of the work decision, which is 'new classical' in spirit. The worker has knowledge of 'going rates' in unregulated, or non-union sectors in which he has the necessary skills to work; he does not need to 'search' for this knowledge. He decides when to enter and when to withdraw from these sectors in a standard 'optimizing' manner, that is he maximizes the present value of his expected welfare, given these wage rates and other relevant prices, including benefits out of work, and taxes etc. in work. Though all workers would like to have a union job, it is assumed that the chances of getting one are not affected by taking a non-union job, so that the union wage does not affect his work decision.

It turns out in this model that the number of people willing to work at *union* wages is irrelevant to the determination of wages or jobs in either the union or the non-union sectors. The reason is straightforward: the union's mark-up over the non-union real wage is determined by its monopoly power interacting with technology and demand conditions; this monopoly power is precisely the power to ignore the desires of non-union members for the better wages within the controlled sector. In practice, of course, this ability would be eroded substantially, the larger the non-union sector. But this erosion depends not so much on the non-union members' frustration as on the enhanced ability of firms to hire non-union members beyond the reach of the union (as in the USA, with firms hiring in the South rather than the unionized North East).

The model therefore implies that the total supply of labour will be dependent on the level of current real wages in the non-union sector ('free market wages'), net of tax and expenses, relative to net out-of-work benefits, on the one hand, and expected future net real non-union wages on the other. In other words, the people who are 'on the margin' of supply in the labour market are in the non-union sector (in 'unprotected jobs'), typically on low wages and in unattractive jobs. Hence the importance in labour supply of replacement ratios (i.e. the ratio of benefits out of work to net in-work income) for low income households, for these are the ones most likely to withdraw into unemployment and swell the statistics under additional pressure.

There are various ways in which the supply of labour could contract as real wages fell. Workers could decide to quit more frequently, taking longer periods between work. For manual men, for whom explicit part-time work is awkward, this would approximate to part-time working over the year as a whole. Workers could take spells of work abroad, and spells on benefits at home. They could do less actual work on the factory premises, so lowering productivity per hour. For example they could choose longer rest periods, hold meetings at work, go absent without leave or simply make less effort. Workers could decide not to work at all until real wages picked up again. They could, for instance, withdraw from the labour market in recessions and return in boom periods. Most drastically they could withdraw indefinitely and change their life style to one of living on benefits and casual, probably undeclared, earnings, on the assumption that real wages are never likely to be sufficiently attractive. To those accustomed to the ways of prosperous Southern areas of the country, such ideas may seem unfamiliar, even outrageous; but it has to be said that they are part of the everyday gossip and 'casual empiricism' of an area such as Liverpool.

Viewed in this way, the distinctions between decisions on duration of unemployment, those on participation in work, and those on work effort or productivity become blurred. There is in essence a continuous decision on more or less or no participation in work and work effort.

This decision is naturally viewed as taken for the fiscal year. For example, someone wanting to work half the time would be best advised to work half the year and be unemployed for the other half (in either order) – that way he uses up his tax allowances. Were he to work for one year and be unemployed for the whole of the next year, he would fail to use and subsequently lose his tax allowances in the second year under the UK tax system operating over our sample period.

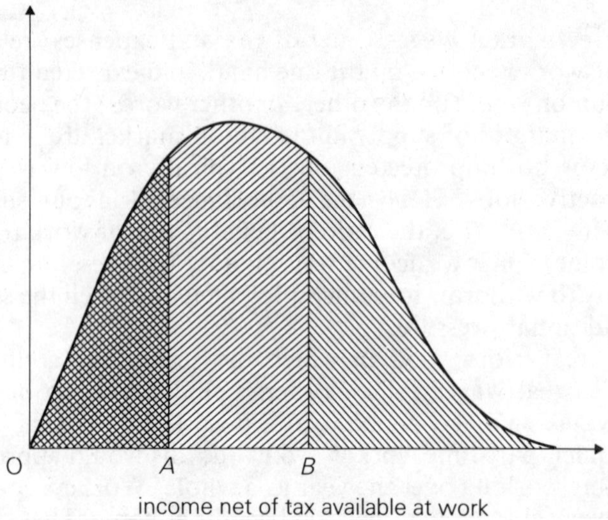

Figure 1.1 Distribution of income and benefit status for a typical household type
A = flat rate benefit 'cut off' point,
B = earnings related benefit 'cut off' point – see text

In the UK we can distinguish three major groups in the bulk of our sample period, according to their benefit status as illustrated in figure 1.1. There are 'flat rate' benefits – that is effectively the minimum period, shown as point *A*. People on net incomes to the left of *A* will face a relative price of work and leisure of unity. The point *A* is properly the wage at which the flat rate benefit level is just attractive enough to make 100 per cent leisure preferable. (What ratio of benefits to net income in work, 'replacement ratio', this will correspond to will differ from person to person. For some it may be below, for others it may even be higher than 100 per cent). These people are likely to be in a situation where they do not work at all and be unresponsive to benefit or wage changes.

Then there was an earnings related supplement (ERS, abolished in December 1981) which raised the benefit/wage ratio to 2/3 for those whose incomes relative to flat rate benefits otherwise put them below this ratio. Their relative price of work will be somewhat more attractive therefore; they accordingly will react to changes in the replacement ratio because of a substitution effect. The group to the right of *A* includes these people as well as those with benefit/income ratios between 2/3 and 1.

Finally, there was a ceiling on ERS, that is, an income above which ERS became a flat rate supplement, shown as point *B*. Those to the right of *B* will have benefit/wage ratios progressively less than 2/3 as income rises; their substitution effect may therefore be smaller than those between *A* and *B*. (At very high incomes the relative price of work becomes lower again with the higher rate of tax. However, this is not of much concern for unemployment.)

Most importantly, as flat rate benefits rise, more people will be drawn into the area to the left of *A* where they may decide not to work at all. Since someone who does not work at all will be unemployed 12 times as long as someone who takes a two-month spell every two years, these people dominate the unemployment stock. In a time-series analysis, we may expect the elasticity of unemployment (under the UK system) to the benefit/income ratio to be very low for a low aggregate ratio (e.g. around 0.5), to rise as the ratio rises, reaching a peak and dropping again towards zero as the population becomes concentrated around or to the left of *A*.

This illustrates the important general point that while the cross-section studies of populations are undoubtedly of great value, they do not necessarily provide ready answers to questions about reactions of populations over time. In this case, to translate cross-section findings into time-series predictions of the effect of benefit changes, one requires to know the income distribution, the location of points *A* and *B*, the reservation wage levels and the elasticity between *A* and *B*. Such a translation is likely to be hazardous at best. A time-series relationship, for all its faults, provides a useful direct estimate of the reactions under investigation.

While labour supply and unemployment depend on non-union real wages in this way, non-union real wages in turn are determined at the level which set supply equal to demand in the non-union labour market. This market is like the free market in 'two-tier' markets, where one market is controlled, and one is free and unrestricted, for example the financial Belgian franc or any Black Market. It reacts sensitively to demand and supply factors in both markets. For instance, a rise in union monopoly power which raises the union mark-up over non-union wages, will raise union wages, with non-union wages constant, and reduce demand for union labour. Those who lose their union jobs will be available for work in the non-union sector and depress wage levels there. As this non-union wage falls, so total labour supply contracts and unemployment rises.

As another example, suppose UK real costs of imported inputs rise, worsening the terms of trade. This has a substitution effect which raises the demand for labour, but an income (terms of trade) effect which lowers the demand for labour in conditions of external current account balance. Suppose, as is likely, the latter effect dominates. Then labour demand falls, probably in both union and non-union sectors. At constant real non-union wages, this will fall entirely on the non-union supply–demand balance; non-union real wages will drop, again lowering labour supply and raising unemployment.

EMPIRICAL WORK ON THE UK LABOUR MARKET – AN ACCOUNT OF THE ESTIMATED MODEL

Our analysis is concerned primarily with the long-run determination of employment, unemployment and real wages, and we assume that in the long run there is no excess supply or demand for labour or goods. Our long-run assumptions are captured in figure 1.2. It shows, first, a supply curve of labour to the UK economy associated with the average real non-union wage, *Wc/P* on the vertical axis; the quantity of labour (*L*) is on the horizontal axis. The supply

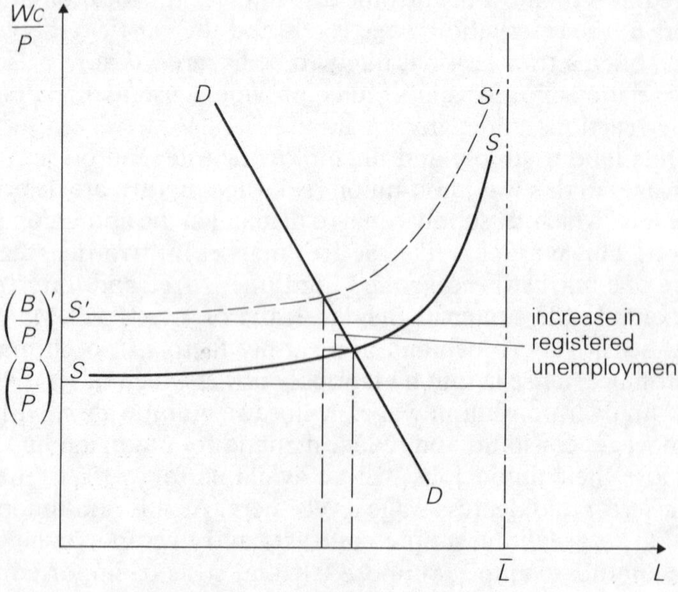

Figure 1.2 Increase in benefits

curve is drawn flat at low wages because the ratio of real benefits (shown as B/P) to real wages becomes critically high for a large section of the population. The *average* non-union wage cannot logically fall below real benefits (in terms of gross real wage equivalent) because if it did no one would be working for a wage less than the average! So real benefits act as a 'floor' beneath real wages, with supply tending towards zero as average real non-union wages tend towards this floor.

At high wages the benefit/wage ratios drop to irrelevance for the vast majority, so that the only effect of benefits is to raise somewhat the length of time spent between jobs in 'search'. At these high wages the supply of labour approximates to what we may call the 'labour force' shown as $\bar{L}$; those capable of working would wish to do so under appropriate terms, and would mostly register as desiring work at unemployment benefit offices.

This supply curve of labour shifts to the left if real benefits rise or if income tax rates rise (reducing disposable wages corresponding to the gross wage shown on the vertical axis), or if the labour force is reduced. We must allow also for the rigidity of the housing market and the dispersion of employment opportunities; a mismatch between population centres and opportunities will shift the *SS* curve to the left if mobility is obstructed by housing.

The demand side of the figure is drawn up on the simplifying assumption that there is a constant union 'mark-up' (the percentage by which unions raise unionized workers' wages above non-union wages) at all levels of non-union wages and other relevant variables. The expositional advantage of this clear over-simplification is that it allows union and non-union firms' demand curves for labour to be put on a single figure. With union real wages uniquely related to non-union real wages, demand for union labour, though truly related to the union real wage, is shown by the D_uD_u curve (figure 1.3). The demand for non-union labour will be related straightforwardly to the non-union real wage. We can add the two demands for labour together to obtain the total demand curve *DD*.

The position of these demand curves – the 'level of demand' – depends on four groups of factors. First there are the international ones: world trade and our terms of trade, which together dictate what domestic demand and output will be, consistent with current account balance at given non-union real wages. An expansion in world trade, for example, would increase demand for British goods from abroad. If these are supplied at higher real wages, the additional export earnings will be available for domestic demand

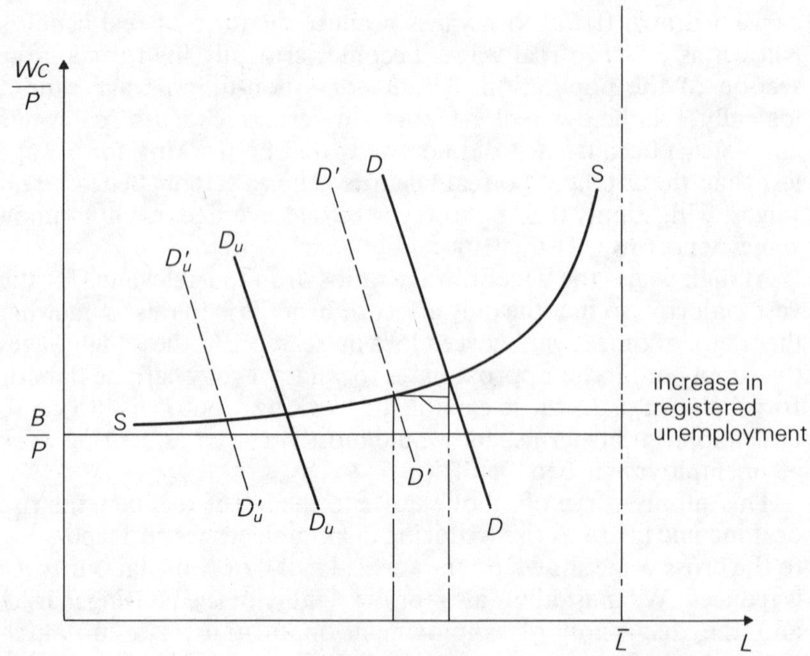

Figure 1.3 The effects of an increase in union power (the dashed lines represent the situation after a rise in union mark up)

to increase also, raising imports by the same amount. Both D_uD_u and *DD* curves shift to the right, and real wages rise, as will labour supply and employment.

Secondly, there are the technological factors which affect the productivity of labour and other costs. A rise in other costs, such as raw material or capital, both of which we assume to be set in international markets, will shift the *DD* curve to the left. A rise in the marginal product of labour will shift it to the right.

Thirdly, taxes on labour paid by firms and other implicit labour costs levied on employers (such as sickness benefits and redundancy costs) will shift the *DD* curve to the left.

Finally, we come to the union mark-up. A rise will shift the D_uD_u curve to the left, since a given non-union real wage will now correspond to a higher union real wage. The *DD* curve will be shifted to the left by the same amount (there will be no change in non-union labour demand at given real non-union wages).

What determines the union mark-up? Our analysis is straightforward enough: each union is a maximizing monopoly which faces the problem of working out an optimal time-path of real wages for its members, given that actions it takes today will have effects far into the future. In principle, therefore, all the factors determining the demand for labour in both sectors and the total supply of labour will come indirectly into each union's analysis. Complicated as this is, the essentials of the solution are clear enough. In particular, the mark-up will rise the less easy the employer finds it to substitute other factors of production, including non-union labour, for union labour. 'Union power' is measured in principle by the difficulty of this substitution, but this is not helpful in practice since this difficulty is unobservable. In practice, we resort to the only available index of union power – the proportion of the labour force which is unionized – and suppose that it is likely to bear some rough relationship to the true measure.

We can put this whole framework together easily enough. Employment and real non-union wages are determined in the long run at the intersection of the supply curve, *SS* and the demand curve, *DD*. Unemployment is the difference between workers who register, $\bar{L}$, and those who are employed. This again is an over-simplification because not all in the labour force register for a variety of reasons – especially lack of eligibility and dislike of the unemployment status. But registered unemployment will be highly correlated with the difference between $\bar{L}$ and employment.

THE MECHANICS OF ESTIMATION

In the short run the economy will not jump quickly to any new long-run equilibrium, for the traditional reason that there are costs of adjusting labour demands (and possibly also labour supplies, though we do not find them important). These costs of adjustment cause both employment and union real wages (and so also average real wages) to move relatively sluggishly; our estimates suggest that adjustment takes about four years to come through.

It is convenient for us to assume that in the non-union sector, day-to-day (as opposed to long-run) supply is always equal to day-to-day demand, hence our model assumes continuous labour market equilibrium, in the sense that this residual market always clears and there is no excess supply. However, this is less important than it seems. Our analysis still has the conventional characteristic: that it takes time to get to the long run. Other analyses which would share our long-run framework, but assumed short-run disequilibrium (excess supply or demand) could well produce similar results. So our analysis does not appear to rest crucially on the assumption of continuous market equilibrium.

What our analysis gives us are two basic equations and one group of equations. These are:

(1) An equation for total average wages (union and non-union) which, using real wages as the supply price of labour, says it depends on the volume of unemployment, real benefits grossed up for direct taxes, the size of the labour force and the unionization rate. To allow for one-year nominal wage contracts over a proportion of employees, the size of inflation forecasting errors also enters the calculations. Unexpected inflation causes workers who contracted in advance to suffer an unexpected drop in real wages. Finally, the last period's real wages enter because of the adjustment costs noted earlier. This is the 'supply equation' in the analysis. (The unionization rate (and so the union mark-up) enters the supply equation though it entered the demand curves in the figure because the figure is in terms of the non-union wage, whereas the estimation is in terms of the (observable) total wage over all sectors.)

(2) An equation for unemployment, regarded as depending on the demand for labour; this is the demand equation in the analysis. Unemployment is related consequently to real wages grossed up for labour taxes on the employer, technological progress, the volume of planned output, and lagged unemployment.

(3) A group of equations determining the level of planned output. These are the equations of the Liverpool macroeconomic model. They have the property that, in the long run, output must be such that there is current account balance. Hence long-run output (and so employment) will depend on world trade and the terms of trade, as well as on the other factors entering the supply and demand curves for labour. Output in the short run depends on the fiscal, monetary and international shocks hitting the economy which cause fluctuations around the long-run equilibrium (discussed in our other work, e.g. Minford *et al.* (1984), and not important here).

THE EMPIRICAL RESULTS – A BRIEF ACCOUNT

In all, we have 'fitted' the model described here to over 1300 pieces of data, a very large set indeed. Our primary work, since it is directly relevant to the estimates of UK policy effects, concerns wages and unemployment in the economy as a whole. But we have supplemented this with disaggregated work on wages and unemployment in 17 industries, and also with work on the regional behaviour of wages, unemployment and working days lost. For full details of these results, see Minford (1983, 1984, 1985a) and Minford *et al.* (1983).

This body of work strongly supports the view that the level of benefits, direct tax rates, paid by both the employee and by the employer, and union power have major effects on the level of unemployment. These effects are substantial. We find that a 10 per cent rise in real benefits would, at current unemployment levels, raise unemployment by nearly 0.7 million; a rise in the fraction of labour force unionized by one percentage point would raise it 0.2 million; a rise in employer national insurance contributions by one percentage point would raise it by 0.2 million; a rise in the standard rate by one percentage point would raise it by 0.1 million. Table 1.1 shows these effects based on the parameters currently in use in the Liverpool model. Table 1.2 summarizes the major findings of our research.

Table 1.1 Effects by 1988 of regime changes undertaken in 1985

Fall of	*Un-employment ('000)*	*Real (%) wages*	*Output (%)*	*Exchequer[a] gain/loss (£ billion p.a. 1985 prices)*
10 per cent in benefits	−660	−1.7	+2.2	+3.0
0.01 in employer tax rate[b]	−190	+0.4	+0.4	−0.5
0.01 in personal tax rate[b]	−90	−0.2	+0.2	−0.75
0.01 in unionization rate[b]	−210	−0.5	+0.8	+1.6

Source: Simulations of Liverpool model (February 1984 version), assuming no tax cuts from 1985 Budget onwards (before these changes).

Notes: [a]Assumed to be met by raising or redistributing 'neutral' revenue (lump-sum tax or transfer). Positive figure is gain, negative is loss, to Exchequer.
[b]Rates all expressed as fractions.

Table 1.2 Major research findings (elasticity of x to y = percentage change in x for 1% change in y)

Direct long-run elasticity of real wages to: (supply of labour)	*Real benefits*	*(1 + Personal tax rate)*[a]	*Unionization rate*	*Unemployment*
Quarterly data, whole economy	0.5	0.5	0.8	−0.05
Quarterly data, average of 17 industry results	0.5	0.5	1.2	−0.06
Direct long-run elasticity of unemployment to: (demand for labour)	*Real wages*	*(1 + Employer tax rate)*[a]	*Output*	
Quarterly data, whole economy	5.4	5.4	−12.3	
Quarterly data, average of 17 industry results	7.0	7.0	− 9.3	
Overall long-run elasticity of output to: (whole model)	*Real benefits*	*(1 + Personal tax rate)*[a]	*(1 + Employer tax rate)*[a]	*Unionization rate*
Quarterly and annual data, whole economy	0.2	0.2	0.4	0.4
Overall long-run elasticity of unemployment to: (whole model)				
Quarterly and annual data, whole economy	2.6	2.6	5.3	4.9
Regional data[b]	n.a.	n.a.	n.a.	2.6

Notes: [a]Percentage change in (1 + tax rate) ≃ percentage *point* change in tax rate (e.g. rise in tax rate from 0.28 to 0.30 is 2 percentage points). So elasticity to (1 + tax rate)is percentage effect of 1 percentage point change in tax rate.
[b]Details in chapter 6, table 6.1.

COMPARISONS WITH PREVIOUS WORK ON THE UK

Unfortunately, it is impossible to compare these findings directly with previous work. The reason is that previous work has all been microeconomic in nature, and hence has supplied 'partial equilibrium' results. That is to say, no estimates have been derived, or for that matter were derivable, for total effects.

Nevertheless, we may compare to some extent the estimates of partial relationships embodied here with those found by others.

On benefits, our supply (wage) equation gives a very high implicit partial long-run elasticity of unemployment to the replacement ratio. How high depends, as our analysis would predict, on the level of unemployment within the sample period. In the sample up to mid-1979, it ranges between 6 and 13, depending on which other variables are included. In the sample to end-1982 when unemployment was much higher, it ranges up to 36 implying a very flat supply curve in these, its lower reaches. Nickell (1979a), Lancaster (1979) and Mackay and Reid (1972) have found elasticities of unemployment duration to the replacement ratio of around 0.6, in cross-section studies of samples of the unemployed. Lancaster went as far as to conclude that an 'elasticity of this order could now be regarded as established beyond reasonable doubt.' Though Atkinson *et al.* (1984) queried an elasticity even as high as this, using *actual* benefit data, this size of elasticity has since been corroborated by Narendranathan, Nickell and Stern (1984) using the DHSS Cohort Study, including data on actual benefits.

A detailed critique of all these studies cannot be undertaken here. The Mackay and Reid study is in any case somewhat dated and uses less powerful methods than those of Lancaster and Nickell. Nevertheless, there is one major issue to be raised with all these studies. They all assume, within a search model framework, that intended (or desired) duration is never long term (or 'infinite'), or in terms of the search model that the offer–acceptance rate never tends to zero. We have suggested above that a person's optimal level of unemployment per fiscal year will depend sensitively on the relative price of work and leisure (as roughly measured by the replacement ratio). For high ratios he may decide to work not at all, or for only brief spells when market wages are exceptionally favourable. Such people are likely to exhibit a very low elasticity to changes in the ratio: this is Nickell's (1979a and b) finding for those with long duration (six months or more), and this finding is repeated in Narendranathan, Nickell and Stern (1984). Yet the conclusion, if our suggestion is correct, is precisely the opposite to that which they draw (i.e. that there is little effect of the ratio on long-term unemployment). It is that at some ratio these people would cease to be long-term unemployed and would participate 'properly' again in employment, having therefore at this ratio a very high ('switching') elasticity to it.

Furthermore, the total effect of the average replacement ratio on average duration across the sample would correspondingly be enormously higher. For suppose there were two equal groups, those with 'normal' duration of eight weeks at a ratio of 0.5, and those with 'medium' duration of 20 weeks at a ratio of 0.8. Their average duration and ratio would be 14 weeks and 0.65 respectively. Now suppose the ratios rise to 0.6 and 0.9; the first group, with an elasticity of 0.6, raises duration to nine weeks, the second responds by planning 'indefinite' duration, say two years (104 weeks) to allow for an occasional sampling of work. Average duration will eventually settle at 56.5 weeks, while the average replacement ratio will have only risen to 0.75; unemployment will have quadrupled in response to a 15 per cent (10 percentage point) rise in the average replacement ratio – an overall elasticity of 20.

In a cross-section study (at least as carried out by the authors cited), the elasticity will be biased downwards by this problem. The reason is that the elasticity of the long-term unemployed (caught in the 'unemployment trap') will be estimated to be very low or even zero, whereas in fact for those of them on the *margin* (of the unemployment trap) it is 'infinite'. In a *time-series* study this problem is overcome because the wage equation picks up the movement of population into and out of the unemployment trap. As explained above, movements in this category of long-term unemployed will dominate overall duration of unemployment, and imply of course a very much higher elasticity. That elasticity must be interpreted correspondingly differently from that in the cross-section study.

Of other earlier time-series work, Maki and Spindler (1975), in a time-series analysis of the UK in the post-war period, found a partial elasticity of unemployment to the replacement ratio of 0.6. This estimate is flawed by the use of the ERS benefit ratio, which only applied to a minority of unemployed, and by the ambiguous status of the estimating equation, which is neither a structural equation nor a reduced form. Also, the most recent re-working of their data by Junankar (1981) shows too that the equation is fairly vulnerable to shifts in estimation period. Holden and Peel (1981) have estimated reduced form equations on UK post-war time series using benefits paid to a married man on average earnings with two children. These give an elasticity of around 0.4 to the replacement ratio. However, since other exogenous variables, such as world trade and unionization, have been omitted and rolled into the error process, the coefficient estimate may be biased. Similar problems and comments arise in the context of the work on the inter-war period by Benjamin and Kochin (1979) and others (see Benjamin and Kochin *et al.* 1982). This type of time-series work has been stimulating and suggestive, but it would appear that it has established only that benefits probably matter for unemployment, not the scale of the effect.

Hence, the work reported here is for better or worse rather different from any of these studies, time-series or cross-section. Of the time-series studies, none has been based on a detailed market model as used here, while the cross-section studies appear to have paid inadequate attention to the problem of long-term unemployment which accounts for the very 'high' benefit elasticity we have found.

Whatever is true of benefits is also true of personal direct taxes, since these are included in the replacement ratios.

On unionization, the previous literature has estimated union mark-ups. These estimates have varied considerably, and have given rise to substantial controversy. Most recently, Treble (1984) has pointed out the tenuous basis for the majority of these estimates, which use a methodology originated by Lewis (1963). If one averages available estimates of this type for the UK mark-up (Parsley, 1980), it comes out at around 25 per cent with a high variance. Insofar as any tentative estimates of the union mark-up emerge from our work, it is of the order of 50 per cent.

Using a sounder method, Treble (1984) reworked the data of Mulvey (1976), who obtained estimates for the UK around 30 per cent, and obtained an estimate of about 40 per cent. This is closer to our implicit figure, but there is still reason to believe it is downward biased. This is because both the union mark-up and the level of non-union wages are likely to vary with the density of unionization. This variation would reduce the estimated coefficient in Treble's work. A proper treatment of the data used by Treble and Mulvey would require an additional equation to be estimated, in order to disentangle this effect from the true union mark-up estimate.

At this stage, we must regard estimates derived by methods such as those of Mulvey (i.e. all those for the UK, as cited in Parsley, 1980) and even Treble as inadequate and downward biased, pending a reworking with a full model. A recent study by Stewart (1983) avoids these problems, but raises others (see Minford, 1984). In any case it is confined to manufacturing, whereas our estimates are for the whole union sector versus the non-union. Our own time-series work here is based on the use of a full model, and there is no reason to believe the results are biased – they do not appear to be challenged by these previous estimates.

A rise in the mark-up of the scale we suggest has since been supported by the updated estimates from Earnings Surveys of Layard, Metcalf and Nickell (1978); according to these, the (unadjusted) differential between union and non-union wages in the UK economy had risen from 9 per cent in 1955 to 43 per cent by 1983 – see figure 1.4.

These comparisons have been for the 'supply' equation (the wage equation in our work), over which there has been sharp controversy. The demand equation – in our work the unemployment equation, in that of others, employment equations – is attended by little controversy; our results are quite conventional.

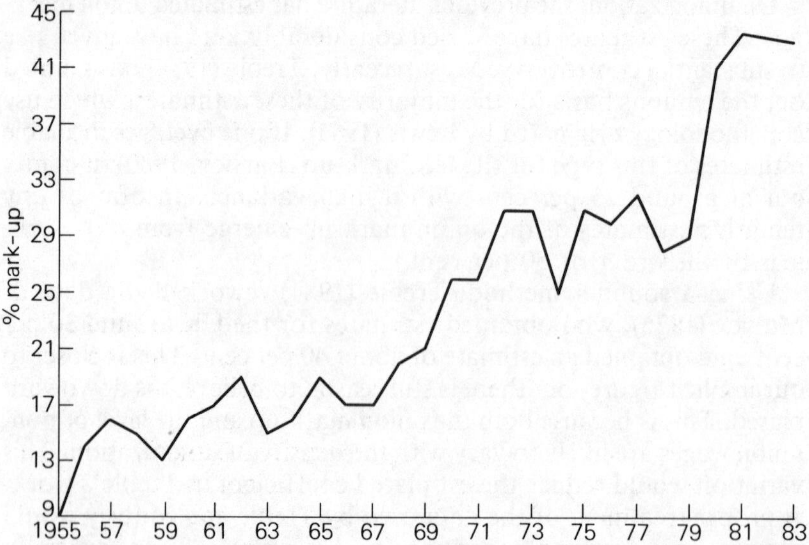

Figure 1.4 Union mark-up (union/non-union wage differential)

Conveniently, two recent papers (HM Treasury, 1985, and Layard and Nickell, 1985) have surveyed the empirical work for the UK and concluded that the total elasticity of employment to real wage costs (assuming final demand is maintained at a 'normal' level, i.e. that consistent with balance of payments equilibrium or current account) is in the range 0.5 to 1.0. The total elasticity in our work is at the top of this range, i.e. around unity, a little above the Treasury's preferred 0.75 and in line with the work of Symons (1985) and Beenstock and Warburton (1984). Taxes on labour paid by the firm are part of wage costs, so that this elasticity is also applicable to the rise in wage costs they cause.

REPLIES TO CRITICS

Criticisms of the first edition fell into three main categories: general, technical, and policy-related. Policy issues are not considered here, but will be dealt with later, together with any relevant criticisms.

Criticisms of the general approach have come from some Keynesian economists and from some who detected an anti-worker, pro-capitalist (even 'Tory'!) bias in the analysis.

The latter point is readily dealt with by counter-example. The interests of low-paid workers will be found to be the most prominent theme in this book – hardly a preoccupation of someone whose concern was only with profits of 'capitalists'. As for Tory bias, first, there is a prominent Tory element, partly represented by the Tory Reform Group, that strongly opposes many of the policy proposals in this book (e.g. Gilmour, 1983); second, proposals such as these would not have, and did not, interest any Tory Government before this one. It so happens that this Government has such an interest. This is to its credit, as a reforming government, but it need not be the only party interested. Indeed, the SDP has shown considerable interest in proposals like these – and it is to be hoped that other parties will see the economic logic behind them. The policy proposals in this book are motivated by the objective of achieving economic efficiency (*given* 'social' aims), in particular reducing unemployment.

This is to take policy proposals as evidence of 'bias' in the analysis. But in fact analysis of any sort cannot be 'biased'; it is either right or wrong, illuminating or not, etc. Whatever the authors' biases, they are immaterial to the force or otherwise of the analysis.

The criticism from some Keynesians has been that 'demand is not taken into account', that unemployment is a problem of deficient demand, and that forces acting on supply are irrelevant because labour has been in excess supply and involuntarily unemployed. Thus if supply-side measures caused more people to *wish* to work (reducing 'voluntary' unemployment), there would be no reduction in total unemployment, no rise in employment, merely a shuffling of the unemployed from the voluntary to the involuntary category.

We would not wish to deny the possibility – even the plausibility in the very short term – of short-term involuntary unemployment, by which is meant that there is excess supply of labour at the market wage, that wage being unalterable in the short term (whether because of contracts or other institutional arrangements) by the excess workers. In this model we have, as it happens, assumed that there is a residual 'non-union' market in which any excess supplies of labour in the economy are eliminated; this 'clears' the labour market. In this sense, we have assumed there is never any involuntary unemployment even in the short term.

This is a powerful assumption and it cannot be checked for correctness by direct observation. You cannot look at the labour market and see whether it is in chronic excess supply or in continuous balance. The assumption can only be tested indirectly by checking the predictive accuracy of models embodying it ('equilibrium' models) against others ('disequilibrium' models).

A full testing of this assumption could not be convincingly carried out on the sample we have at our disposal here. A limited test which is moderately favourable *is* reported, however, and probably it would require repeated samples to convince economists one way or the other about the UK's labour market. Thus we cannot claim to have established that there is no short-term involuntary unemployment.

But the point is that this does not matter for our analysis here, because this is long term. Even someone who believed in a short-term disequilibrium model with involuntary unemployment would not wish to deny that supply-side variables could affect wages over the medium and long term, even if not in the short term. He may query how powerful the effects are, but not their existence in principle. This is because even a disequilibrium model will tend over time towards equilibrium, in which of course supply has an influence.

What is more, such a person would not even write down a wage equation which was different in principle from the one we have written down in this model (see for example Nickell and Andrews

(1983) or Layard and Nickell (1985) which from a disequilibrium viewpoint arrive at a wage equation of the same general sort as ours). A Keynesian would be free to interpret our wage equation as a 'disequilibrium' one, if he so desired.

Only a Keynesian who believed that supply never equalled demand for labour, or only over an exceedingly long period (say of more than 5 to 10 years), would take issue with us on this. Yet such a belief is, as far as one can see, impossible to justify theoretically – for what institutional constraints could prevent wages moving to clear markets over such a long period? – and quite implausible. As a result it hardly has any adherents.

To sum up this rather complicated argument then, for an analysis of long-term unemployment (or the 'trend' in unemployment) such as that given in this book (a) it makes no effective difference whether one believes there can be short-run disequilibrium or not; (b) the assumption of long-term equilibrium (voluntary unemployment) made here would be very widely accepted.

There is one last point to clear up. It is no part of our thesis – or of any equilibrium analysis for that matter – that demand 'does not matter'. On the contrary, unemployment is caused, in the short and medium term, by shocks to demand (such as deflationary policies). How much unemployment at any one point in time can be ascribed to this source is an important question which this book indirectly addresses by asking how much is due to underlying or long-term factors. In short, the point made in this book is that these factors, mainly non-demand factors, *do* matter.

We turn now to technical criticisms, that is, those concerning the variables chosen to determine wages and unemployment and the soundness of the empirical results. These have been dealt with in detail in two journal replies (Minford, 1984, 1985a), so what follows is a non-technical summary.

Professor Steve Nickell of Oxford University (Nickell, 1984) has criticized our treatment of productivity in the model. He argues that in the wage equation there should be an explicit variable to proxy (expected) productivity since this influences firms' ability to pay. To this we have no objection, having included a number of proxies which turned out to contribute not at all to the explanation. However, his particular suggestions for proxies, the capital/labour force ratio and the price of imports relative to that of British goods, are objectionable because they are both endogenous variables (that is, they respond to the same causal pressures as do wages, employment, output, etc.). Their inclusion in the wage equation will induce a bias particularly in annual data where simultaneity is more important than in quarterly data. Indeed, when included in annual data they do seriously distort the results, eliminating the impact of benefits and 'attributing' much of the rise in real wages to a rising capital stock (a pretty suspect result when one considers that rising wages are likely themselves to lead to a rising capital/labour ratio). However, this equation exhibits bad statistical properties (the errors in it are very badly 'autocorrelated' or non-random). Furthermore, when included in quarterly data – on which the results are the most clear and reliable, there being much more of it in the sample – Nickell's variables make no significant difference.

Dr Brian Henry, and two colleagues (Henry, Payne and Trinder, 1985) of NIESR have argued that in the quarterly wage equation, on which they rightly focus in preference to the annual one, the proxy for union power, the unionization rate, is insignificant if the sample is extended to 1982. They argue from this that there is no evidence for a union-induced effect on real wages. But, first, we would certainly

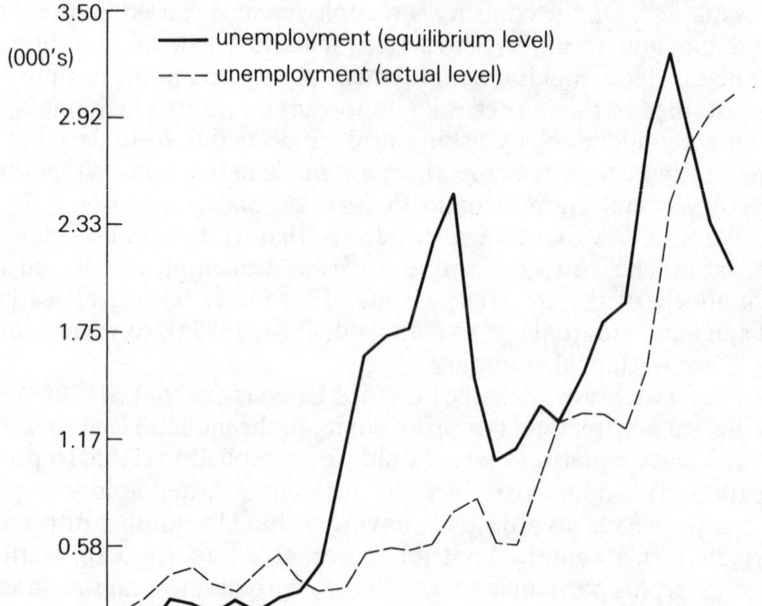

Figure 1.5 Unemployment, actual and equilibrium

expect the relationship to *shift* after 1980, both because of the passing of the new trade union laws, and because union membership dropped (dramatically) for the first time since the war; in particular, the lags in effect could well lengthen as unions evaluate and adjust to the new environment. Secondly, they used a revised series for union penetration which suggests a lag of 8 quarters in effect in the original sample; with *this* lag, the extended sample result is no different. Nevertheless, it is quite likely that the lag *will* lengthen further when the sample is extended more. Thirdly, there is fortunately another series available to proxy union power, the estimate of the union mark-up produced from earnings surveys by Layard, Metcalf and Nickell (1978, updated data courtesy of the authors and shown in figure 1.4). When this is used, the (significant) relationship does not shift when the sample is extended, which is what you would expect, since it is a direct measure of what unions have actually *done* in wage bargaining. In sum, it is obvious that unions have driven up real wages as their power increased up to 1980. Quite *when* the drastic recent reduction in their powers will work through to reduced union mark-ups is something our sample cannot tell us and a matter of judgement at this point.

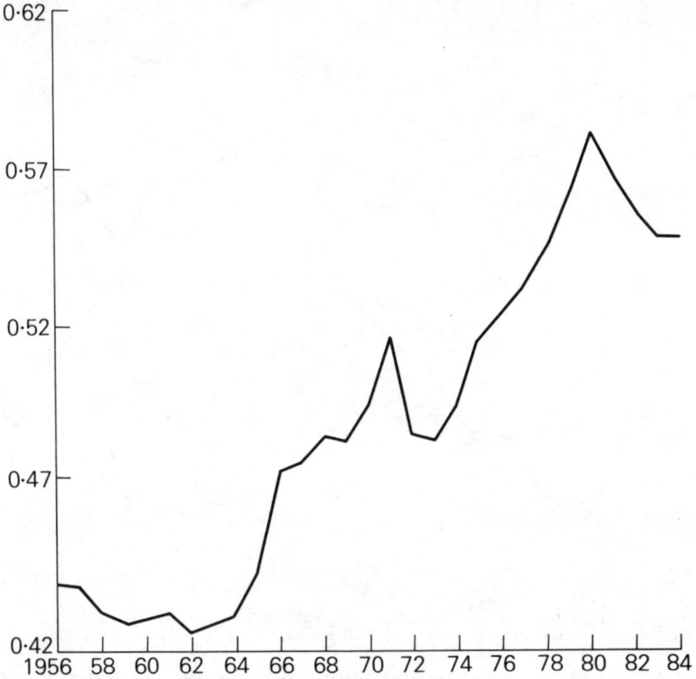

Figure 1.6 Unionization rate

THE EFFECT OF UK POLICY ON UNEMPLOYMENT

We can use the estimated annual relationships within the Liverpool model to compute the effects on the natural rate of unemployment, real wages and output of various permanent changes in taxation, benefits and unionization – shown in table 1.1 above. (All tax and benefit changes are offset notionally by lump-sum transfers, leaving net government revenues unchanged. These, which include the effect of changes in output, are noted in column 5.)

It can be seen that per unit of revenue cost, cuts in national insurance charges paid by firms are more effective in reducing unemployment than cuts in the standard rate, while to equal the effect on unemployment of a 10 per cent cut in real benefits, it would require cuts in NI charges costing the Exchequer nearly £5 billion per annum more. However, the effectiveness of a cut in taxes on employees in reducing employment would presumably be increased

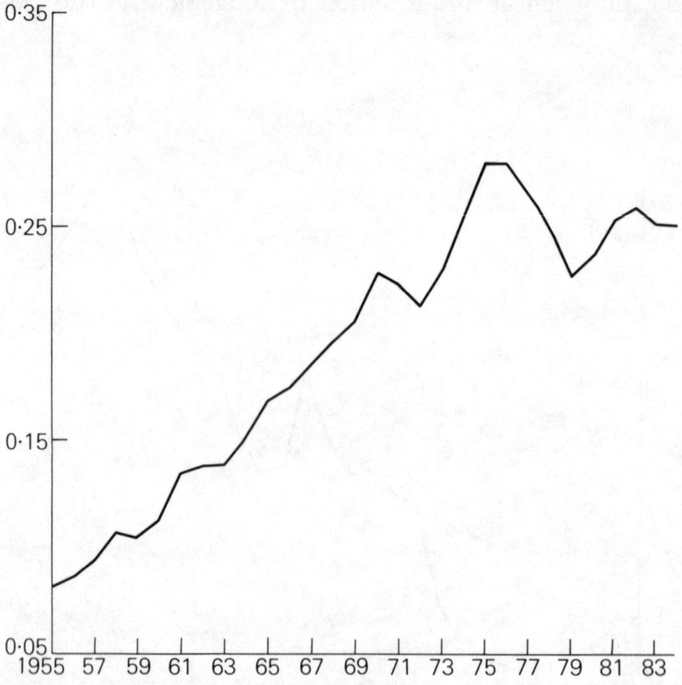

Figure 1.7 Employees' tax and national insurance as a proportion of average earnings

the more it was concentrated on the lower paid. One may presume that, if totally concentrated on those at the bottom end, each £ of tax cut would have an effect on unemployment comparable with that of a £ of benefit cut. At present most of those in the 'unemployment trap' would pay significant tax if they were working.

Finally, we may use these equations to compute the natural rate of unemployment. Figures 1.5 to 1.11 show the model's 'prediction' for this from 1955 to 1984, as well as the behaviour of the 5 key determining variables. The natural rate of unemployment in particular is set at 13.5 per cent in 1980 (about 3.25 million), though it has fallen since. The date at which it began its dizzying rise can be set fairly precisely at 1965, that is at the beginning of a period of Labour Government after 13 years of Conservative Government. This led to a sharp rise in union power, in benefits and taxation. Between 1970 and 1973 taxes were cut and the rise in real benefits was halted by the previous Conservative administration. However, the cut in taxes was unsustainable because it led to very

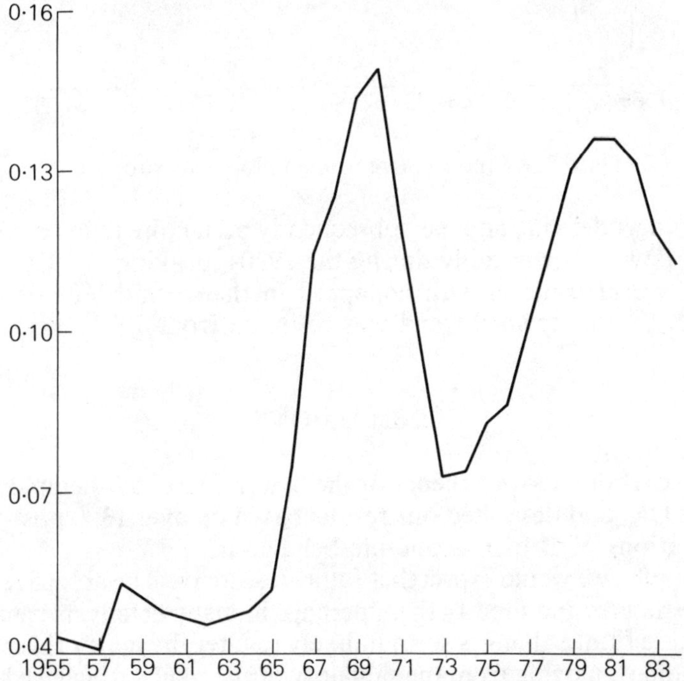

Figure 1.8 Employers' national insurance contributions as a proportion of average earnings

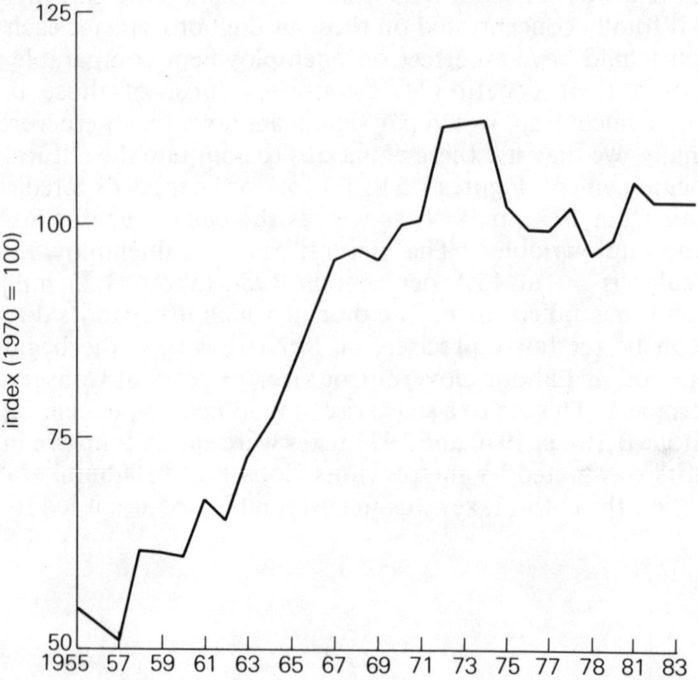

Figure 1.9 Index of real unemployment support

large budget deficits, and has subsequently been more than reversed. Union power rose steadily during the 1970s, peaking in 1980, and finally world trade growth collapsed in the second half of that decade. So the upward trend was resumed from 1973.

CONCLUSIONS

We have set out above a theory of the 'natural rate' of unemployent for the UK, and described our results based on over 1300 post-war observations of British economic behaviour.

Naturally, we would expect that future research will be able to refine these estimates and modify them perhaps in many details. Nevertheless, these future changes seem unlikely to alter the major thrust of our findings, judging from the similarity of the results which we have obtained from the different parts of our study, i.e. the whole economy (quarterly and annual data), industrial data and regional data.

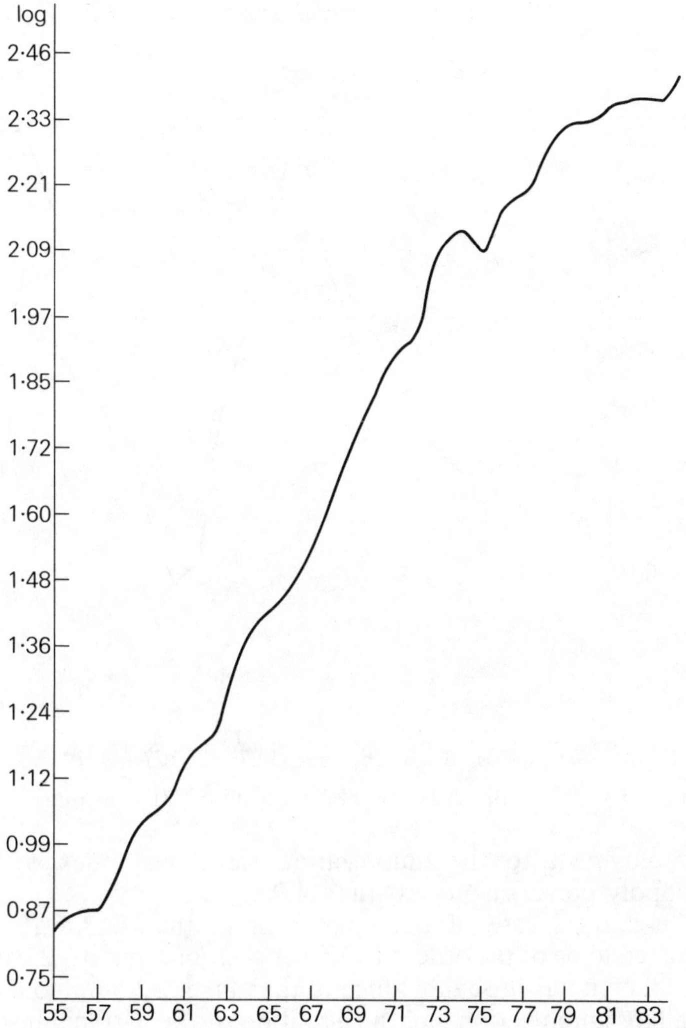

Figure 1.10 World trade volume

These findings were that there is a significant and powerful total elasticity of real benefits on unemployment (operating through higher real wages) of the order of 2.6. This is substantially higher than other post-war estimates insofar as these are comparable. Tax rates on employers and employees have analogous impacts, though the elasticities are much lower. Finally, and perhaps most strikingly, we find that in the past two decades union monopoly power has increased significantly and caused a substantial rise in real wages, with corresponding unemployment. The total elasticity of

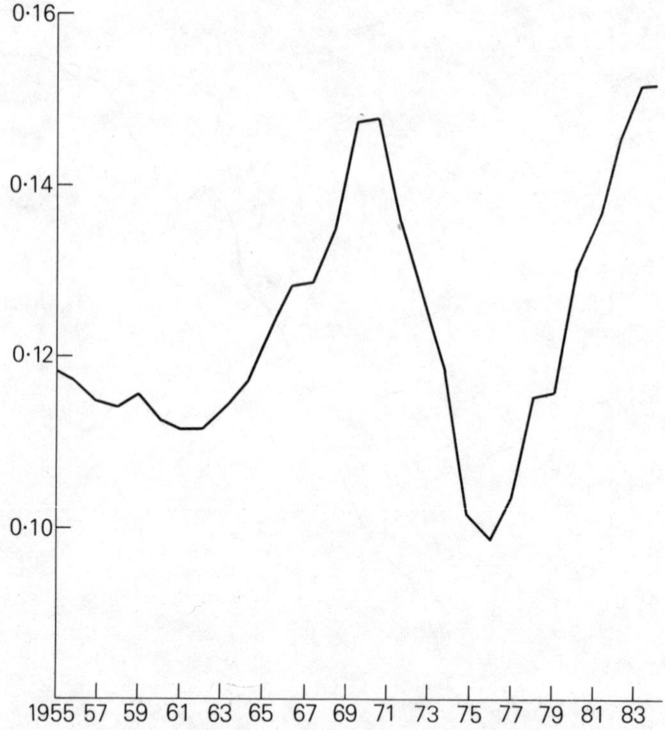

Figure 1.11 Net indirect taxes (as a fraction of GDP at market prices)

unemployment to the unionization rate (our index of union monopoly power) is no less than 4.9.

The natural rate of unemployment in the UK in 1980 was estimated to be of the order of 13.5 per cent, or around 3.25 million. Since then it has probably fallen to the range 2–2.5 million, owing to falling unionization and the abolition of the national insurance surcharge. Our analysis suggests that it can be lowered substantially further by additional measures to reduce real benefits, labour tax rates and union monopoly power.

In the parts that follow, we go in detail into the facts related to each of these major policy areas and suggest policy proposals to remedy the problems.

2

The Tax/Benefit System

The account in the previous chapter of the causes of unemployment stressed the role of benefits and their interaction with taxes, among other factors. In this chapter we describe in some detail how the benefit and tax system of the UK works at present, and in particular how it affects incentives to work at all, on the one hand, and, once in work to work for more pay on the other.

Incentives to work (rather than to go or remain on the dole) are conveniently measured by the 'replacement ratio', the ratio of net income on the dole to net income in work. If a person has a replacement ratio of, say, 80 per cent, this implies that, by taking a job, he would only receive 25 per cent more for doing the work involved than for doing nothing. The ratio can therefore be thought of as a marginal tax rate on the act of working (the marginal reward is only 20 per cent of the net income apparently paid). People with high replacement ratios are colloquially often said to be in the 'unemployment trap' in the sense that it will not pay them to work and so they are trapped. What is 'high' is a matter of judgement and it will of course differ from person to person, but over 70 per cent is frequently taken for purposes of illustration (70 per cent is considered a high marginal tax rate by most economists).

Some caution is necessary in using the replacement ratio. In our analysis the *average* replacement ratio plays no causative role. To understand the effects of benefits one must take account of the whole system (e.g. is it a ratio or flat rate system? Does it give support that is limited or indefinite in time? Does the rate fall over time?) and the strength of unions is crucial. For example, powerful unions will drive up wages in the union sector, non-union wages will be driven down by those displaced and replacement ratios in the non-union sector will worsen, driving workers onto the dole. Yet *average* wages in the economy will rise, *raising* the average replacement ratio.

Nevertheless, a description of the present state of replacement ratios is useful as a rough guide to the extent of the population whose behaviour will be seriously influenced by benefits according to the model of long-term unemployment we set out in this last chapter.

We also consider the present state of incentives to work for more pay, a related problem affecting many of the same people who suffer from poor incentives to work at all. These incentives are measured conveniently by marginal tax rates at different pay levels. It is a feature of the UK tax-benefit interaction at low wages that extra taxes plus benefit withdrawal cause very high marginal tax rates, at points even exceeding (and by a substantial margin) 100 per cent. This feature is colloquially referred to as the 'poverty trap' for obvious reasons.

THE 'UNEMPLOYMENT TRAP'

Estimates of Replacement Ratios

The calculation of replacement ratios is bedevilled by the problem of non-take-up. Non-take-up of benefit entitlements may occur for a variety of reasons, including stigma effects, ignorance, and the transactions costs of take-up. However, it seems wrong to allow for non-take-up by simply recording benefits actually taken on average. The reason is that economic analysis is concerned with decisions by people on the margin, that is weighing benefit and costs which are finely balanced. It seems likely that such substitution effects as we observe – actions by those on the margin – will be carried out by people conscious of the marginal choices confronting them; for they have the strongest incentives to know.

It seems better to calculate *entitlements*, as if everyone is rational and well informed, and then to allow the data to determine, through the estimated elasticities of response, how far these entitlements affect decisions. This has the advantage of consistency with the assumptions of the economic models typically used, based on maximizing behaviour. Take-up rates can then be regarded as reflecting people's decisions, given their tastes and attitudes, just as their unemployment duration and labour force participation reflects those decisions. The take-up problem worsens the unemployment trap, because the take-up of benefits by the unemployed is high (for supplementary benefit it is 75 per cent among nonpensioners generally, and presumably close to 100 per

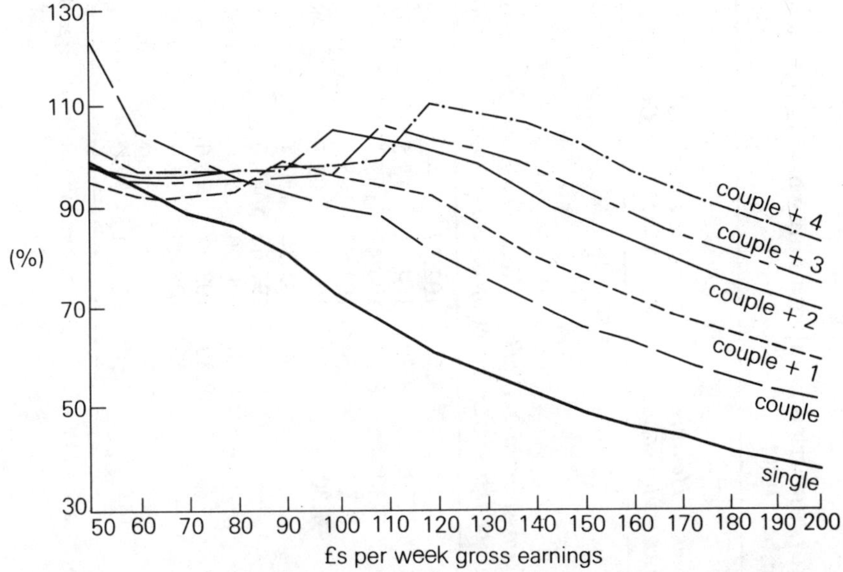

Figure 2.1 Replacement rates for six household types, December 1984

Assumptions used for Figure 2.1

Housing costs: Single £16.50 p.w.; couple £18.00; couple + 1 £19.50; couple + 2 £21.00; couple + 3 £22.00; couple + 4 £23.00. Plus water rates £1.50 p.w.

Ages of children: couple + 1:4 years; couple + 2:4,11; couple + 3:4,7,11; couple + 4:4,7,11,14.

Work expenses: £8.50 (see text).

Passport benefit (with SB and FIS): free dental, optical and prescription charges £1.60 p.w. per adult; free school meals £2.50 per school-age child; free welfare milk and vitamins £1.60 per eligible child.

cent among the unemployed since 72 per cent of *all* unemployed now receive this benefit) whereas take-up by low-paid workers is low (about 50 per cent for Family Income Supplement among all those eligible, and among recently unemployed men it is as low as 12 per cent of those eligible according to Davies *et al.*, 1982).

On the basis, then, of full entitlements we have calculated the November 1984 replacement ratios for single persons and for married men with non-working wives, by size of family and income. The calculation is based on supplementary benefit rates (including relevant 'passported' benefits) for the unemployed, since this is now the basis on which the overwhelming majority of the unemployed are supported (less than 30 per cent receive benefits that are not 'topped up').

Table 2.1 Replacement ratios and marginal tax rates for a married man with non-working wife and two children, December 1984

Unemployed Income (£p.w.)

Supplementary benefit	*Child allowance*	*Child benefit*	*Housing (rent)*	*Benefit*[a] *(rates)*	*Water rates*	*Heating allowance*	*Passported benefits*[b] *(FSM)*	*(FMV)*	*(FDOP)*	*Total benefits*
45.55	10.25	13.70	15.50	5.50	1.50	2.10	2.50	1.60	3.20	101.40

Employed Income (£p.w.)

Earnings	*Tax*	*NI*	*Child benefit*	*FIS*	*Housing (rent)*	*Benefit*[a] *(rates)*	*Passported benefits*	*Work expenses*	*Net income*	*Marginal tax rate*	*Replacement ratio*
50	—	4.50	13.70	25.00	14.43	4.94	7.30	8.50	102.37	—	0.99
60	—	5.40	13.70	20.00	13.18	4.54	7.30	8.50	104.82	75.5	0.97
70	2.80	6.30	13.70	15.00	11.93	4.14	7.30	8.50	104.47	103.5	0.97
80	5.80	7.20	13.70	10.00	10.68	3.74	7.30	8.50	103.92	105.5	0.98
90	8.80	8.10	13.70	5.00	9.43	3.34	7.30	8.50	103.37	105.5	0.98
100	11.80	9.00	13.70	—	8.00	2.90	—	8.50	95.30	180.7	1.06
110	14.80	9.90	13.70	—	5.10	2.00	—	8.50	97.60	77.0	1.04
120	17.80	10.80	13.70	—	2.20	1.10	—	8.50	99.90	77.0	1.02
130	20.80	11.70	13.70	—	—	—	—	8.50	102.70	72.0	0.99
140	23.80	12.60	13.70	—	—	—	—	8.50	108.80	39.0	0.93
150	26.80	13.50	13.70	—	—	—	—	8.50	114.90	39.0	0.88
160	29.80	14.40	13.70	—	—	—	—	8.50	121.00	39.0	0.84

Notes: [a]Assumes Rent of £15.50, Rates of £5.50. [b]FSM = free school meals; FMV = free milk and vitamins; FDOP = free dental, optical and prescription charges.

Work expenses of £8.50 per week are deducted from work income, and family income supplement with housing benefit added to it. Our work expenses figure includes £5.65 for fares to work, as in the DHSS tax/benefit model tables (November 1984). We have also allowed £2–3 for other work costs, i.e. additional expenditure on clothing and on food taken outside the home. This may well err on the low side, but there is no firm information. A notional allowance is made in these figures for fringe benefits. Subsidized canteen meals are frequently provided by an employer (15 per cent of the DHSS study obtained them). This is reflected in our low cost of food outside the home.

The picture presented by these calculations is a grim one from the point of view of incentives to participate in employment (see table 2.1 and figure 2.1). The replacement ratios are such that, should a person 'work the system', incentives to have a job are, on the whole, rather small for the family man. Even for the single person, the replacement ratio reached 0.8 at just under 58 per cent of average male manual earnings. Since the bulk of single persons are young and so have earnings well below the average, this is more damaging than it might sound.

Table 2.2 Percentage of workers by household type with replacement ratios higher than those shown in November 1980

Replacement ratio	*Single men and women*	*M*	*M+1*	*Married men*[a] *M+2*	*M+3*	*M+4*	*Weighted average*
(A) *Long-term ratios*							
0.6	30.0	59.1	63.3	67.6	76.1	87.0	56.6
0.7	16.7	37.5	40.8	46.2	59.3	78.3	37.2
0.8	9.9	19.3	23.4	27.8	39.9	67.4	21.7
0.9	6.5	9.0	12.8	16.0	25.6	45.7	12.2
1.0	4.8	3.5	7.2	7.1	15.1	26.1	6.3
(B) *Long-term ratios, 1984*[b]							
0.6	38.5	65.1	66.9	68.9	74.7	85.9	61.2
0.7	24.5	44.5	45.3	47.3	58.7	76.1	42.2
0.8	13.9	25.1	25.6	28.9	38.2	58.7	24.9
0.9	9.0	11.9	14.1	12.4	22.8	40.2	12.9
1.0	6.3	4.5	7.8	7.5	14.2	23.9	7.0

Source: GHS data tapes 1980 and Liverpool tax/benefit program.
Notes: [a]Wife assumed not to be working.
[b]Extrapolated from 1980 GHS data and NES 1980 and 1984.
Percentage of working households shown in each category.

It is difficult to estimate how many workers are affected by high replacement ratios, since so many different factors interact. However, we can use the GHS 1980 to obtain an estimate of the distribution of gross weekly earnings across each (non-retired) family unit. Our calculations are shown in table 2.2. Using the GHS shares for these households, the proportion of workers whose long-term replacement ratio is around unity or above is 6 per cent, while 22 per cent have a ratio of more than 0.8. This applies to the employed only. The percentages would be higher if the unemployed were included. Kay, Morris and Warren (1980) found that the proportion of the unemployed with a ratio of 0.8 or more was three times that of the employed, in which case the percentage overall would be 27 per cent. This indicates that there is a substantial proportion of the workforce with high replacement ratios. This picture is virtually unaltered both on balance and in detail if one looks at the short-term replacement ratios (not shown).

THE POSITION OF MARRIED WOMEN

The picture presented above assumes that in family households married women do not work. However, in 1982 (GHS) 27 per cent of wives of working men had full-time jobs, and another 35 per cent had part-time jobs; far fewer wives of unemployed men had jobs (only 15 per cent full-time, 14 per cent part-time).

The optimizing problem faced by the household is clearly a complex one, involving the work/home time preferences of each partner and total household income at each combination of full- and part-time work by each. Nevertheless, it may be reasonable to divide the problem into two separate stages: the husband's decision to work, assuming his wife does not work, and secondly, the wife's decision to work, full- or part-time, given the husband's decision. The justification would be that the wife is likely to move in and out of the labour market at different times in her lifecycle. A typical pattern would be full-time when just married, not at all when the children are young, part-time when they are at school, and finally full-time when they leave home. The husband has to take a decision about participation on a full-time job for a long period of time. Therefore the household's average life-income is likely to be dominated by the husband's earnings.

On this basis, the replacement ratios for married men shown in figure 2.1 (and table 2.1) and table 2.2 would not be seriously misleading.

We now turn to the choices facing married women, the remaining section of the potential labour force. Table 2.3 documents the retention rates they face, that is the proportion of extra gross income retained by wives. The top half deals with the situation when the husband is working. The retention ratios for full-time work are around 46 per cent with dependent children at average earnings, but rise to around 60 per cent without children. In the calculations, we have made an allowance for child-minding of £18 per week for a child under five when both parents are working full time. This may be on the low side. But most importantly, we cannot know what premium households place on wives' home time when there are dependent children. It seems quite possible that these ratios provide insufficient incentive for wives with children, especially those with low incomes. According to the GHS, they push wives with

Table 2.3 Retention ratios of married women November 1984[a]

	Number of children				
	0	*1*	*2*	*3*	*4*
Husband working					
Husband and wife[b] both on average manual earnings, full-time	64.1	45.8	45.8	45.8	45.8
Both on 75 per cent of average manual earnings, full time	65.1	40.8	36.4	32.4	28.6
Husband on average earnings, wife part-time £50 per week	67.1	31.1	31.1	31.1	31.1
Husband unemployed					
Wife on average manual earnings £98 per week	18.1	13.2	12.8	15.1	12.5
Wife on 75 per cent of average earnings, £74 per week	6.1	13.0	9.3	12.2	8.7

Source: Liverpool calculations.

Notes: [a]Additional income kept by wife as a result of working, long-term, i.e. compares net household income after one year with wife working, against what net household income would otherwise have been.

[b]Average weekly manual earnings: male £160, female £98.

children mainly into part-time work where retention ratios are higher (because of no expenses for child-minding); 36 per cent of these wives had part-time work in 1982, only 14 per cent had full-time work, leaving 49 per cent who did not work at all. Working wives are most common as one would expect, among families with no dependent children, where 40 per cent worked full-time, 27 per cent part-time, leaving only 33 per cent who did not work at all.

The bottom half of table 2.3 shows how the retention ratios fall dramatically when the husband is unemployed; the reason lies in the loss of the husband's supplementary benefit. Consistently with this, we saw earlier that 70 per cent of unemployed men's wives did not work in 1982.

POLICY PROPOSALS FOR THE UNEMPLOYMENT TRAP: A CEILING (OR 'CAP') ON BENEFIT INCOME RATIO

There are two aspects to the policy debate over benefits. There is on the one hand the understandable and widespread desire to provide an income 'safety net' for the least well off in society. On the other hand, there is the objective of maintaining incentives to work, so that society should not unnecessarily support those who could support themselves.

As economists, we restrict ourselves to comments on efficiency in meeting these potentially conflicting objectives. The obvious point is that income support can be given to *both* employed and unemployed, with a minimum differential in favour of income in work. For example, higher benefits to (or lower taxes on) the lower paid can be achieved, at some cost to those on average earnings and above, by changes in tax structure, without cutting benefits to the unemployed. The question is whether people will vote for the higher tax burden necessary for this to be done.

It would seem therefore right to separate two issues very clearly:

(1) minimum support levels;
(2) appropriate minimum differentials between in- and out-of-work income.

If one could obtain agreement that, as a matter of principle on efficiency grounds, the benefit ratio to net work-income should for no individual exceed, say 68 per cent (as for family heads in West Germany) or some such figure, it would then be possible to have a rational discussion of appropriate tax and support levels, trading off the welfare of the less well-off (including those likely to remain unemployed) against that of the average and better paid. One would visualize this as a running discussion, with support levels altering according to general social attitudes.

The crucial policy point to make is that the current system of unemployment support is dangerously inefficient because it does not limit replacement ratios as work-incomes fall. The minimum reform to it that we would wish to see is the introduction of a 'maximum replacement ratio' override (a benefit ratio ceiling) on the level of total net benefits paid out (similar to, but we would hope administratively simpler than, the old 'wage stop'). This could in principle be combined, if people wish it, with a more generous provision for the low paid in work which enables the living standards of the unemployed not to be seriously damaged.

Simulations of the Effects of a Cap on the Benefit Ratio

The introduction of a 'cap' on the benefit ratio would change the operation of benefits on the labour market quite fundamentally. The effect is illustrated in figure 2.2.

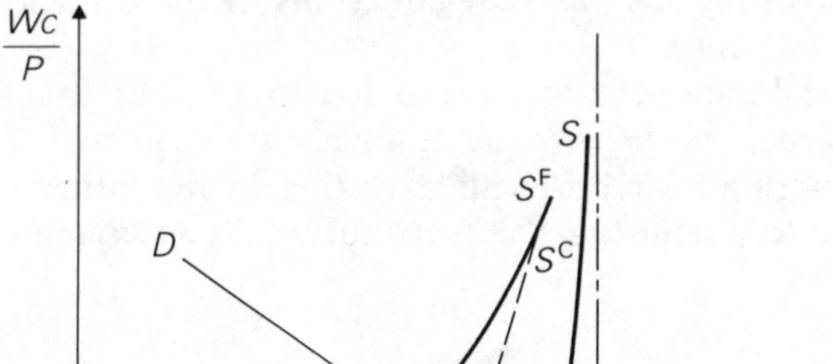

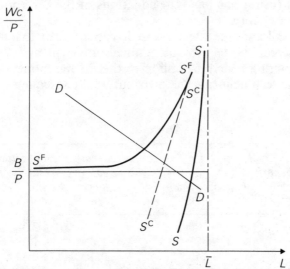

Figure 2.2 The supply of labour under different benefit regimes (S^cS^c is the supply curve with capped regime, SS the supply curve with no benefits, and S^FS^F the supply curve with flat rate benefit B/P).

Under the flat rate regime, the supply curve of labour is flattened substantially (or 'truncated') as wages fall towards the flat rate benefit level B/P. Hence as demand falls for the economy ('demand being defined as the output sales the economy can sustain, without going into external current account deficit), so unemployment rises and wages fall little.

Under the capped regime, the supply curve (S^cS^c) shifts to the left of the no benefit supply (SS), because workers now receive some ratio of benefits to wages which induces them to work less; as wages fall, a higher proportion of workers receive the maximum ratio and so the leftward displacement becomes greater. But the displacement never becomes a truncation as with the flat regime (S^FS^F) because, as wages fall, so benefits fall too (if not, in the aggregate, quite in proportion). Hence the downward pressure on wages as demand falls encounters very much less resistance from benefit levels than in the flat rate case, and there is correspondingly very much less effect on employment and unemployment.

Our estimates for the UK are derived for a flat rate regime and are unlikely to be fully appropriate for a capped regime. Nevertheless, we may get some notion of the order of magnitude by using them, provided that we treat them cautiously. Table 2.4 shows estimated *total* long-run effects on unemployment, real wages and output (using as a basis the equations of the Liverpool model discussed in chapter 1).

These are long-run effects, and it can be seen that a cap at 0.7 has a sizeable effect, reducing unemployment by 0.7 million, and contributing nearly £4 billion to the PSBR, money available for tax cuts to ameliorate the distributional consequences of this measure.

Table 2.4

	Long-run effect compared with present situation, on			
Maximum benefit ratio or 'cap' set at	*Unemployment ('000)*	*Real wages (%)*	*Out-put (%)*	*PSBR*[a] *(£bn 1985 prices)*
0.7	−700	−1.8	+2.3	3.8
0.8	−375	−1.0	+1.2	2.1
0.9	−140	−0.4	+0.5	0.8

Note: [a]The effect on the PSBR is assumed to be eliminated by lump-sum transfers back to the taxpayers; the column shows the 'tax-cuts' made possible and assumed to take place.

Table 2.5 Time lags for benefit changes to affect unemployment

No. of years	*Percentage of effects*
1	35
2	70
3	90
4	100

The time for these effects to come through on unemployment would be, taking the model at face value, as shown in table 2.5.

Hence for example a 0.7 cap if instituted in November 1985, would bring unemployment down by 0.5 million by March 1987 reaching 0.7 million by November 1989. These lags arise within the model largely because of firms' adjustment costs in taking on extra labour. There seems no particular reason to believe that these costs would alter significantly when the benefit regime changed or to alter these lagged estimates therefore.

We defer consideration of distributional consequences until we have considered all the policy measures which may be necessary. At that stage we evaluate how it may be necessary to handle distributional aspects in this overall package.

ADMINISTRATIVE ASPECTS OF THE CAP

The proposal is made here to limit total individual social security benefits so that, in all cases, out-of-work net income would be noticeably below in-work net income. In the past somewhat similar schemes became known as 'wage stops'.

In the past, schemes relating one form of income such as, for example, out-of-work or a social security based one, to another, such as past earned income, have existed. All have now been terminated except one aspect of one scheme which continues today. The national assistance and supplementary benefit schemes contained a wage stop and these were abolished in 1975. Unemployment benefit (UB) did have an earnings related supplement which augmented UB in the short term for middle and higher income earners, but this scheme terminated in 1981. The present family income supplement (FIS), which is an addition paid to earned income for low wage workers is set for a year on a previous month's earnings, and so relates one set of earnings with another. Rent and rate rebates have somewhat similar linkages. There are, of course, difficulties and objections to such schemes, but many of these arise because of the complications built into them. If the proposal is kept simple and fair, many difficulties disappear. The concept under review here is quite simply a proposal to limit total net social security benefits to 70 per cent of previous net earned income.

The proposed scheme would be to place a ceiling on the total net unemployment benefits package, so that it did not exceed 70 per cent of recent in-work net income. Recent acceptable evidence of pay slips would be combined, if relevant, with other benefits, for example FIS, rent rebate, child benefits and other FIS 'passported' benefits, so as to arrive at a net in-work income figure. Mandatory tables similar to those for PAYE or a set tariff would assist here in establishing the FIS and other potential additions, and also in relating them to out-of-work income, starting with UB and child benefit (CB), and if appropriate supplementary benefit (SB) and other 'passported' benefits, as well as a credit for not having work expenses. These would then be established on a tax-paid basis, so as to reach a net out-of-work income figure, which would be subject to a 70 per cent maximum of the relevant in-work income level. This maximum would then be indexed to the retail price index (RPI) with annual upratings as for other social payments.

Those unemployed at the time the cap came into force would have their work-income computed as follows. Previous pay slips would be produced to establish previous gross income. This would be uprated to the present by the RPI, and also adjusted for *current* tax rates, work expenses etc. This would then be used to set the 70 per cent ceiling.

Some workers currently unemployed, particularly those long-term unemployed, would probably be unable or unwilling to produce acceptable evidence of previous pay (e.g. a payslip, a letter from a previous employer, evidence of occupation and colleagues' earnings). In these cases, some simple fall-back procedure is required. We suggest that net previous wages be deemed equal to current benefits plus 10 per cent (corresponding to the approximate effect of the tax cuts). Benefits for these people could thus drop 23 per cent, creating an incentive to produce acceptable evidence.

Wives' earnings, if any, would be disregarded in the calculation of the husbands' in-and-out-of-work income, and the cap amount. The wife's benefits would similarly be subject to the cap, disregarding the husband's earnings or benefits. This will ensure that the incentive for each partner to work is maintained, in general. The only exception could be where the man is unemployed and loses supplementary benefit when his wife works. In this case, even though the wife's benefits out of work may be low, the loss of household income when she gives up work may be small, i.e. her 'retention ratio' is low. The incidence of this case, however, should be substantially reduced by the cap, since many unemployed men will receive less supplementary benefit than they do now, so the loss of it caused by the wife working will be correspondingly lower for them.

Young people and others joining the labour force will not be subject to the cap, since they have no previous earnings. However, as argued below under the 'workfare' and denial of benefit scheme, they should be subject to tougher conditions for benefit receipt so that the choice facing unemployed school-leavers is between a place on the Youth Training Scheme or unsubsidized idleness.

The administrative advantages of such a scheme would be:

(1) it would be fair, plain and simple;
(2) it would relate to an individual's own circumstances; his incentive to rejoin the active workforce would rise;
(3) in-work benefits, some of which relate to family size and circumstances, would continue to exercise a significant influence on income received;
(4) there would be no undue discrimination against those with large families or high housing costs;
(5) the use of the most recent work-income figures would avoid some major disadvantages in past wage-stop schemes, e.g. relationship to an individual's potential earning capacity, its high error rate, forecasting future income, etc.
(6) there would be little scope for dispute as to figures etc. and therefore no need for any burdensome appeal procedure.

Possible administrative disadvantages would be:

(1) the scheme fails to cope with any particular hardship, physical or mental handicap problems or any exceptional needs;
(2) for the unemployed without evidence of pay the relevant base income would be arbitrary;
(3) it could increase civil service staff numbers and costs;
(4) it could arouse some controversy as wage-stop did for a decade (1965–75) and activate or divert pressure groups to fight the scheme.

Previous wage-stop schemes have been terminated for various reasons, but the climate may now be judged right for the introduction of a similar measure, namely a ceiling on benefits. There are considerable economic advantages in terms of the labour market and public expenditure. There are administrative advantages and disadvantages of such a proposal, but the balance here clearly lies in favour.

A 'WORKFARE' SCHEME AND THE PROCEDURES FOR DENIAL OF BENEFIT

The placing of a cap on benefit ratios is designed to exert market pressure on unemployment by making people willing to take jobs at lower pay. Hence it has its effect via the general level of wages (or equivalently of productivity and work practices input by workers for the same wage). The only way to bring unemployment down is to alter the general market situation in some such way.

There is a case, however, for strengthening these pressures by tightening up the procedures for obtaining benefits, and in particular making benefits contingent on accepting, if no other is offered, a job designated by the state (from a 'workfare' pool of community and other jobs). In principle, the state should only provide benefits where the unemployed can get *no* job, however unpleasant or low paid. The practice however appears to be very different and this difference has been especially marked since the separation of job centres from benefit offices. The worker 'shops' for a job in the 'job centre'; if he cannot find one he likes, he claims benefits and typically gets them (the rate of denial is extremely low – in 1980 about 0.5 per cent of the unemployed).

It has been suggested that the state sets up 'community work schemes' and that the unemployed be offered places on such schemes, benefit being conditional on acceptance of such places if offered. The problem with such ideas is that they are expensive to the state – involving supervision, equipment and other costs – and that the jobs involved have a very low value to society (otherwise they would already have been undertaken). However, as a last resort of benefit, they are of some use.

Let us designate such a pool of jobs 'workfare' jobs. It would then seem useful to include all existing jobs notified to job centres (often private sector but also public sector), in this pool; the 'community' jobs would then be there as a last resort, in the total absence of normal jobs. (With strict controls on pay and conditions the cost of such a last resort scheme could be kept within bounds – Ashton, 1984 – by contrast with the lax regime proposed by Layard, 1984.)

The denial procedures in each area of the country could become tougher the longer the individual's period of unemployment; beyond six months it could become sufficient for benefit denial to refuse any job offered by workfare. Furthermore, repeat spells of unemployment, however short, could also attract such criteria. Finally, there could be the differentiation of these criteria by age – for workers below 25 years of age, acceptance of a workfare job after three months of unemployment could be a condition of further benefit. There would be a demonstration effect on low-wage vacancies; as firms got to hear of people filling them, more would come on to the market. At present it is a pointless expense to advertise jobs at low wages which are marginally competitive with benefits.

In general, new instructions should be given to benefit officers to keep close liaison with Manpower Services Commission (MSC) job centres and evolve from their experience operating procedures which implement these tougher denial provisions. The objective should be to open up the low-wage non-union employment sector, so reinforcing the downward pressure on real wage costs.

Administratively, such procedures will require the re-integration of MSC job centres (where the workfare pool of jobs will be primarily located) and unemployment benefit offices. Their separation now is clearly seen as an error. The simplest way to do this would be to place DHSS officials currently dealing with unemployment (and supplementary) benefits in the job centres. The unemployed must attend regularly at this job centre as well as whenever required by the workfare scheme – i.e. to be presented with a selection of jobs, acceptance of which is a condition of further benefit.

TAX THRESHOLDS AND THE LONGER TERM

Setting a cap on benefits will only alleviate and not solve the 'unemployment trap'. A full solution would require, in principle, the total abolition of state benefits for the out of work (then unemployment insurance would be a private decision, such that any effects on supply would be individually chosen and so welfare-optimizing).

But the effect of this, on its own, would be to depress the wages of low-paid workers substantially; and this would, besides being obviously politically unattractive, draw many more workers into dependence on state benefits in work and so into the poverty trap. Even the cap, on its own, has a (lesser) effect of this kind. Therefore, it is necessary to draw the reforming net wide, to include tax thresholds and the means-tested benefits system itself.

By tax in this context we mean both income tax and national insurance contributions (by employers and employees; it is strictly immaterial in economic theory who pays the contribution). It is sometimes stated (for example, on a number of occasions by the Prime Minister, Margaret Thatcher) that national insurance is not a tax but *insurance*, entitling the insured to certain rights (sickness, unemployment benefits and of course a pension are the main ones). This is correct under certain strict conditions (which Beveridge himself intended to apply quite generally). These are that the insured person is *not* eligible for supplementary benefit. To the extent that he is so eligible, the 'insurance' element in his payment diminishes, for he gets the benefit or part of it whether he pays his national insurance or not. For the low paid, the insurance element is absent or negligible because whatever they pay, they will receive supplementary benefit (and no more). Hence the link between contribution and benefit is totally broken for these people, and the contribution for them becomes a pure tax. To give a practical example, if they are out of work, they will not pay national insurance, and they will regard its payment if they take a job as a straightforward reduction in their welfare (since it brings them no corresponding future benefit).

Raising tax thresholds – in this general sense of income tax – would counteract the depressive effect of benefit reduction on the net of tax wages of low-paid workers. They would then require – and under a reformed system receive – less state benefits in work and the poverty trap would affect less people. The full effect will depend exactly on how a reformed system of in-work benefits would work. We turn to that next, deferring to the next chapter a detailed consideration of the economic effects of a radical reform package.

MEANS-TESTED BENEFITS AND THE 'POVERTY TRAP'

Strictly speaking it is possible to consider the poverty trap – the very high marginal tax rates (MRTs) on low-paid workers – as an issue with no bearing on unemployment. For the poverty trap only affects those already working.

However, this is too narrow a view for several reasons. First, such high MRTs may well affect the supply of hours and so the level of under-employment. Second, they may affect the quality of the labour supply by discouraging training which would raise earnings. Third, they will tend to hold people at lower income levels, where they will have higher replacement ratios than otherwise. So more people than otherwise may elect to remain unemployed, for any given benefit system, because the population is more skewed towards those with higher ratios. In practice, therefore, there is a high coincidence between those 'at risk' from the two traps.

Estimates of the effects of the poverty trap on labour supply are, however, hard to come by. We surveyed the evidence briefly in Minford *et al.* (1983), Appendix C. There we found that there is evidence of incentive effects among workers facing high MRTs, but that the elasticities to marginal real wages are typically quite small (0.1–0.3), in our view quite implausibly so. In the context of MRTs between 80 and 200 per cent, as occur in the poverty trap, they are virtually useless.

Few people, in any case, regardless of political views would disagree that these MRTs must be reduced. Disagreement only arises as to the distributional effects that should be accepted as a consequence of reduction.

FACTS ABOUT THE UK TRAP

Figure 2.3 shows net against gross pay for single persons and married men with non-working wives. The problem of low incentives is most acute for married men with children. Figure 2.4 shows the MRT for a married man with two children. Net income remains static between £50 and £90 per week and then dips before starting finally to rise above this level at £140 per week. Here the MRT falls at last to 39 per cent (standard rate plus NI) having reached 181 per cent at £100 per week. Similar patterns are displayed for other families and the patterns are only slightly better for single people and childless married couples (see figure 2.3).

The problem arises because of the interaction of FIS (with 'passported' benefits), rent/rate rebates, and the tax system. Each of these is 'means-tested' in a different way, and it is the unintended overlap of the three means tests that creates the problem. Table 2.6 shows this summarily.

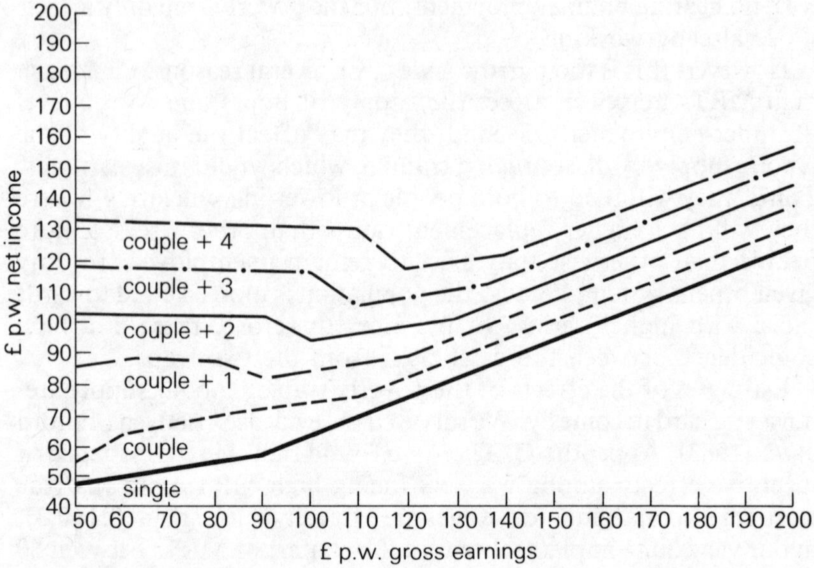

Figure 2.3 The poverty trap: net incomes for six household types (for assumptions see figure 2.1)

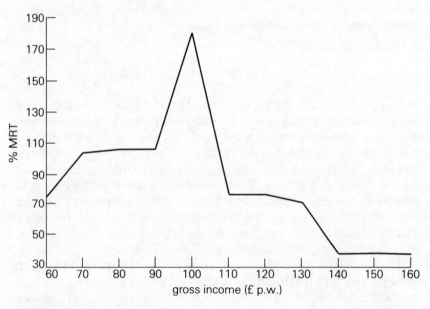

Figure 2.4 Marginal tax rates for a married man with two children
Source: table 2.1

Table 2.6 Certain sources of income of married men with two children, wife not working (£ per week)

Wages	*FIS and passported benefits*	*Housing benefit*	*Taxes and NI*
80	17.30	14.42	13.00
100	—	10.90	20.80
120	—	3.30	28.60

Married women do not face such problems, provided their husband's work and joint income exceeds the FIS level; in this case, they will face a 39 per cent MRT. However, if the husband is unemployed, then the wife's MRTs are similar to those just seen, as her additional earnings cause her to forfeit first FIS, then housing benefit. Of course, it is as we saw unusual for wives of unemployed men to work at all, because of the very low retention ratios they face through the loss of their husband's supplementary benefit.

POLICY PROPOSALS FOR THE POVERTY TRAP

The major proposal for eliminating the poverty trap is the 'negative income tax' (espoused among others by Milton Friedman), according to which work-income would be substantially supplemented by some percentage (the marginal tax rate) of its shortfall below a defined 'poverty level'. This percentage is not typically proposed to be the same as the marginal tax rate on income above the poverty level.

NIT abolishes the high MRTs while retaining acceptable distributional effects. Figure 2.5 illustrates one such case where the NIT is 66 per cent below, 33 per cent above, this level.

Objections have been of two sorts. First, some people have a preference for transfers in kind rather than in cash to the poor, to ensure consumption patterns are constrained in a 'desirable' way. Secondly, NIT has been argued to be administratively impossible before the tax system is computerized. The previous Conservative administration abandoned it for this reason. However, computerization is now imminent and NIT could be phased in to fit in with it.

In practice, FIS and rent/rate rebates, which are both cash transfers, dominate the current UK system; passported benefits are significant but have very low take-up rates. Even if they were

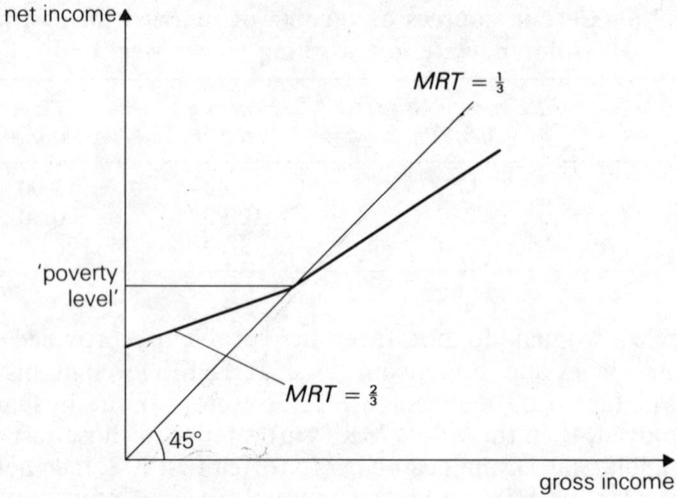

Figure 2.5 Negative income tax illustrated

retained on the grounds that money for prescriptions, dental work etc. should be tied to these things, the replacement of FIS, housing benefit and tax/NI by NIT would be a very substantial improvement. In the next chapter, we set out a detailed NIT system which deals with this set of problems.

CONCLUSION

In this chapter we have identified the faults in the tax and benefit system – summarized by their effects, the poverty and unemployment 'traps'. We have also identified three main elements needed in reform:

(1) limiting the level of and terms of benefits for the out-of-work;
(2) rises in tax thresholds;
(3) replacement of means-tested benefits to low-paid workers by a negative income tax.

We turn in the next chapter to a detailed consideration of how these reforms might be put into effect.

3

Reform of the Tax/Benefit System and How to Pay for It

SECTION I: SOME PRINCIPLES

Any proposals to 'reform' taxes and benefits cost money. This means inevitably that, to be credible, measures must be proposed also to raise the money involved. In this chapter we partially reprint and update an earlier study (Minford, 1984) in which a complete package of public sector reforms, with no net PSBR cost, was sketched out.

The purpose of this chapter is to analyse the mechanisms with which we are trying to achieve our social objectives by state expenditure and to enquire whether we could design mechanisms that achieve the same objectives better. Our purpose is not to attempt to persuade anyone, least of all politicians or the British public, to change their objectives. Some may wish to do that, and all of us have varying ideas about social objectives at different times. But they lie outside the scope of our discussion.

Briefly, we shall simply assume that the British people care about the poor, the disabled, the sick and the old; that they wish to achieve civilized and widely shared standards of education; that they wish the realm to be adequately defended, law and order to be preserved, economic infrastructure to be maintained, and other equally obvious purposes. We shall also take it as axiomatic that they would like more rather than less of all these desirables but that, with the finite resources of the economy, *given* the mechanisms of production and consumption, they recognize the necessity to allocate priorities as these resources expand and contract and that they are fully capable, through the political process widely defined, of this exercise in allocation. Give the people the information about what they can have, and they will choose wisely and in the general social interest.

Our focus is thus on the mechanisms of production and consumption which condition people's choice. They are the proper focus for the economist, since it is likely that others will neglect them – out of technical ignorance – while the economist may see something useful that could 'add to the cake' from which they are choosing.

THE EFFICIENCY OF THE GOVERNMENT EXPENDITURE MECHANISM

There are three aspects of 'public expenditure' which require to be distinguished:

(1) Much state expenditure involves public *production*. The state provides the capital and the management, and hires the labour for such products or services as primary and secondary education, the National Health Service, and the nationalized industries. Obviously, not all state expenditure goes on government produced goods and services; one example is the defence goods industry which is very largely private, another is the universities, which are privately owned and run though heavily subsidized by the state.

(2) Much state expenditure involves state *purchase* on behalf of the public to whom the goods and services are provided at prices different from those they would have paid if they had bought them privately. Examples of government purchase from the private sector are defence products for the armed forces, drugs and equipment for the NHS, roads and their maintenance, council houses and maintenance. Where the state (local or national) owns the production, it is usually the main or only customer in its role as government purchaser. The prime examples here are primary and secondary education and the NHS. But in nationalized industries this is not so, as the private sector – companies and individuals – are the major customers. Finally, a lot of state expenditure does not involve public purchase, notably cash transfers (such as pensions, supplementary benefits and debt interest), which go straight into people's pockets for them to spend in the open market. These are best thought of as part of the tax/transfer system by which the state distributes income both *within* one generation and (by borrowing and deferring tax) *between* generations.

(3) State expenditure invariably requires *taxation*, whether present or future (if funds are borrowed). It is usual in discussing state expenditure theoretically to assume that this taxation takes

the form of 'lump sum transfers' (i.e. a poll tax – the only sort of tax which causes *no* economic inefficiency or 'disincentive effect'). But in practice no modern government makes significant use of poll taxes, for the obvious reason that they are very 'regressive', hitting the poor as hard as the rich (or harder relatively to income). Rather, governments have used income and expenditure taxes (including national insurance fund contributions). They have also used inflation, which taxes people according to their holdings of non-indexed financial assets, such as money, government bonds and occupational pensions (how much depending on how far ahead the inflation was anticipated). Borrowing without default (either explicit or implicit via inflation) can only defer taxation, but in practice because of the effect on interest rates, it often leads to inflation as a way of easing the debt burden. Whichever of these routes is chosen as an alternative to poll taxes creates a loss of economic efficiency which, of course, must be studied as part of the debate on state expenditure.

We now evaluate the efficiency dimension of each of these aspects.

State Production

In principle we can visualize the state being a producer of 'widgets', operating alongside competing private producers (who thus deprive it of monopoly power) and enjoying no subsidy (or equivalent privileges such as preferential tendering for government contracts). But this is very rare. For once the state *is* a producer of widgets, its direct interest, as a corporate entity consisting of managers, tax gatherers, employees, public sector unions and politicians, becomes the maximization of its returns (broadly defined to include non-monetary returns such as prestige, power and security of tenure) by hedging the company around with protective devices. The most effective device is monopoly power, which in practice is enjoyed by the vast majority of state producers. Examples are nearly all the nationalized industries, schools and the NHS (a monopoly of 'free' medicine, best treated as a different product from private medicine under present institutions).

But monopoly is not always so readily to hand. When the Government took over British Leyland (BL), it was unable to confer on it a monopoly of cars, as the British consumer would not have tolerated it. The state can then subsidize the producer or erect a tariff (or equivalent) barrier, which is the same as simultaneously subsidizing the producer and taxing the consumer by equal percentages. In the case of BL, the Government *both* gave a direct, overt subsidy (which still continues) *and* installed a covert tariff barrier by sanctioning a producers' cartel to raise UK prices. The Japanese, who might not have co-operated with the European multinationals operating this cartel, were coerced by the British Government into accepting 'voluntary' quotas and, since they could not compete for extra business, were content to let their car prices rise in line. This cartel still continues, though it has come under attack and the present Government has agreed in principle that it should end.

The cost to society – the residents of the UK, its 'consumers' and 'taxpayers' – of such protective devices can be measured by the well-known technique (due originally to Alfred Marshall), that of 'consumers' surplus' lost, that is, the pure waste of resources due to the *inefficiency* fostered in their use. There is nothing controversial about this method of measuring losses; all economists accept and use it. Although a variety of more refined measures have been developed in recent years, as well as new and ingenious ways of measuring it in practice, we are interested here only in a rough idea of the orders of magnitude and will stay with Marshall's formulation, as applied, e.g. by Harberger (1964).

First, monopoly power. The cost to society is illustrated in figure 3.1. The monopolist raises price above the competitive equilibrium and in so doing wastes resources. While the appropriateness of this measure for *private* industry has been questioned (Littlechild, 1981) because of the *dynamic* nature of private competition, the questioning does not apply to state monopolies where competition is almost invariably removed.

In the UK, the openness of the economy has meant that, if tariff and equivalent barriers were eliminated, foreign competition might often be sufficient to eliminate monopoly power in the markets for goods. Indeed UK policy in general has been to ensure that trade barriers come down on the products of the private sector, but this policy has been applied only loosely – if at all – in the state sector, since much of government production is of non-traded goods and services (education, medicine, rail and road transport, electricity). Where imports could have meant competition, as with coal and BL, they have been restricted. In the state sector, therefore, monopoly is likely to be serious. As for the size of welfare loss, the elasticities of demand probably lie in a low range (perhaps 1.5–3.0), given the limits on even indirect competition. This suggests sizeable welfare loss, ranging from 10 per cent to 30 per cent of turnover.

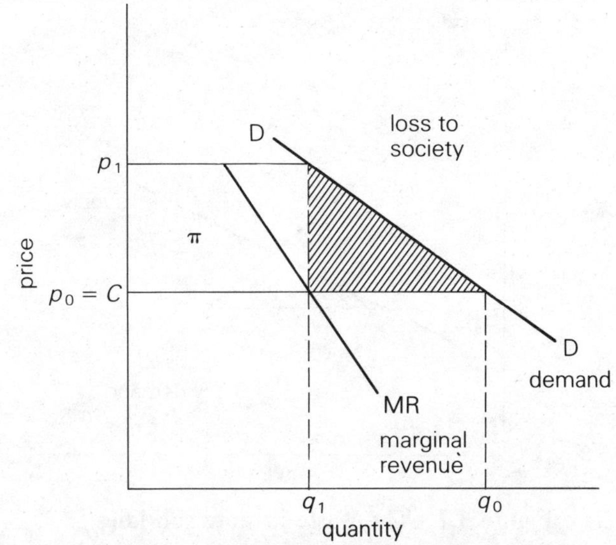

Figure 3.1 The waste in state monopoly

The monopolist sets marginal cost, *C* (inclusive of normal profit), equal to marginal revenue, MR, reduces output from q_o to q_1, raises price from p_o to p_1. The loss to society shown in the shaded area represents the difference between what people would have paid for each extra unit (over and above q_1) and what it would cost the monopolist to provide it (i.e. his marginal cost), these differences for each extra unit are then added up to give this area. The monopolist's excess profit is shown by the area marked π. It turns out that an approximation to the loss of surplus as a proportion of the monopolist's revenues is 0.5 of the monopolist's excess profit rate on sales $= 0.5\pi/p_1q_1$ and this in turn is equal to 0.5/(the price elasticity of demand). For example, a monopolist whose elasticity is 2.5 (i.e. a 1 per cent rise in price would reduce demand by 2.5 per cent), would cause a social loss of one fifth of the value of his operations (with excess profits of 40 per cent of sales). He is wasting this much of the resources he controls.

The costs of national loss from subsidies and tariffs to state producers not protected by monopoly can be calculated analogously. Figures 3.2 and 3.3 illustrate the loss for the usual case of a good entering the international trade. These losses can be simply explained. The producer subsidy induces more production resources

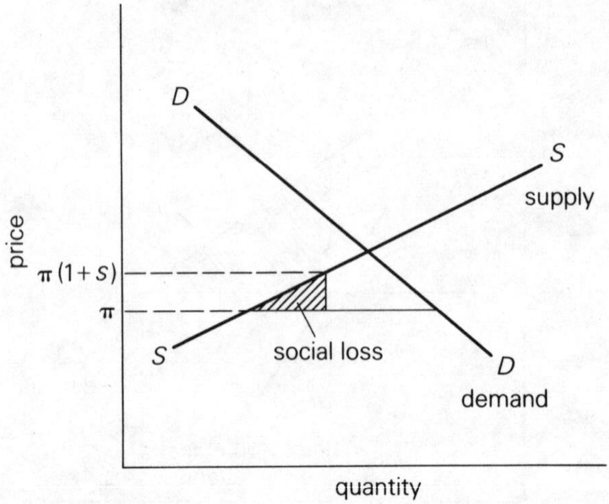

Figure 3.2 The waste in state subsidies

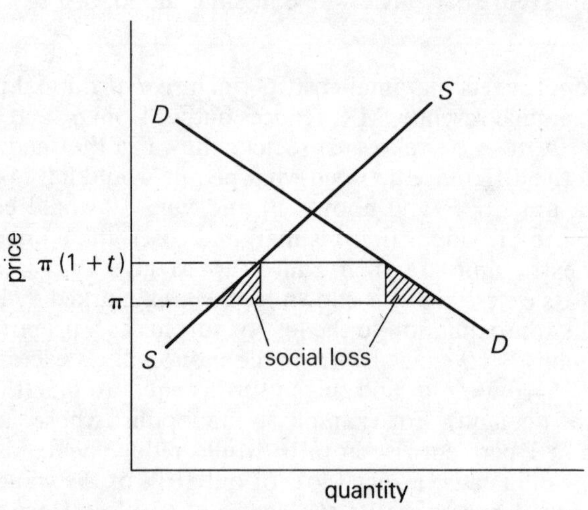

Figure 3.3 The waste in state tariffs

s and t are the subsidy and tariff rates respectively; π is the world price which would prevail on the domestic market for producers and consumers alike if there were no intervention. With a subsidy (figure 3.2), the price received by producers rises to $\pi(1+s)$, and they move resources into the industry. The cost to society for each extra unit

continued on next page

continued

is the difference between the price required by the producer to cover his marginal costs (as shown by the *SS* curve) and the cost to society of buying the produce abroad at π. Adding these extra costs up for the extra units involved gives the shaded area.

With a tariff (figure 3.3), not only is all this happening, but consumers also pay over the world price at $\pi(1+t)$; in addition to the cost above, there is the cost to society from consumers reducing their purchases. On each unit reduction, the loss is the difference between what that unit was worth to them (i.e. what they gave up by not buying it) and the world price at which they could have obtained it.

The approximation to these sources of social loss are:

$0.5 \times$ price elasticity of supply $\times s^2 =$ loss due to subsidy (as a proportion of production).
$0.5 \times$ price elasticity of imports $\times t^2 =$ loss due to tariff (as a proportion of imports).

Again, there has been a lot of work on these sorts of costs, especially on tariffs and international trade. Elasticities of import demand for commodities (at the level of industries, such as 'footwear', 'rubber products') in the range of 1–3 are typical (Stern, Francis and Schumacher, 1976).

to enter the subsidized industry, thus wasting resources since they could produce more profitably elsewhere. A tariff not only subsidizes the producer of the protected commodity in this way but also raises the price to the consumer over the true (world) cost, so diverting demand and reducing the consumer's welfare.

Of these sources of waste in state production the main one is probably the monopoly element. It is not unreasonable to suppose – as discussed earlier – that between 10 per cent and 30 per cent of state production is pure waste, mainly as a result of monopoly power. The value added in government production is around one-third of GNP, so the waste here could be from 3 per cent to 10 per cent of national income, or some £9 to £30 billions (the second figure exceeds the cost of the NHS). The UK evidence from privatization and deregulation to this date has already shown significant savings, see table 3.1; for example, on contracted out local authority and NHS services savings have been running at around 25 per cent deregulated and long-distance bus fares have fallen 40 per cent in real terms.

Table 3.1 Some effects of privatization and deregulation

(a) Privatization

Company	*Performance since privatization/ deregulation*
British Aerospace	Sales at record levels; orders doubled.
Cable and Wireless	Pretax profits more than doubled.
Amersham International	Turnover up 20%; pretax profits up 22%.
National Freight Corp.	£8.5 m profits 1983/4 – previous year only broke even.
Britoil	Post-tax profits up 35% in 1983
Assoc. British Ports	Profits up from £1.5 m to £6.8 m in first half year following privatization.

Contracting out (sources: Public Service Review, and press reports)

(i) National Health Service ancillary service: Savings to District Health Authority estimated at £9.4 m a year, including:

Authority	*Savings £p.a.*
Medway	357,000
N.W. Surrey	210,000
Huntingdon	200,000
E. Surrey	150,000
Redbridge	143,000

(ii) Local Authority services: Savings to local authorities estimated at £15 m a year including:

Authority	*Savings £p.a.*
Wandsworth B.C.	2,600,000
Merton B.C.	1,800,000
Wirral B.C.	1,400,000
Ealing B.C.	1,300,000
Kent B.C.	1,100,000
Cambridgeshire C.C.	700,000
Dudley B.C.	600,000
Southend B.C.	600,000
Eastbourne B.C.	500,000
Milton Keynes B.C.	488,000

(Estimated percentage savings on contracted out: about 25%)

(b) Deregulation

Transport Act (1980)	Between 1980 and 1983 fares on long-distance bus services fell on average by 40% in real terms. Seven hundred new services introduced.

continued over

Table 3.1 (continued)

Hereford bus experiment	The trial deregulation of bus services in Hereford resulted in lower fares on the most popular routes and more frequent buses for suburban commuters. Subsidies fell by a third.
Oil and Gas Act 1982	Since the Act, 70 wells have been drilled in the Southern Basin of the North Sea (to July 1984), compared with only 8 in the previous 3 years.
Health and Social Security Act (1984)	The ending of the monopoly in the dispensing and selling of spectacles has resulted in cut-price glasses being available in Woolworths, and more competitive pricing in many opticians.

The Cure in Principle for the Waste Caused by State Production

Long experience of political pressures shows that, if something is produced by central or local government, it is very hard to avoid the addition to it of substantial monopoly power or protection. It is utopian to think that production could remain 'public' and yet be disciplined by competition. The only remedy is for production to be private and, simultaneously, for any residual monopoly power to be broken up, any protection to be removed – in short, simultaneous 'privatization' and competition.

This process has no necessary implications for the existence of the 'welfare state'. Defence *production* is mainly private but its products are bought by *government*. In some countries (such as Argentina) the defence industry is government owned, and the government has to spend *more* resources on defence (or get worse quality) to allow for the waste involved in state production. Thus, if the total resource budget for welfare spending were to be maintained, privatization and competition would certainly *increase* the value for money – probably rather substantially – of that unchanged spending by cutting out the waste in *production*.

Once this crucial conclusion is fully grasped – and it has not been in much recent debate – it should become common ground between defenders of total welfare spending *per se* and those who wish to see less of such spending by the state (for reasons to be examined below), that, if nothing else, privatization *and* competition (from now on 'privatization' for short) should be pushed ahead. Coal, gas, electricity, railways, hospitals, schools, car producers, and all the other now state-owned production units should compete for the private and government customers' business as private *production* units (see also Beesley and Littlechild, 1983, for a useful discussion).

The details may have to be different in each industry to allow for technological characteristics. For example, it would make little sense to allow two telephone companies to offer a parallel set of telephone lines. A better solution is to sell a franchise for operating and maintaining a single network for a limited period, at the end of which the franchise would be resold to the best contender. This is an example of a 'natural monopoly', of the concept of which much play was made when nationalization was first introduced in Britain. A natural monopoly is one where for technological reasons (economies of scale) it is most efficient for only one company to operate. But, as has now widely been explored in economic analysis and case studies, and as the example shows, *potential* competition – in the sense of 'contestability' or the threat of new suppliers – can be effectively preserved even in these cases (Baumol, 1982). Often competition can be strengthened beyond the point of the example given by carefully separating parts of the operation that have economies of scale from the bits that do not and limiting the franchise arrangement to the natural monopoly parts. To follow the same example, the telephone *lines* should not be duplicated and their operation and maintenance could be franchised, but telephone *services* (i.e. installing and maintaining telephones, operating switching networks, sending messages) could compete freely in significant numbers on these lines.

We return below to the detailed possibilities for privatization in a variety of major services now produced by the state. At this stage we note the principle that society must benefit from privatization in a way that meets the approval of all sections of *consuming* opinion, including those who desire *more*, not *less*, welfare spending.

Why then is it retarded? The answer is obvious: producer pressure groups are likely to be damaged, and see no chance that society will recompense them for their loss of producer privilege under privatization, and so oppose it. For when producers have monopoly power, resources are transferred towards them at the expense of the consumer. In the process the pure waste we have evaluated occurs, because the way in which producers achieve this transfer is by raising prices and so driving a wedge between the true competitive costs of the product and its value to the consumer.

There is a paradox here. Society – i.e. consumers – could 'buy off' these producers, give them all they now get in resources as a gift from the taxpayer, and in return demand that they cease their monopoly practices. As a result society would at least recoup the pure waste we have isolated, even if consumers, other than those in these producer groups, would not get back the transfer.

But of course this procedure is in principle dangerous and in practice impossible. It is dangerous because it implies propriety in the exercise of monopoly power; in principle monopoly power is not acceptable and rightly so since it damages society. Were society to legitimize it *post facto*, it would encourage monopoly further.

It is also impossible for two reasons. First, because it is improper, producers exercise it *covertly* while claiming they do no such thing. Their actions are 'in the public interest' because of the 'special circumstances' of the industry, because 'competition would cause instability'; and there are other such specious arguments. How then can society ask them, in return for a gift, to do that which 'they are not doing'? There is no overt basis for buying them out, or making a 'deal'.

Second, how could society – supposing it achieved this arrangement – police it? It is practically impossible to make reliable estimates of the true internal costs of a corporation without competitors, for it will conceal or pad them.

It follows that a policy of 'bribing the monopolists' is useless; but indeed the experience of those who have dealt with protection gangs would have confirmed this already. The bribe is taken and the screw is left as tight, or tightened if the bribe is regarded as a sign of weakness – Danegeld, in short.

So producer groups will resist, the public in general will (apart from the producer minority) unanimously wish for them to be overcome, and government has the difficult – but ultimately necessarily rewarding – task of pressing ahead with privatization against producer obstruction. The present experience of British Telecom and the threatened difficulties over NHS ancillary work (such as laundry) are classic illustrations.

The principles could not be clearer, and it is to the credit of this Government that privatization has been vigorously embraced. But there is a long, long road to travel yet in implementation.

We now turn to the second aspect of state expenditure, consumption, where the Government has shown much less clarity of mind and firmness of purpose, and the academic and public debate is hopelessly confused.

State Consumption

We now have to ask the key question, is there waste or justification for the state to buy goods and services (such as medicine, doctors' services, education, armaments, bridges and roads) on behalf of the public, using their taxes, rather than let individual consumers/taxpayers buy these goods and services with their own untaxed money directly from the producers?

There is one type of product or service for which government purchase can be justified under certain circumstances, viz. something which, once bought and installed, can give an extra person pleasure or benefit at 'low' or zero cost ('low' means smaller than the average cost of buying it) whatever the direct cost of utilization or indirect cost of inconvenience to other users. The classic example is a park; once bought and set up, extra people can enjoy it (at least up to the point where congestion sets in) without imposing costs on the park budget or on other people using it. Arguably, therefore, it pays society for the park to be used up to the point where an extra person doesn't use it because he has better things to do and not because he can't pay the price. It should in other words be free because it costs society nothing for an extra person to use it. The park is said in this argument to be a 'public good' because, if its use was privately bought by individuals at the average cost of park provision from a private operator, it would be under-used; thus it is 'natural'or 'right' that society should buy it and provide it to taxpayers free.

In practice, the argument is viable but must be used with care. *Many* goods have the feature that, once bought and installed, their marginal cost of use is at times lower than their average cost of installation. Once bought and flying a route, aeroplanes can carry an extra passenger for nothing. They are clearly not public goods (Seldon, 1977, has a fairly comprehensive discussion of private goods which masquerade as 'public'). Even when governments buy aeroplanes, as, unfortunately, they do mainly for prestige reasons, they hesitate (except in some lunatic cases) to give seats away in this manner. The reason is that for much of the time planes are full and full prices ought to be charged. To vary prices according to capacity is too complicated and hence expensive (in information costs, for example) to operate. Hence airlines are classed as private goods.

Furthermore, many other goods, while 'public' to a limited degree, are not public enough for the *state* to be involved in their provision.

A squash court has 'public good' qualities, in the sense that extra people can use it at little additional cost, but it is not necessary for the state to buy it and pass it on to a group of local people. Instead, the efficient method of purchase is through a private club. A club comes into existence to deal with just such a localized 'public good'; it charges an 'entrance' fee to a group of users large enough to be willing to finance the building of a squash court, and then it levies a user-cost fee for each game on the players in the club.

The advantage of a private club is that it has a strong incentive to search out people who will benefit and so contribute to the fixed costs of the operations. Those excluded would not contribute and so would not benefit sufficiently to cover *average* costs per person. Clubs will also often offer an 'occasional use' membership or guest fee for people who like to be casual users; this fee will usually be set at marginal cost. There can be a justification for the *state* taking over the club activity only if there is a significant number of users who are unwilling to pay the entrance fee but willing to pay more than the user-cost fee for an occasional game of squash or whatever. The objection to the state taking over, which has to be balanced against this potential justification, is that everyone will have to pay for a facility that only a few more may use. This can clearly lead to under-provision, since the mass of people will have no interest in creating the facilities.

The question one must ask about state provision of goods with 'public good' qualities is therefore: Is the state the 'natural club' for this product? And this boils down to whether its benefits are sufficiently widely spread, either directly in the sense that everyone will or may use it, or indirectly in the sense that everyone enjoys the availability. For example, air/sea rescue facilities may give the public in general pleasure because they want people not to perish in sea crossings, mountaineering, etc. This is the question and it must be posed very carefully and answered by those in the debate. A few examples of fairly obvious 'public goods' (*full* status) are: defence, police and economic infrastructure such as trunk roads and sewers. But we will attempt a finer discussion later in this chapter.

Having attempted to define public goods in principle, we now discuss the cost to the public if a *non*-public good (henceforth a 'private' good) is provided free (or at a subsidized rate) to the public and financed by taxation.

We can use the same Marshall technique as above for measuring this waste in public consumption. The possibility is illustrated in

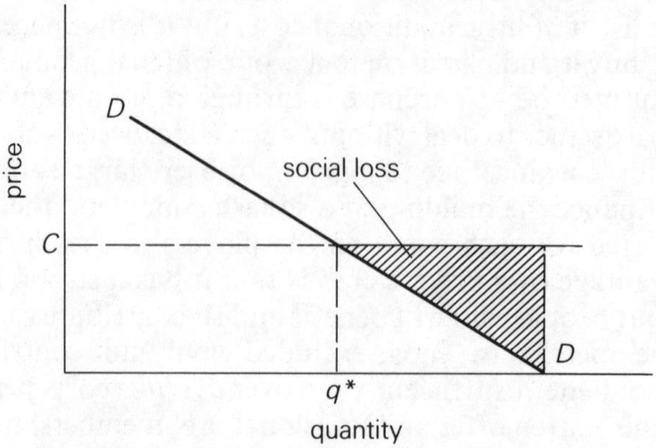

Figure 3.4 The waste in state consumption

The loss is the difference for each extra unit over q^*, the optimum number of units, between the cost of the service and the extra benefit to consumers as given by the *DD* curve. The approximate value of this loss as a fraction of the costs of production is

$$\tfrac{1}{2} \times \frac{\text{the price elasticity of demand } (\eta)}{1+\eta}$$

This is potentially a very large number. For example, if the elasticity of demand is one, the waste would be a staggering 25 per cent of production.

figure 3.4: here we assume that the state provides *all* that people want of the good.

As figure 3.4 makes clear, the cost of this over-provision could be massive. It is for this reason that the state would typically *ration* goods that it provides free. This conclusion introduces a modification of the problem. Now some goods may be rationed to amounts *less* than consumers would want at cost price, while others may be rationed to *more* (figure 3.5).

We can simplify the problem if the state allows private purchase as well as public. In this case under-rationing (figure 5a) will not arise because the private sector will fill the gap between government provision ($\bar{q}$) and private demand at the full-cost (q^*). In the UK a typical case is plastic surgery, where the state rations *below* what people are prepared to pay for at cost price, and the private sector steps in at the margin.

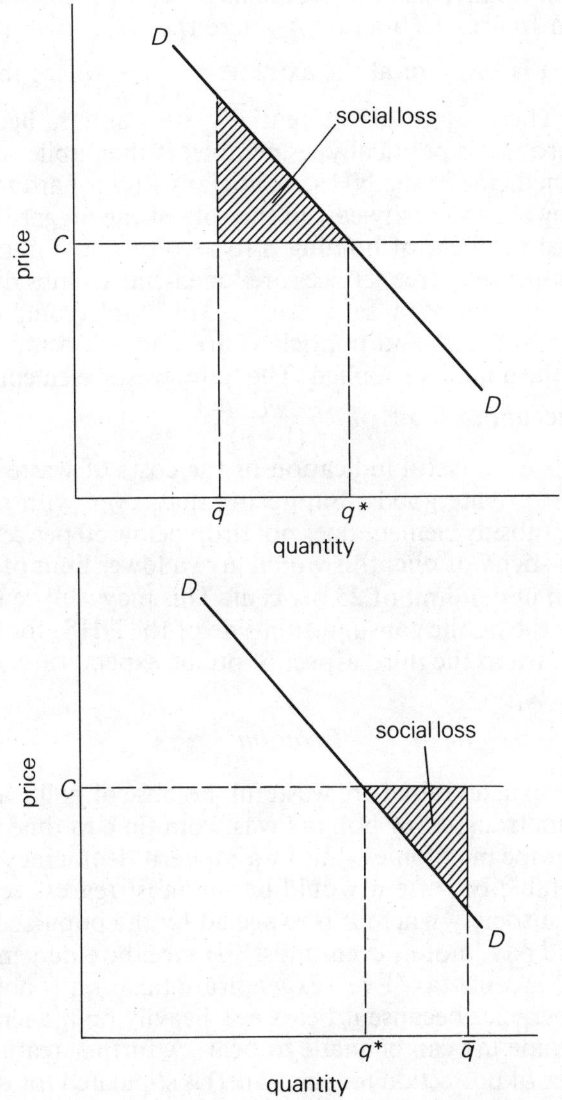

Figure 3.5 The waste in state rationing

The waste here is hard to evaluate because we have no obvious measure of how the ration translates into the subsidy or tax the public is receiving. In principle, the approximation as a proportion of public expenditure is:

$$\tfrac{1}{2}\eta T^2 \text{ or } \tfrac{1}{2}\eta S^2$$

where T is the implicit tax rate, S the implicit subsidy rate.

It follows, finally, that the problems of state purchase arise with the cases in figures 3.5b and 3.4 where the state 'over-provides'; here the cost is $\frac{1}{2}\eta S^2$ or at the extreme $\frac{1}{2}\frac{\eta}{(1+\eta)}$ where there is no rationing. These costs are potentially substantial, because the rationing process is politically vulnerable; if the public *want* more expensive medicine in the NHS, politicians find it hard to deny it, because they are too easily cast in the role of the niggardly villain. The political problem of holding S to zero or a low number is in practice insuperable; free services are 'open-ended' subsidies, in the sense that demand at a zero price is 'infinite' (compared with Exchequer resources) and politicians are under constant pressure to increase the quantity supplied. The 'pure waste' element will tend towards the upper limit of $\frac{1}{2}\frac{\eta}{(1+\eta)}$.

This gives us a useful indication of the costs of waste in public provision of private goods. Supposing that, even with rationing, the implicit subsidy element does not drop below 50 per cent. Then, given an elasticity of one, this would give a lower limit of 12½ per cent, and an upper limit of 25 per cent. This may well be the range of waste on the public consumption side of the NHS, for example.

We now turn to the third aspect of public expenditure, taxation.

Taxation

In practice, all taxes raised are wasteful, because of political factors. A 'lump-sum transfer' or poll tax was from time to time practised in some European colonies, but in a modern democracy it would be unacceptable because it would be the most regressive form of taxation in a society where it is expected by the populace that the 'rich' should pay 'more', even 'most'. Hence the emergence of the 'graduated' income tax. Even expenditure taxation is not liked in many democracies because it bears less heavily on higher incomes than an income tax can be made to bear. A further feature is that a high degree of protection (or safety-net) is stipulated for the poor – presumably because most people feel there is a significant chance of slipping into that category. The result of this general tendency is that marginal tax rates on labour input (i.e. personal effort) are typically high in two main areas of the income scale – high and low incomes: high because high earners have to carry a bigger burden of tax, and low because the desire to protect low incomes implies that extra work for the poor brings little extra income.

The effects of these high marginal tax rates are well documented, less indeed at the top end of the income scale, where evidence is more elusive (perhaps because it involves individuals rather than large groups) than at the bottom end in the 'poverty trap' and 'unemployment trap'. Chapter 1 details recent evidence for the UK from our own research on post-war behaviour for the economy and for 17 individual industries. It suggests that on average across the whole economy a 10 percentage point fall in marginal tax rates on working among the poor unemployed, whether it comes from lowering taxes on the low-paid or benefits of the unemployed, would reduce unemployment by 0.7 million (a rise in *employment* of 3 per cent).

If one accepts that a reduction in government expenditure would lower taxes on the low-paid, and even facilitate a reduction in unemployment benefit, because *post-tax* wages that the unemployed could then obtain in the labour market are higher, the gain to society from lower spending is swelled very substantially. Suppose we allow that every 1 per cent reduction in state spending (about £1½ billion) would permit a fall in *marginal* tax rates on the low-paid (because of skilful distribution of the gains across the tax structure) of 2½ percentage points, employment would on this evidence rise by about 0.7 per cent and output by about 0.5 per cent. This means in effect that, at present tax rates, some 60 per cent of the *total* cost of any extra government expenditure is wasted in collecting the taxes to pay for it; or, in other words, the inefficiency cost of extra taxes is now up to 60 per cent of their yield. It follows that there is a strong absolute case for government expenditure cuts simply to avoid Exchequer outlays and regardless of the other, more subtle, arguments above. Of course, as these bad taxes are reduced (high marginal tax rates on low and high income groups eliminated), this factor will disappear from the calculation. But at present it must be rated as of very high importance in the debate.

PRINCIPLES FOR ACTION

Let us consider what an 'ideal' system would look like. Transitional arrangements can be considered at a later stage in the light of this analysis. Too much discussion considers incremental changes in expenditure of a few percentage points from the system we have. These bring little improvement but create practical difficulties, so providing an easy excuse for their rejection.

Let us enumerate our objectives:

(1) *efficiency* in production wherever at present the state sector is a producer;
(2) optimum provision of *public goods*, which can only be provided by the state;
(3) for private goods, *efficiency* in *consumption* wherever government is at present a consumer;
(4) to ensure that the poor have 'good' education, 'good' health care, and are at all stages of the lifecycle supported above 'subsistence' income, while preserving incentives to obtain work and, once in work, to work for higher wages. Call this objective, in short, *the efficient relief of poverty*.

In the next section we consider in more detail what can be done to achieve each objective.

SECTION II: APPLYING THE PRINCIPLES IN DETAIL

We now proceed to go through in a measure of practical detail each government programme, using as a basis the 1983 Public Expenditure White Paper (Cmnd. 8799. More recent White Papers on Public Expenditure became available after this study had been completed, but the analysis remains unaffected.) We shall get a national target saving for each programme, where possible by heads, and a timetable for it. Decisions on government spending require a long lead time, and the sensitivity of almost every product, service or benefit requires a long transition period. The proposals are therefore all notionally targeted for 1990, with implementation to begin in 1985–6. This framework is convenient for discussion and presentation.

We examine the major programmes in approximate size order of spending and potential economies.

Health, Social Security and Education

We treat these services as one group since they are conceptually related in the 'welfare state', for which our proposals form a package.

Spending in the UK on these services was projected for 1985–6 as shown in table 3.2. We are therefore talking here about roughly half of the planned total of government expenditure of £132.3 billion.

Table 3.2[a]

	£ billion
Education	15.6
Health	16.5
Personal services	2.8
Pensions	17.1
Unemployment, sickness and other social security	22.0
Total	74.0

Note: [a]Includes allocation of Northern Ireland expenditure.

What we propose in general is that the state privatizes government production and replaces its consumption by Negative Income Tax (NIT), conditional on adequate private insurance or other forms of payment. We now discuss each of the services (pensions, health and education) in turn – without reference to NIT – and then turn to social security and NIT ('the efficient relief of poverty').

Pensions

State pensions consist of a basic pension and a recently introduced earnings-related pension. Clearly, society must insist that everyone has some minimum pension sufficient to avoid dependence on society. But we can say at once that on this principle the earnings-related element is no business of society's; it is the individual's choice. So this element can be abolished without delay before it grows too far. People who have contributed to date can have their actuarial entitlement (based on their contribution record) transferred at state expense to a private scheme of their choice or else in cash.

The ultimate object is to transfer *all* pensions, including the basic state pension, into private schemes, financed by private contribution. This transfer is a massive operation and the provision of pensions will have to be undertaken by a number of large institutions. We envisage that the state will allow any institution, profit-making or non-profit, which is licensed to offer pensions, to provide the state minimum package, either on its own or as a part of a bigger package. Market competition will ensure the best terms for individual buyers. On transfer, DHSS offices will have a list of companies or institutions offering the state package at minimum cost, which they will show to the transferring individuals.

The transition problem is that older people will pay more than younger people for a new private pension of given size. Yet the older people will have paid more in taxes and national insurance contributions towards their pension entitlement. To take an extreme example, someone of 65 would have to pay a massive amount for his private 'pension'. In effect, he would have to pay it to himself – not a viable idea.

We suggest that a standard pension plan contribution over working life (say, from 18 to 66) be computed, giving real contributions in each year. Everyone over 18 is then deemed to have participated in such a plan since the age of 18. The state rebates to the pension institution the difference between the contribution a person should make and the standard contribution. The person pays only the standard contribution. This implies that the state in effect pays the economic cost of that part of the pension which the individual would already have contributed if he had been paying on an actuarial basis. Each person may have paid less or more than this in taxes, etc. But as a UK citizen he is *entitled* by the system to this pension, no more, no less, however much or little he paid. Therefore he was deemed by that arrangement to have paid the economic cost. The rebate scheme is just insofar as it involves no retrospective reallocation of rights.

Two important elements remain to be decided: the pensionable age and the nature of indexation in the compulsory 'state package'. At present, pensionable age is 60 for women, 65 for men. But changing working habits and rising life expectations are making these unrealistically low. Most men reckon to work beyond 65, most women beyond 60. Indeed, it is unclear why women who have a longer life expectancy than men should have a *lower* retiring age. It seems appropriate to review these age limits; our supposition is that both men and women should have a pensionable age in the state package of 66.

The question of indexation is really one about what society means by a 'subsistence' or 'minimum' pension. Presumably the concept of subsistence for a pensioner is relative to the real income he(she) will experience during his working life; this will be his 'conditioning'. Society wishes to ensure by compulsion that no one in retirement drops below a living standard which would have been regarded as a minimum by someone of his generation. But since the pensions will be provided privately, they are contracts drawn up at the time of taking out the pension, and the payout cannot be varied from the contract terms. Furthermore, since individuals can always *increase* their contributions and pension if they wish, but cannot *reduce* them, because it is compulsory, the minimum should be set so as not to assume growth in real earnings which may not take place. This suggests that the state package be indexed to prices, so that the final benefit payable is a fixed *real* amount in purchasing power. Pension institutions can easily cost such a package given the existence of indexed bonds. As growth did or did not occur, the minimum package would be revised in real terms (and younger contributors could 'top up' their packages) on a rolling basis. The likelihood of *negative* national economic growth is fairly low, and so low-paid contributors are unlikely to be forced to pay *more* than they can be expected to afford.

These suggestions would ensure that everyone had an acceptable minimum pension and could voluntarily have any higher pension he wished to pay for. Since people would be paying for their own pension, there would be no political pressure to 'raise pensions' – at least of the sort that now obtains. There could be genuine concern about possible pension under-provision by individuals acting freely; this would cause debate about the 'minimum package'. But such concern would be carefully weighed against the obvious personal cost of higher contributions. So the 'free good' element would disappear from the discussion. Pensioners themselves would have *what they paid for* and would not therefore feel cheated. Pensions in short would have been taken largely out of the political arena.

It is sometimes maintained – by Keynesian economists for the most part – that there is a 'problem' with pensions, that they are a transfer to an inactive group which must be paid for in practice by economically active citizens, whether by taxes or via savings channelled into pension funds. In a pay-as-you-go system, pensions in principle are financed by taxes; so resources are 'extracted' without raising interest rates. In a contributory system, as proposed here, pensions are financed by invested funds so that at the moment of payment the pension funds may be net withdrawers of funds from the pool of savings. This puts upward pressure on interest rates, and vice versa if contributions exceed pension payments.

But this macroeconomic approach misses the crucial point that, under the contributory scheme, people save for the pension *they* wish – at least subject to a minimum. This will increase general

Table 3.3 Pension savings (£ billion)

	1985–6	*1990*	*2010*	*2040*
Current pension bill	—	1	4	15
Raising retirement age	1.3	2.2	1.7	0.1

Assumptions:

(a) *Retirement age:* Life expectancy of males 74, females 78; so average reduction in female retired cohorts = 6/18 and of male = 1/9. Overall reduction in pension bill by raising retirement age ≃ 14 per cent, reached in 6 years, diminishing as numbers covered by state pensions fall.

(b) Because 'rebates' are unfunded, pensions paid out by the state are unchanged initially, but gradually fall as the private element in pensions builds up. By 2040, the retired are all on private schemes.

economic welfare by eliminating over-provision. Interest rates will be moving to equate marginal returns on investment with the marginal sacrifice of postponed consumption. For example, periods of high savings (with contributions larger than pension payments) will generate additional investment that will mature later in the periods of low savings and thus even out the swings in interest rates. In the pay-as-you-go system, economically active people are compelled to provide the resources. Interest rates and the capital market are not allowed to perform their function of smoothing out net demands on resources over time. Instead, tax rates vary over time so that a wedge is driven between the rates of transformation of output and consumption over time. (Of course, if the pay-as-you-go pensions are financed by borrowing, there is no *macro*economic difference for any given pension stream; but there is still the *micro* difference that people cannot decide on the pension level for themselves.) Another possibility is that people anticipate their future tax liabilities (i.e. the taxes required to pay future pensions) and save up to meet them. In this (unlikely) case funded private and public pay-as-you-go pensions have the same effect, generating exactly the savings expected to be required to pay the pensions. The other advantages of private pensions still apply.

The fiscal savings of our proposals are now calculated on the assumption that pensions are indexed to their current purchasing power value (table 3.3).

Health

The ultimate objective here is to have everyone covered by a minimum standard of 'comprehensive' health insurance. The insurance policy would specify a minimum medical expenditure per year below which no claim would be paid to the insured (the same effect could be achieved by a 'no claims bonus'). For serious illnesses amounts above this minimum would be reimbursed 100 per cent (provided the expenses were incurred in a 'no-frills' manner). For illnesses of intermediate expense there would be a sliding scale, with some degree of co-insurance by the insured person.

With everyone insured in this way and paying cash for treatment by doctors and in hospital, health provision would be privatized, but in such a way as to create competition in *each* geographic area. So that no one consortium of companies could have a monopoly of the hospitals in any area, hospitals would be sold off in 'lots' from assorted areas. Doctors' practices are, of course, privately owned, but current 'demarcation' of patients would cease, and patients would be able to switch doctors freely. New practices could be set up at will, and without licensing by restrictive medical panels; and they would, of course, be subject to the truth-in-trading laws governing all consumer activities.

As with pensions, there is a transitional problem that older people will pay more for insurance than younger people, even though they have contributed through taxes, etc. Again, a system of rebates will be required in the transition. A standard package would be used as a yardstick for the rebates for people who must pay more because of advancing age. Similarly, those who cannot obtain standard terms because of chronic sickness would be rebated. Some would effectively be non-insurable, and here the rebate would amount to meeting the bills as if they had been insured in the standard way.

With these rebates, there would be no 'cash flow' problem as with the pension case (where the rebated pensions were consequently 'unfunded'), because illness (unlike age) is a chance occurrence. A competitive health insurance industry will charge premiums which generate a cash margin over the cash outflows on medical bills. With a stable population structure there is no reason for these outflows to vary systematically over time. In effect, the health insurance industry would immediately take over all medical bills to the extent of insured risk, and individuals would pay the uninsured element. The state would now immediately pay less than before insofar as individuals are: (a) paying the uninsured element; (b) paying for their own insurance. The rebates would therefore be the residual cash cost left to the state. In effect, the state would continue to pay the health bill for the chronically sick and the aged at the time of the changeover, as well as a proportion of the bill for the middle-aged.

The fiscal savings in this case would be of the (very rough) order shown in table 3.4.

Table 3.4 Health savings (£ billion)

1985–6	*1990*	*2010*	*2040*
4	6	12	16

Assumptions:
State subsidizes households' insurance to the extent that their premiums exceed the 30-year-old rate. Average premium income from 14 million households (at least £300 p.a. average per household based on rates quoted in table 3.6) would contribute £4.0 billion initially; this assumed to be initial reduction in health cost to be met by state. Ultimate reduction, reached by 2040, is total health bill which for simplicity we assume constant at 1985–6 levels.

On the production side, privatization side-steps the need for a massive government reorganization of NHS management (sensibly suggested by Griffiths, 1983) in the context of continued state provision. The new private owners of hospitals will themselves take the action necessary to be profitable in the face of stiff competition. The trouble about attempting further NHS reorganization is that the whole process can be blocked by numerous powerful pressure-groups. New management may have an impossible task so long as hospitals remain under government control and thus politicized. Selling off hospitals, though not politically easy, is a self-contained operation which, once carried out, guarantees future efficiency. Privatization is indeed far from unpopular with the employees in many cases; and the incoming owners can offer incentives to them to co-operate.

Education

In education the objective is to have everyone pay for their own school and university fees, and to make primary and secondary education compulsory as now. At the same time we wish to have education services competitively provided in the private sector. As with pensions and health, the poor will be looked after by the negative income tax.

There appear to be rather limited transitional problems on the consumption side, unlike pensions and health. The reason is that parents who have to pay school fees will benefit for most of their working lives from the lower taxes which will result from the transfer of the education bill to private pockets. Students who now pay university fees, whether by cash or via loans (as is most probable), will receive the 'pay-off' from their university education in their future income stream.

The problem of transition is therefore really one of ensuring political acceptability by changing gradually. A sudden shift in the environment could cause straightforward cash flow problems for people whose current incomes are low relative to their future incomes. The disturbance to financial plans, caused by a shift in government policy, should be reasonably cushioned by the government. We therefore propose a simple 5-year transitional period, with people paying one sixth of the fees in the first year and full fees in the sixth year (1990).

More dificult in most people's eyes is the process of privatization of schools. Universities are already non-governmental (although non-proprietary), and competition can easily be introduced by allowing them freedom to fix their own fees and to advertise, neither of which they do currently.

Schools are at present state-owned and the teachers in them have no management experience; the management function is carried out by the local education authority. The exceptions are of course, the private schools of which there are far more since the abolition of direct-grant status.

The move of these direct-grant schools into the private sector is revealing. Most have made the transition smoothly, despite having been substantially controlled by local authorities previously through their control of most income. There is no reason to believe that management expertise cannot similarly be injected into (or found within) state primary and secondary schools. Many headmasters and staff would no doubt welcome the freedom to manage their affairs in the profitable and efficient manner implicit in a move to the private sector.

The procedure to follow would be similar to that with hospitals. To ensure competition, no one education 'firm' could own more than a small proportion of the schools in any catchment area. The schools system could be sold to private firms in diverse 'lots', and not necessarily all at once, but rather spread out over the transition period or even longer.

Some local authorities would, no doubt, refuse to co-operate. This co-operation could not be withheld indefinitely in the face of parliamentary authority, but while it continued to be withheld the parents in that area would have the freedom to pay school fees to *any* school, including those outside the local authority's control. In itself, this ability to escape would create competitive pressure on the authority to provide a good school service. *Any* private firm would be free to set up a new school in the area to compete with the local authority should *it* feel there is a market because the authority's schools are poor. If planning permission were withheld, the firm could appeal to the Department of Environment. Thus, even where there is local authority non-co-operation, privatization would be made effective.

Some critics of school privatization argue that the best schools will 'cream off' the best pupils and the worst schools will get the 'worst', becoming 'ghetto' schools. This misses the point that competition will create incentives to produce good schooling for *all* parts of the market, from those with vocational or artistic bent to those with high academic abilities, from children with handicaps to those with exceptional gifts. Parents with 'different' children will look for a *good* 'different' school. A firm which can provide that sort of school will capture the market. Schools will, of course, tend to specialize in particular markets (academic, vocational, artistic, handicapped, etc.), but there will be competition in *each* sector to ensure high quality.

'OK', the critics go on, 'but what about standards? Your good low-level-ability school will not give an adequate grounding in basic academic skills – the 3Rs and so forth'. It is true that there will have to be inspection of schools, to check that they satisfy the standard of education society wishes to be achieved. The Schools Inspectorate of the Department of Education and Science already performs this function, which would thus be continued. (That part of the Inspectors' Report dealing with compulsory 'basic' standards would be mandatory, other parts would be for information and advice only.) But the problem at present is that, *without* local competition, a school criticized by the Inspectorate can avoid reform. In the new environment, it could not, because the inspectors' report would alert parents who would withdraw their children to a local rival.

The fiscal effects of these plans are obvious enough. State expenditure on education is assumed to be phased out over the five-year transitional period, saving £3.5 billion in 1985–6 and the full £16 billion from 1990 onwards.

Government (i.e. local education authority) involvement in the *production* of education could continue patchily across the country for much longer, depending on the mechanics of disposing of schools to private education firms. But there would be little incentive to prolong state ownership of schools once competition had become significant, because the management pressures on local authorities – to be able to compete effectively – would be too great for them. They would have a strong incentive to sell out.

A last word about universities. It is sometimes said that, by charging university fees to students, the study of 'non-vocational' subjects – such as English or the Classics – would be discouraged, even eliminated. This will not necessarily be so; and to the extent that it seems socially desirable to preserve aspects of our culture, an explicit subsidy to threatened subjects can be voted by Parliament and distributed in the most cost-effective way to relevant universities. That neglect of non-vocational subjects will not necessarily occur is nevertheless plain. Universities win prestige from their scholarship across a wide range of subjects. *No* university wishes to be a single-subject place, for the benefits from intellectual cross-fertilization are lost. Not *all* universities will wish to have *all* subjects in their portfolios, but it will generally be optimal for some at least to offer any given subject, even if it is not 'commercial', for reasons of intellectual prestige and cross-fertilization. The 'vocational' subjects, such as law, will tend to make large profits which will be used to subsidize prestige subjects. The indirect return to the university from the prestige so attained justifies the cross subsidy.

Personal Social Services

The provision of direct social services is regarded by many as something that the family should undertake. When the state provides these services, there is serious concern that families feel morally justified in abandoning their responsibilities to the state. This is an unhappy situation. For if families do *not* carry out their responsibilities, and if charities *cannot* cope with the resulting burden, society is unwilling to let the victims of this neglect suffer, and rightly so.

There is an analogy here with education. Suppose parents refuse to send their children to school, preferring to spend their money in some other way. Does society then pay for the children to go to school? If it does, it risks undermining the whole basis of parental responsibility. If it does not, the children may fail to be educated, at least until the parents have been compelled to fulfil their legal obligations.

We do not have to be impaled on the horns of this dilemma. In education it is clear what society should do. It takes legal action against the parents *and* it pays for the children to be educated, while deducting the school fees eventually from parental income through court action.

An analogous solution applies to social services. Society rightly feels that elderly parents and relatives, for example, who cannot manage on their pension plus any special assistance (disability allowances, etc.) are the responsibility of the next-of-kin to help. The same is true of handicapped children. The logical action to take is therefore for such responsibilities to be made legally mandatory, just as child-battering or child-neglect are penalized by the law. Neglect of these family responsibilities would be actionable by the state.

At the same time, neglect *will* occur, either temporarily while legal action is being taken against people responsible, or even permanently if no responsible agents can be identified or found. In these cases of neglect, social services will be necessary, just as police are necessary to maintain law and order. These activities are a public good, for society's interests as a whole are damaged by the neglect.

Some economies in consumption of these services should be possible with this legal approach. As elsewhere there is no reason for these services to be produced by government. There would be no difficulty in privatization as the existing staff would largely find employment in the new private firms.

Possible savings from this would be modest but worthwhile. We suggest 7 per cent (£200 million) in 1985–6 rising to 20 per cent (£600 million) by 1990.

Social Security, Family Benefits, and Unemployment Benefit

We come last, but by no means least, to what we have labelled 'the efficient relief of poverty'. So far we have notionally changed the welfare state into a private service, with people paying their own bills and private firms producing welfare services. But we have stressed throughout that this structure would be subject to provision for the poor by a safety net; they would be able to pay for these services by the provision of negative income tax. They would also be compelled not to forego these services, for the payment of NIT would be conditional on their purchasing them (besides the law being available to compel compliance).

We now investigate how this poverty relief would be established. In many ways it is the most difficult problem to resolve efficiently. At present, society makes a complete hash of it, the symptoms of which are the 'poverty trap' and the 'unemployment trap' described in chapter 2.

Let us begin with the allowances for the poor *in work*.

Our basic idea is simple. A 'subsistence' income is defined for each type of family; this is a true *minimum*, and it is important that it exclude all items not necessary for survival, otherwise the whole system will become hopelessly expensive. Then there is a 'poverty threshold' income defined in relation to social views of the income *above which* help would *not* be willingly given by society. It is also the threshold for ordinary income tax to start. Then the NIT does two things: it never allows income to drop below subsistence and, for incomes less than the poverty threshold, it supplements them by 70 per cent of their difference from that threshold. No *other* benefits of *any* sort – cash or kind – are payable, other than NIT. Hence the marginal rate of tax for the poor will never exceed 70 per cent (unless they are below *subsistence* in which event it will inevitably be 100 per cent). There is thus both relief of poverty and an improved incentive to work harder and better oneself.

The complications arise in 'calibrating' this system so that it is both generous enough to fit society's objectives and not too expensive. This is really for society to decide. Fortunately we have evidence of society's wishes objectively before us in the shape of the family income supplement. We propose to use the FIS rates to calibrate our system, adjusting them for the extra costs of health, education and pension which people will now have to find.

The aim at this point is to use the opportunity of complete restructuring of the personal welfare and tax system:

(a) to abolish or at least reduce to insignificance the 'poverty trap' in which poor people in work face very high marginal tax rates;
(b) to raise significantly net income *in* work for people close to the unemployment trap (whereby taking work will involve little or no gain in income) so as to reduce unemployment;
(c) to simplify the tax/benefit system and so reduce administrative cost.

The method will be simplicity itself. First, we will 'tidy up' the *existing* system of family income supplement, housing benefits and 'passported benefits' by replacing it with a *cash* system of income transfers for people currently in receipt of these benefits. Second, we will abolish the personal national insurance contribution (really an income tax) and raise tax thresholds and child benefits sufficiently to offset the extra costs of buying health insurance etc., *and* to overcome the poverty and unemployment traps. Finally, we will 'dovetail' the cash transfer system into the tax system by making the cash transfer into a negative income tax of 70 per cent below the new tax threshold.

The proposed changes, with their direct Exchequer costs, are thus (the figures all apply to the situation prior to the 1985 Budget):

(1) Replace family income supplement, housing benefit and all benefits in cash and kind ('passported benefits') payable to people receiving FIS, by a *cash* transfer.

(2) Abolish personal national insurance contribution. Revenue cost: £9.7 billion.

(3) Raise single tax threshold from £39 to £79 per week and married tax threshold from £61 to £124 per week. Revenue cost: £16.7 billion (=30 per cent of £2080 p.a. × 11.4 million single taxpayers, +30 per cent of £3275 p.a. × 13.2 million married tax-paying couples, minus allowance for those taken out of tax net, some 5 million single, 2.5 million married, set at, say, £3.3 billion on assumption that on average they had taxable income half-way between old and new thresholds). Other thresholds to rise by the same £s per week: £0.3 billion (15 per cent, difference of average marginal rate from standard rate, × £3275 p.a. × 0.7 million mainly married higher tax payers).

(4) Raise child benefit from £6.85 to £22 per child per week. Revenue cost: £9.8 billion (£788 p.a. × 12.5 million children). This rise in benefit counterbalances the extra cost per child of education and health insurance borne by parents as a result of our reform proposals.

(5) Converting cash transfer, equivalent of current rate as in (1), into 70 per cent negative income tax. Revenue cost: £0.5 billion, the estimated amount of unclaimed in-work benefits.

The total cost of these changes is £37.0 billion. In effect we are 'returning the welfare state to the people', reimbursing them for the cost of paying their contributions but increasing their incentives to work by the higher efficiency with which the whole operation is financed.

It should be clear from the scale of the changes that the poor are *not* being short-changed. On the contrary, the changes make them better off, for the most part substantially. Table 3.5 shows the impact on typical households.

Those on 25 per cent below average incomes are some 18 per cent better off, while those on the *very lowest* incomes have their incomes maintained. Families in between have intermediate income increases. The general rise in incomes for those in the vicinity of the unemployment trap is of the order of 20 per cent, a substantial improvement. People on average incomes have a rise of about 22 per cent, which is around the peak percentage increase. As incomes rise above average, the percentage increase steadily declines. Those with an egalitarian view may declare that this is 'unacceptable'. If so, they have failed to understand that to improve incentives for the poor, the arithmetic *requires* a larger improvement for people on average incomes unless the general marginal tax rate is to rise. Many would regard such a rise however as undesirable on economic grounds. A marginal tax rate (disregarding indirect taxes) of 25 per cent appears to be a desirable aim for the generality of people. At rates much above this it would appear from the size of the black economy (Matthews, 1982) that people's respect for the tax system and general law declines, even if their formal incentives may not be excessively damaged.

We have taken into our calculations here a cut in the standard rate to 25p financed (tables 3.10 and 3.11) by the indirect revenue gain to the Exchequer which results from higher employment and output. We also assume for the same reason the abolition of the higher rates of tax. Nevertheless, there is a higher marginal tax rate for low earners because they are being *subsidized* by the system (and a lower marginal tax rate creates worse problems of incentives for the very poorest, since a steeper 'rate of descent' of net income implies that the 'poverty level' is reached sooner, and at this point the marginal tax rate reaches 100 per cent). Low earners *have* to pay these tax rates as the price of receiving their income subsidy.

Finally this leaves us with the issue of benefits for people *out of work*. Here the key problem is ensuring that available jobs are taken and that low-paid jobs are not prevented from being created and willingly taken by the competing amount of unemployment benefit. Chapter 1 implies that there *are* jobs at *some* rate of pay available

Table 3.5 Overall effect on post-tax[a] income in work ('disposable' basis paying health costs, etc.) £ per week

Income pre-tax	*Single now*	*After*	*Difference*	*Married (M) now*	*After*	*Difference*	*M+1 now*	*After*	*Difference*	*M+2 now*	*After*	*Difference*	*M+3 now*	*After*	*Difference*
160	109	133	24	116	138	20	123	144	21	130	153	23	136	159	23
150	103	126	23	110	130	20	117	137	20	123	144	21	130	151	21
140	97	118	21	104	123	19	110	129	19	117	136	19	124	144	20
130	91	111	20	98	115	17	104	122	18	111	129	18	120	136	16
120	85	103	18	91	110	19	98	116	18	108	123	15	118	130	12
110	79	96	17	85	107	22	96	113	17	106	120	14	116	129	13
100	73	88	15	84	104	20	94	110	16	104	117	13	126	129	3
90	66	81	15	81	101	20	91	107	16	112	114	2	127	129	2
80	63	73	10	79	98	19	97	104	7	112	113	1	128	129	1
70	61	70	9	76	95	19	97	101	4	113	113	—	128	129	1
60	59	67	8	73	92	19	98	98	—	113	113	—	129	129	—

Note: [a]counting 'minimum' cost of health, pension and education costs, as tax *after* change. 'Now' and 'After' show post-tax incomes before and after the change, followed by the difference. 'Now' includes all benefits in cash and kind to which household is entitled. All calculations assume the wife does not work (wife's income – net of her earned income allowance – would under our proposals be aggregated into household income and marginally taxed at 25 per cent or 70 per cent if subject to NIT; the current situation is very complex).

Assumptions in table 3.5
Quotations for private pensions at age 66 (worth indexed £1930 p.a.) and for full health insurance obtained from J. D. Ward and Co., Financial and Insurance Consultants, 55 Lincoln's Inn Fields, London WC2; pensions from Standard Life; health insurance from BCWA. Premiums for indexed pension of £2000 p.a. taken at age 18: £158 p.a. (man), £234 p.a. (woman). For education, costs based on 1983 White Paper per pupil expenditure as follows: primary £800 p.a., secondary £1200 p.a. These costs are averaged over age 0–15 for each child (i.e. approximately £700 p.a.).

For health, BCWA 'Extra Security Scale' for Company-Group-Non-Contributory scheme is used; it gives full refund of hospital or nursing home charges up to the amount charged by a London Post-graduate Teaching Hospital and full refund of all surgeons', anaesthetists', specialist physicians', home nursing, radiotherapy, and all other consultation charges. The premiums charged per person enrolled from age 18 are raised once at age 30 and then remain constant for the rest of the person's life. These premiums are averaged here (with a weight of 0.25 for below age 30) to give: single £97 p.a., married couple £193 p.a., family £227 p.a. In addition, an allowance must be made for visits to the doctor and for the cost of births; these are assumed to be included in insurance with premiums covering average cost as follows: based on average prescriptions issued per head in 1981 (6); doctors' time including overheads at £20 per hour, ¼ hour per visit, 6 visits per person per year = £30 p.a.; also allow £20 p.a. for prescriptions. According to the DHSS, the average birth cost £855 in 1980/1, say £1100 in 1985 prices; averaged over an earning lifetime of 47 years this is £23 p.a. These costs are then: single £50 p.a., married couple £100 p.a., married + 1 £173 p.a., married + 2 £246 p.a., married + 3 £319 p.a. In the pension quoted above, £130 p.a. per person is included to cover the cost of continuing these premiums.

When all the charges people would have to pay after the change are added, we have the data shown in table 3.6.

Table 3.6

(£ p.a.)

	Health insurance	*Pension contribution*	*Education charge*	*Total*	*(£ per week)*
Single	147	196	—	343	(7)
Married	293	392	—	685	(13)
M + 1	400	392	700	1492	(29)
M + 2	473	392	1400	2265	(44)
M + 3	546	392	2100	3038	(58)

continued on next page

continued

These 'minimum costs' are deducted from people's incomes after adjustment for tax/NIT to determine their disposable income after the changes proposed. Before the change disposable income does not have to meet these charges, since the welfare services in question are provided free at the point of purchase (apart from minor charges which have been removed from the extra costs people will have to pay). After the change, the tax thresholds are: single £79 per week, married £124 p.w. Marginal tax rates are 25 per cent *above* the threshold, 70 per cent (NIT) *below*. Child benefit is £22 per child per week.

for the unemployed to do. Our estimates suggest that at rates of pay only 10 per cent below existing market rates, unemployment would effectively disappear. In other words, 2.25 million more jobs exist at rates of pay up to 10 per cent below the rates workers will not now willingly accept. These jobs are not taken (and in many cases potential employers do not even bother to advertise them because of the waste of time and money) because they are too low-paid relative to benefits. Consequently society loses the work and resources that these unemployed *could* do in return for its support of their incomes.

This is lunacy. The community has a right to expect people to work if they can. It will subsidize them if they are low paid by family income supplement or negative income tax *in work*, but at least it gets back from them in return what they *can* contribute to society.

Therefore our principle will be to create inducements for the unemployed to take the jobs that potentially exist at lower wages. That is their contribution as a condition of society's support.

We propose one main way to do this in the first instance, which will be to put a ceiling on benefits receivable as a fraction of previous work income (net of tax, work expenses, etc.). That ceiling would be set at 70 per cent, so providing in general at *least* a 30 per cent incentive to work.

In the longer term we would go further and make unemployment insurance a private matter, to be taken out at personal expense in the market, subject to some minimum cover the state would insist upon. The date for this substantial change in regime is set at 1990, since it is a particularly radical departure, requiring considerable further public education.

Throughout the Victorian period and up to the First World War, unemployment insurance was private, normally provided via trade unions and other voluntary institutions; unemployment fluctuated in a range of 2–10 per cent; averaging around 6 per cent. There is no evidence that the state is better as an insurer than private firms as the problems of checking on fraud are compounded by the difficulties encountered by politicians in this sensitive area. The 'moral hazard' associated with people being voluntarily 'unemployed' for particular jobs is well known and insurers have ways around such problems (coinsurance, escape and fraud clauses, etc.). The state is not particularly efficient in enforcing such devices, witness the ludicrously low rate of benefit withdrawal for improper claims over the past decade, when there is considerable evidence of widespread fraud (black economy, 'foreigners', etc.). (Parker, 1982, gives details of how the state creates moral hazard; Beenstock and Billington (1982) discuss a market-based unemployment insurance system.)

Some say that the proposals would cause 'hardship'. The unemployed are unwilling to take low-paid jobs for which society pays a subsidy in order to ensure that the low-paid have an adequate income in work. The unemployed are therefore *better off* than at incomes at which society feels it appropriate to support people in work. They must be better off unemployed, otherwise they would be willing to take these jobs.

Their living standard would of course be *reduced* if their unemployment benefits were cut; but society has determined appropriate support for people in work. It is no part of its obligation to maintain people in *higher* living standards than that.

These changes to unemployment subsidy, moreover, will occur at a time when taxes on people in work are being cut; therefore net incomes in work will be higher than before (as we have seen by some 20 per cent for those close to the unemployment trap). This implies that the changes will improve the potential incomes of the unemployed if they decide to work – a very relevant improvement in the opportunities facing them.

The direct fiscal savings from this change are fairly modest as its main objective is to get people back to work. This itself, however, causes a substantial indirect fiscal saving estimated later. The estimates of direct savings are £1 billion in the period 1985/6 to 1990, and £6.8 billion in 2010.

Our assumptions are:

(1) 70 per cent ceiling operates from 1985/6 to 1990, with average reduction in benefit of 15 per cent (projected payments to the unemployed in 1985/6 are £6.8 billion including estimated payments in Northern Ireland);
(2) unemployment is held constant at 3 million for these calculations, in order to illustrate the 'worst case' where unchanged policy prevents the recovery of employment; and
(3) by 2010, unemployment insurance is privatized, so that the whole of unemployment benefit is notionally shown as saved, though of course the unemployment projection for 25 years ahead is meaningless.

Nationalized Industries

The external financing requirements of these industries are projected in the White Paper at £1.8 billion in 1985/6. This includes the special grants on current account, notably money to British Rail and to the National Coal Board uneconomic pits (£1 billion in 1983/4). These financing requirements would disappear under privatization, except for the remaining infrastructure elements. But these would be extremely limited under the plans described earlier, and tolls might be collectable from many of them. The saving under this heading would therefore be a very large proportion of the total, and we set it initially at £1.5 billion in 1985/6 rising to £2 billion by 1990.

Industry, Energy, Trade and Employment

The White Paper budget here in 1985/6 is:

	£ billion
Industry	1.1
Energy	0.3[a]
Trade	0.3
Employment	3.3
Other	0.1
Total England	5.1
Wales, Scotland and Northern Ireland	0.7
Total UK	5.8

[a]excludes support for uneconomic coal pits, dealt with above.

The energy expenditure and £0.4 billion of Industry is devoted to support for science and technology. The justification is presumably that companies either cannot see the economic returns in the exploitation of science and technology or that they accrue also and separately to society. Both propositions are dubious.

Companies will always *suggest* they cannot fully exploit opportunities because that strengthens their argument for state money. But on what grounds, *if* such opportunities are profitable, would the state be more likely to know this? It is, after all, the business of these companies to know!

And the 'social return' argument is hard to see for *exploitation* (rather than research itself). It is valid only if the exploitation involves the potential creation of *new* knowledge with returns *beyond* the industry, for society would then benefit from its free dissemination beyond the immediate beneficiaries. But some of this expenditure appears not to be in this category. The promotion of 'awareness' of robotics and information technology is particularly silly, reminiscent of Harold Wilson's 'white heat of the technological revolution'. Technology will be applied by a business if it is profitable. The producers of new equipment will bombard that business with advertising without any help from an over-zealous government. We propose a sizeable cut in these subsidies, reducing them to the support of true general research and development that therefore society should undertake.

Regional support of £0.7 billion accounts for the rest of the Industry budget. Regional policy is better carried out by increasing labour market flexibility. General rises in tax thresholds accompanied by a ceiling on unemployment benefits would do more for the regions in the long run. Selective 'bait' to projects is neither effective nor durable. In the context of our proposed programme of tax/benefit cuts, this regional support should be eliminated.

The Trade budget of £0.3 billion operates regulation and makes miscellaneous grants to shipping, tourism, and civil aviation. But none of these expenditures has any merit except that on regulation, which includes the important watchdog agencies such as the Monopolies and Mergers Commission (MMC). The rest can either be charged for by the industries concerned or is uneconomic. A cut of £0.2 billion is feasible here.

The biggest budget is Employment. The bulk is special programmes operated by the Manpower Services Commission to subsidize labour. These programmes have served as palliatives while taxes, benefits and union power have caused massive labour market distortion. But they are very much less effective than general cuts in taxes and benefits (and, indeed, other measures, discussed in chapters 4–6, reducing union power and other labour market distortions). When these are brought in as planned here, this programme can wither away. A phased cut of £2.8 billion on this account is suggested, which leaves some money to operate some central services and to operate the redundancy payments scheme. The Advisory Conciliation and Arbitration Service (ACAS) and some other labour services could be charged for or privatized (job centres, in particular). Hence the cuts suggested here are as shown in table 3.7.

Table 3.7

	£ billion	
	1985/6	*1990*
Industry and energy	0.4	0.8
Trade	0.1	0.2
Employment	0.4	2.8
Total England	0.9	3.8
Wales, Scotland, and Northern Ireland	0.2	0.5
Total UK	1.1	4.3

Housing

Total housing expenditure (net of sales) is projected at £3.1 billion. It is not broken down, presumably because of the difficulty in predicting how local authorities will use their discretion. In 1983/4 about half went on subsidies to rents and housing associations, the rest on building (net of sales).

It makes little sense to build new council houses while selling off existing ones at a loss and probably also running new ones at a loss. More generally, the principles we have already pursued suggest that subsidizing council house rents and building such accommodation is wasteful. It would be better to allow the private rental sector to operate freely (see chapter 6) and to use Negative Income Tax to help the poor who cannot pay those rents.

It follows therefore that this housing programme should go into *surplus* as sales exceed building and as subsidies are eliminated. This would have to be coupled with freeing the rented sector from existing controls. Hence we target this for 1990 with a gradual build-up to allow progress on this front. With sales projected at £1.3 billion in 1983/4, a surplus of £1 billion is realistic.

The saving here is set at £600 million in 1985/6, rising to £4.1 billion by 1990.

Transport

£1 billion of this is British Rail subsidies already dealt with. The remaining budget is projected at £3.6 billion in 1985/6, and much of this is infrastructure (mainly roads) which *should* be in the public sector budget.

About £½ billion goes on transport subsidies other than to British Rail (mainly for local buses and undergrounds). The justification for these subsidies is said to be to relieve inner urban congestion, but this can be dealt with, e.g., by taxes on car parking space and there is no reason to make a *current* loss on these services. A saving of this order therefore is feasible here; thus £200 million in 1985/6 rising to £500 million in 1990.

Agriculture, Fisheries, Food and Forestry

The agricultural industry has done extremely well out of the British taxpayer and consumer by domestic subsidies and the Common Agricultural Policy (CAP). The Government is committed to bringing down the cost of the CAP sharply in EEC negotiations. That cost is now so high (the resource transfers to our EEC partners have been estimated by the Institute of Fiscal Studies (Morris, 1983), at £3.6 billion p.a., mostly due to the CAP) that it calls into question the whole basis of the EEC if we do not succeed in this objective. An industrial free trade area with strong political links allied with NATO commitments would seem to be a strong candidate for consideration as an alternative to the EEC, and such a deal has been reported to be on offer before. We leave this possibility aside at this stage since EEC changes are under negotiation and may make more drastic suggestions unnecessary.

The domestic subsidy to agriculture is itself running at an amazing £0.9 billion in England and another £0.4 billion in the rest of the UK. There is no *economic* case for this expenditure. The case may be social or environmental, but it is not entirely obvious, given that agriculture is so heavily supported anyway under the CAP. It is a very profitable industry indeed for the efficient. *Prima facie*, the subsidies should be eliminated.

Allowing for some special cases, cuts of £1.0 billion by 1990 are suggested. The Forestry Commission in particular should be abolished and its assets sold (both scenically and economically it is a disaster).

The saving on agriculture therefore is projected at £400 million in 1985/6 rising to £1 billion by 1990.

Defence

At £18.3 billion for 1985/6 this budget is prodigious and increasing rapidly (up 27 per cent from 1982/3 in cash terms). We have no intention of discussing strategic issues here, and refer the reader to the Omega Report on defence (Adam Smith Institute, 1983), which calls for cuts of £1.25 billion, mainly by reorganizing the NATO commitments into a more flexible force, with fewer units stationed expensively and unproductively in West Germany and more use made of volunteer civilian reserves. The Falklands element too at £0.5 billion per year should be reducible. Since the new Argentine regime is also concerned about its massive military budget, negotiations should now make de-escalation possible. Defence purchasing and organization are also criticized in the Omega Report as unwieldy and expensive. That they are so immune to public scrutiny would suggest such a case. More efficiency must be a source of savings, the extent of which we can only guess. The same report sets it at £0.9 billion (roughly 20 per cent on R&D, training, repair facilities and administration) but it could well be much more.

It would seem that savings of £2 billion could be a conservative target for defence by 1990, rising from £1 billion in 1985/6.

Environmental Services

In a total £3.8 billion in the White Paper budget, £0.5 billion goes for water, £2.4 billion for local services (dustbins, parks, etc.) and the rest in various forms of support for regional 'environmental development' (such as clearing urban dereliction). Water services should be charged for or privatized. This also goes for many other local services (refuse collection has begun to move this way).

A partial list of other services which could be contracted out (with probably substantial gains in efficiency) includes architectural, legal and accounting services, public relations, printing, computing, office cleaning, plant nurseries, management of parks, gardens and sport facilities, cemeteries and crematoria, golf courses, public baths, and laundries. Construction work is partly privatized and could be contracted out entirely. This is also true of emergency services, where independent contractors could undoubtedly provide a cheaper standby service than is currently offered. There is increasing experience of privatization of some of these services by some councils. This experience suggests possible cost reductions of up to 50 per cent.

A possible saving from privatization in these areas would be £1 billion (around 40 per cent) by 1990 rising from £400 billion in 1985/6.

'Environmental development' is really a euphemism for providing more park land in urban areas, and as such, it is a 'public good'. The question really is, *how* beneficial is such provision? There is already a lot of open space (other than Green Belt) inside many of the rundown inner urban areas. Upkeep in the face of chronic vandalism is expensive, and *too much* open space is hard to police and frightens off users, besides preventing commercial development. Much will be learnt from the Liverpool International Garden Festival and, more importantly, its aftermath when the festival site is turned over to the city. We do not yet know the long-term benefits to the environment. This programme therefore will have to to be reviewed sceptically, expensive as it is. A modest cut here is suggested, of the order of £0.2 billion in 1985/6 (and 1990).

Savings on the Environment can therefore be substantial: £0.6 billion in 1985/6 rising to £1.2 billion by 1990.

Other Government Spending

This includes overseas aid, law and order, arts and libraries, and common services. Much overseas aid expenditure has been shown (Bauer, 1982) to be of little or even no value to the common people in recipient countries, so the taxpayer should feel little compunction about reducing it. Higher charges or the introduction of charges for the remaining services is possible. Police can charge economically for their *ad hoc* services (such as policing football matches and marches), libraries could charge for lending books as they do for records, and so on.

Arts subsidy is argued to be a 'public good'. We have culture which must be preserved for society's sake, over and above the pleasure each performance gives. We accept this argument, up to a point. With high taxation, patrons are in less supply. But first, this will change under our proposals. Secondly, sponsorship by industry is growing. Third, 'culture' ought to be based on what people want and will pay for; Arts Councils can breed cliquery in place of true culture. Cuts in these subsidies therefore are possible without endangering our culture.

Activities that support UK commercial operations abroad and that are most efficiently performed by government as an overhead activity (the Export Credit Guarantee Department (ECGD), commercial Consular services, etc.) should continue but be provided on a commercial basis.

We suggest cuts in these programmes (totalling £12.5 billion in 1985/6) of £500 million in 1985/6 rising to £1 billion by 1990.

'TAX EXPENDITURES'

There is a remaining category of expenditure which is not shown explicitly in the budget accounts. This is 'tax expenditure' – allowances given against tax liability (which reduce tax revenue) and not, of course, state expenditure in the true sense. One main element of tax expenditure stands out.

This element is mortgage tax relief, worth £3.5 billion. Understanding of how this subsidy operates is limited. Some people appear to believe that it benefits all home-owners, and therefore argue on political grounds that this relief should be maintained, since the home-owner is a floating voter and we wish to encourage a home-owning democracy with a property stake in our society.

It does not work like that. Since the planning system limits the supply of land for house building, mortgage tax relief bids up the price of this land and that of the stock of houses on it. The effects depend on the structure of tax relief and are complex. Broadly speaking, the present structure – in which tax relief is limited to £30,000 – works as follows (chapter 6 discusses further). For people contemplating acquiring a house or a larger house (piece of land), those on middle and lower incomes now will pay less (net), and those on higher incomes will pay more (net). This is because the tax subsidy favours the 'middle/lower' income household (with mortgages up to £30,000) while the rise in land prices will be fairly evenly spread across all groups. So if the political aim is to help 'new entrants' to house-ownership, it will be partially achieved. However, their gain is much less than would be a direct subsidy limited to them alone (equal to mortgage tax relief as they now get it) because the rise in land and house prices is larger under the present system (the *lower* the limit on the size of mortgage eligible, the more new entrants are benefited).

For people *with* a house, the effect is to give them a capital gain (equal to the present discounted value of the tax relief plus the rise in price of their house). This feature of mortgage tax relief makes it politically hard to be reversed, especially the resulting *fall* in house prices.

The capital gain itself, of course, creates no distortion. Distortion – since land for building is a relatively fixed resource – mainly arises insofar as one group of people is subsidized relative to another.

This subsidy (to new entrants to the market) is a deliberate political act, although somewhat frustrated by the general rise in land prices. There is thus no significant loss to economic welfare from the arrangement, and it could reasonably be left alone as, at worst, a minor problem. The political objective, to subsidize *new* entrants, indicates that the limit on eligible mortgage size should be gradually reduced in real terms. This would increase the effective subsidy to this group. A saving of £0.7 billion should be possible on this basis by 1990, a reduction of 20 per cent over 5 years.

There are many other distortions in the *tax* system, which would take us too far from our main topic, expenditure. The Meade Report (Meade *et al.* 1978) identified one such major distortion – the taxation of savings and the capricious rebating of this tax through, for example, tax relief on pension contributions. A move to an expenditure basis for tax would eliminate these distortions, and there are also other ways of dealing with them. They should be placed on the agenda and dealt with as opportunities arise. But for our purpose here we assume that no net revenue savings will emerge.

Accordingly, we have identified here about £0.7 billion of savings on tax expenditures.

THE OVERALL PICTURE OF SAVINGS IN THE BUDGET

Table 3.8 identifies savings in the budget in 1990, the target year.

Table 3.8

	£ billion
Health	6.0
Education	16.0
Pensions	3.2
Unemployment benefits	1.0
Personal social services	0.6
Nationalized industries	2.0
Industry, etc.	4.3
Housing	4.1
Transport	0.5
Agriculture	1.0
Defence	2.0
Environment	1.2
Other government programmes	1.0
Total programmes	42.9

Against this table 3.9 identifies tax changes which by 1990 would cost:

Table 3.9

	£ billion
Personal national insurance contribution abolition	9.7
Raise tax thresholds	17.0
Raise child benefits	9.8
70 per cent negative income tax	0.5
Minus saving on tax expenditures	−0.7
Total	36.3

These are the *direct* savings and costs to the Exchequer. The *net* direct saving is £6.6 billion. On top of this, there will be indirect savings as employment and output rise owing to increase incentives, these we quantify below. This saving could be used to reduce the national insurance contribution (NIC) by firms, or the rates of personal tax, or to finance some additional infrastructure spending as justified by cost/benefit calculations. It is difficult, without knowledge of marginal projects on offer in infrastructure, to rank these *a priori*. But of *tax* reductions the next highest priority in our view is the reduction of NIC, since it penalizes labour (unlike VAT which is a neutral tax). Like direct personal taxes, it is therefore a tax on jobs, which is damaging when labour is in excess supply. Currently this stands at 10.25 per cent. Its gross yield is projected in 1985/6 at £10.1 billion.*

As a working assumption, we allocate £2 billion per year to additional infrastructure and the rest to the reduction of NIC. Any surplus revenue after the abolition of NIC is allocated to the reduction of personal tax rates. Roughly we find that the spare revenue (after indirect effects) is sufficient to *eliminate NIC*, to reduce the standard rate of income tax by 5p to 25p, and to abolish the higher rates of tax.

On this assumption, we can calculate the *indirect* effects on the budget of our tax/benefit changes. These effects come about because of the stronger incentives to employ labour and to take jobs. We estimate them in table 3.10.

The rise in output by 1990 is set at about 11 per cent per annum. The additional saving from this is £15 billion (by 1990), so making possible changes (over those listed in table 3.9) whose direct cost is as in table 3.11.

Table 3.10

	On output (%)	*Indirect effect on revenue (£ billion)*[a]
Rise in tax thresholds and child benefits, abolition of personal NIC	+2.0	2.9
Unemployment benefit ceiling	+2.4	3.5
Abolition of employers' NIC	+5.0	7.0
Abolition of higher rates of tax and reduction of standard rate to 25p	+1.4	1.6
Total	+10.8	15.0

Note: [a]Assuming marginal tax rate of 0.4, and money GDP pre-charges = £335 billion.

*We do not deduct from this the element paid by publicly-owned bodies, in order to keep equality of treatment across the different taxes. *All* tax cuts have some effect on public sector costs which might reasonably be deducted, and wages *fall* with cuts in other taxes, so decreasing slightly the relative price of government services. In the case of NIC, government pays less NIC but real wages *rise*; the net effect on the relative price of government services is comparable. Rather than include all these amounts which, besides being complicated to calculate, are very small relative to the margin of error of our calculations, we prefer to omit them all.

Table 3.11

	£ *billion*
Extra infrastructure spending	2.0
Abolition of NIC (employers')	10.1
Abolition of higher rates of tax	4.0
Reduction of standard rate	5.5
Total	21.6

The overall programme now balances in its effect on the budget in 1990.

We do not attempt a calculation of the 'improvement in welfare' from these changes. Indeed, even if we interpret this as the Marshall measure discussed earlier, the number of detailed assumptions required to make the calculation is beyond existing knowledge, let alone our resources here. In the first place, there is the better utilization of national resources generated by the rise in annual output of about 11 per cent. This corresponds to the crude resource loss from unemployment. On top of this we would also be saving the consumers' surplus from waste in state production, state consumption, and the distortions induced by the tax/benefit system. In view of the arguments and orders of magnitude discussed earlier, a saving of the order of 11 per cent of GDP – approximately equal to the extra *output* generated by changes – would appear to be a minimum estimate. *Jobs* created by these changes would be of the order of 2½ million, enough to bring unemployment to the numbers of the 1950s. This perhaps is the most relevant measure for practical purposes to most people.

CONCLUSION

The object of this chapter has been to review the functions of the state sector and to identify the scope for reorganizing its activities to eliminate economic waste in achieving society's objectives. Our quest has been solely for improved economic efficiency.

Our starting point was the wish to eliminate the unemployment and poverty traps in order to get the labour market to work more effectively and bring unemployment down. In principle we could have found the revenue needed to tackle this problem by increasing *average* tax rates (while reducing the marginal tax rates on those in these traps). However, this 'solution' would raise marginal tax rates on people higher up the income scale than the low-paid, possibly as high as 60 per cent (including indirect taxes). This would cause economic inefficiency (work disincentives) on a scale we cannot estimate but which could be substantial. Perhaps partly for this reason it is a solution which is also highly unpopular.

Instead, we have looked for economies in the public sector that *raise* the efficiency of the economy overall. These economies have mainly involved privatization of production and consumption on a large scale. Private producers replace public sector production, private consumers buy directly from private producers without public sector intermediation. Increased efficiency comes about because (1) competition produces lower private sector costs, (2) consumers can decide directly on their consumption patterns and (3) marginal tax rates are lowered across all income groups.

We have offered some estimates of the gains but they are very tentative *except for* those related to the effects of increased labour market incentives on unemployment and output, where we have used our own research. Nevertheless, apart from these substantial effects, we can be sure of the beneficial *direction* of the other effects and even our very tentative arithmetic suggests they could well be substantial.

4

The Problem of Union Power

THE ARGUMENT RECAPITULATED

It is not original to suggest that unions create unemployment. It has been a widespread claim by those economists who have urged more freedom for market forces. What they have generally had in mind was that unions raise wages for *unionized* workers, some of whom as a consequence will lose their jobs (or equivalently other non-unionized workers will fail to get jobs in unionized industries). The workers displaced will find it hard to gain employment in the non-union sectors because of the limited opportunities there, and will for the most part be unemployed.

Two elements have been lacking in this argument. First, there has been some vagueness about why workers would not find jobs in the non-union sector, since they would drive non-union wages down there until there was full employment. Second, the order of magnitude of the unemployment which could result from union power has not been indicated; this is obviously very important because if the magnitudes are trivial, the ordeal by fire required to reduce union power would not be politically attractive.

The findings of this book are two-fold. First the operation of a tax and benefit system prevents wages in the non-union sector from dropping much, because benefits are 'flat rate' (i.e. regardless of previous earnings) after six months, and for low-income jobs they may be so close to net earnings that the jobs would become unviable and unattractive for workers if wages fell very far. Hence the non-union sector has only a small ability to absorb workers displaced by the union sector. Second, upon estimating relationships which incorporate the role of the tax and benefits system, we have found that the substantial rise in union power since the early 1960s has raised unemployment by about one million. This is a round number probably at the upper end of what politicians and practical men may have suspected, but, if correct, it must weigh heavily in the political scales against the fuss involved in reducing union power.

This work is bound to be controversial at this stage because it challenges much wishful thinking. But it will be a long time before all the additional evidence has been sifted – particularly the immense amount of potential information in the Family Expenditure Survey – which may settle all the interlocking issues involved. But by the time such research has been done, it may be too late to take the necessary action. Already the tide of union power has swept in irresistibly. Some recent events have suggested it may be receding. But who can tell what access of strength it may gain in the next economic upturn and beyond? Now may be the last major opportunity available to politicians to push the tide out once and for all. To lose such an opportunity on the chance that our estimate of the effect of union power may be much too high would be a dangerous gamble. Compared with it, the risk that the highly unpopular union movement will be able to resist successfully and damaging by the necessary legislation to cut its powers seems a risk substantially less to be feared.

The basic ideas related to the effect of union power have been described above. But it seems worthwhile briefly to recap on this point.

A union exists to raise the wages of its members to an 'optimal' amount, given, first, that higher union wages mean fewer union jobs, and, second, the wages that their members could get in the non-union sector. The union typically determines an optimal union wage which is some way above the non-union wage. A monopolist raises his price to the point at which his profits are maximized; this point will be above that which would have been set by free competition and will reduce the size of the market – so with a union monopoly.

Workers who lose their jobs as a result of their monopoly power will then seek jobs in the non-union sector. These additional supplies of labour force wages down there, until supply is equal to demand. But at this point we note that the social security system guarantees a minimum income regardless of work and that taxes apply to workers with very low incomes. As wages in the non-union sector fall, they become progressively less attractive (after tax) to workers forced out of the union sector. Some, perhaps many, will not be prepared to take the jobs on offer for such rewards. They will go on the dole. The major way in which supply is equated to demand in the non-union sector by falling wages is through the contraction of supply. Demand rises as wages fall, but the tax and social security system imparts a 'floor' to wages, which causes major withdrawals from the labour market as wages get too close to this critical level. Consequently wages cannot fall enough to create much additional demand.

This analysis is sometimes criticized on the grounds that the resulting unemployment is labelled 'voluntary'. Many people feel, rightly, that unemployment is a tragic misfortune and cannot be regarded in any meaningful sense as voluntary. Consequently they feel inclined to dismiss the analysis. But such a feeling is inspired by a complete misconception. There is nothing in the analysis to suggest otherwise than that unemployment is unpleasant and degrading. The point of the analysis is that the alternatives to unemployment, non-union jobs at non-union wages, are even less attractive. What is more, workers who take jobs in the non-union sector would, of course, prefer to work in the better paid union sector. It is a technical convention in economics to call the decisions of these people 'voluntary', because they are doing their best even in poor circumstances, but they could just as well be described as involuntarily forced out of the union sector.

No amount of re-labelling, however, will avoid the basic problem society faces: how to create permanent jobs for pay that people will accept. The analysis clearly indicates that one major way to do this is to reduce the power of unions to raise union wages. As union wages fall, the demand for union labour rises, people are withdrawn from the non-union sector, non-union wages rise and more people are prepared to work in it, so unemployment falls.

A POLICY FRAMEWORK

Monopoly power in the labour market from the union side now rates as a major allocational issue. Monopoly power in goods markets was the major allocational issue in the post-war period, resulting in important legislation such as the Restrictive Trade Practices Act of 1956, new institutions such as the Monopolies Commission and tax changes like the successive tariff-cutting 'rounds'.

In British history the trade unions have been the instigator of major social reforms. Once they were a 'countervailing force' in an economy where major employers held the whip hand in negotiations. But their historical role as social reformer is no longer relevant. The need for a countervailing force has disappeared in an economy where employers' monopoly power has been heavily curtailed by the stronger competition in goods markets and the emergence of industrial relations institutions such as the industrial tribunals. It is hard to escape the conclusion that the public interest requires measures to deal with labour market monopoly power in an analogous way to goods market monopoly power. A corollary is that, since the power is vested in the unions by exceptionally favourable laws, it is no use hoping that non-legal measures, such as incomes policies, 'confrontations' or exhortations, will have any effect on the problem. Only changes in laws and institutions which take away union power wil remove its effects on unemployment, output and the interests of non-unionized workers.

THE PRESENT SITUATION

A fairly full account of the history and present state of union legislation is attached in Appendix A. Since the first edition of this book, dramatic changes have been introduced which have gone a long way towards the proposals we made then. Unions have lost a large part of those privileges that put them above the common law of the land.

The exact situation is complex and cannot be summarized without risk of serious inaccuracy. Its very complexity indeed is now a reason for going to the full extent of our legal proposals, which would reintroduce the simplicity prevailing before the 1906 Act.

Broadly speaking, unions have now lost immunity for almost all secondary action and even for 'primary' action (i.e. against their own employer) that is not for reasons connected with wages and terms and conditions of employment, or is not supported by a secret ballot of its striking members. All closed shops will now have to be supported by an 80 per cent majority of the workforce, as from November 1984.

The results of the closed shop ballot have yet to be seen. The problem is that the ballot gives no vote to those *outside* the workforce who might wish to gain entry to it. Nor does it give expression to the public interest in free entry. It is quite likely that many closed shops will be 'legitimized' by such ballots, against the public interest.

The results to date on the reduction of immunities are much more encouraging. A large number of cases have now been brought under the new laws, and the success of these actions has indirectly encouraged the wider use of the common law in industrial relations (notably, in the case of the 1984/5 miners' dispute).

The main disappointment has been the unwillingness of many private employers to use the law, apparently encouraged by the CBI in the interests of 'good industrial relations'. A similar attitude has been evidenced by public sector employers. Whatever tactical or other reasons may be put forward for such unwillingness, it was perhaps to be expected that it would take time for the use of the law to be widely accepted. The risks of using a new instrument are always present, and they are most likely to be taken by those with most to lose from inaction. That has tended to be the early pattern, the lead being taken by small private employers with no established union ties and facing union threats to their very existence. The classic example was Mr Eddie Shah and his Stockport Messenger Group against the National Graphical Association. The large private employers by contrast have learnt to survive with union power. Like an established club owner, they do not wish to upset the resident protection gang. As for public sector employers, their action has been inhibited by a fear of politicizing disputes, spreading them to other unions, and compounding resistance.

However, public attitudes to the laws have been highly favourable. Even among union members there is a large majority in favour of the balloting provisions. The public has appeared to wish public sector employers to be *more* active in the use of the civil law instead of relying on attrition in facing up to strikes. The recent decision of Austin Rover to use the law to break a strike – highly successfully as it turned out – is evidence of a new attitude emerging.

The largest private employers are likely to remain cautious for some time. But, if the laws are available, their shareholders will want to know why the opportunities to increase their profits, by lowering wage settlements and raising productivity, are not being taken. Take-over bids will emerge for these managements.

Nevertheless, in the civil law as it affects the private sector, there may in certain cases be a serious problem of enforcement, namely that it may well be in nobody's individual interest to take legal action that is in the public interest.

This has been recognized in the law governing monopolies and restrictive practices – i.e. by firms in the goods market. In civil law, it is not possible for consumers of a product to take the supplier(s) to court for damages from monopoly practice. We therefore do not rely on such private actions to curb monopolies and restrictive practices. Instead we have a Monopolies Commission, whose job it is to report on practices that are referred to it by the Secretary of State for Trade as being potentially damaging to the public interest. In the light of that report, the Minister may bring an order in Parliament regulating or forbidding these practices and ordering whatever other action is necessary. From this point disobedience becomes a criminal matter, for the Attorney-General.

It is natural to think of extending this mode of action to monopolies and restrictive practices in the labour markets (incidentally by extending it in this way it embraces actions and situations *not* involving unions.) The Monopolies Commission is at present empowered to investigate labour markets; but no labour market situations have ever been referred to it by the Secretary of State for Trade. We take up this point below as part of our proposals for reform of the legal framework governing the labour market.

PROPOSALS FOR REFORM

The immense power wielded by unions in the British economy is plain for all to see. As a result of that power, the thinking of policy makers has been conditioned to accept labour market monopoly. Such acceptance has led most people involved in policy discussion not to question the basis of such things as union immunities under the common law. This acceptance is highly dangerous to constructive reform, and has bedevilled all earlier proposals.

We begin from the basic conception that the labour market should be free of all restraints on competition, except those for which a positive case based on the public interest can be sustained. Any action which causes workers to act in combination in order to fix the terms of their employment is a restraint of competition. Such actions include the calling of strikes, the denial of work to non-union workers (the pre-entry closed shop), and the enforcement of union membership on all workers in an industry (the post-entry closed shop). Similarly, any action which causes employers to act in combination for the same purpose is a restraint of competition. This includes most conspicuously concerted bargaining by employers' associations.

It may be said that such a conception is Utopian and has no hope of implementation. It would certainly be opposed by a variety of groups with vested interests; the unions of course, and some employers who would fear transitional disruption. We would certainly accept that full implementation of free competition in the labour market could not occur rapidly and might never come. Our point is, however, that it should be the ultimate aim of all actions taken in this area. The rate of progress will depend on a variety of pressures, but the aim must be clear for any progress to occur. With that aim we do not believe rational men can disagree, in the light of the damage to the British economy inflicted by labour market imperfection.

With this aim in mind, we make three sets of proposals, for implementation at the earliest possible moment in whatever order is most expedient.

(1) The actions of unions should be subject to the common law *without exception*, that is, all union immunities under common law should be repealed. The common law upholds contracts between employer and employee and recognizes the 'tort' of inducement to breach of contract. Union immunities from such tort cases allow them to call strikes without fear of action for damages. Strike calls are a *prima facie* restraint of trade and should not therefore be given immunity by society, since society's interest lies in competition. If unions and employers wish to sign contracts with clauses explicitly permitting strike calls under specified circumstances, then this could freely be done. The lack of immunities would not prevent it and would in fact stimulate the bringing of industrial action within the framework of the contracts. Any such contracts, however, would be potentially subject to investigation by the Labour Monopolies Commission proposed as (3) below.

(2) A 'status provision' should be legislated which would invalidate any contract between employer and worker contingent on the union status of the worker. Such a provision – analogous to a variety of similar provisions already in existence under common law – would render null and void any closed-shop agreements, explicit or implicit.

(3) A Labour Monopolies Commission (LMC) should be set up under an extension of existing competition legislation, which would enunciate the 'public interest' in labour market competition. This Commission would be an independent body with power to investigate any apparent breach of the public interest, to publish a report about it, and to bring a case, based on its report, to the common law courts requesting that remedies to uphold the public interest as suggested by the report be mandated by the courts. The Commission's independence would ensure, as with anti-trust actions in the USA, that no *political* intervention is necessary, or for that

matter possible, on the part of any future government hostile to competition. Its power would cover breaches by both sides of the labour market, so that the proposals overall are seen to be completely even handed between employers and workers. The powers are sweeping and would institute over a decade a body of case law with substantial impact on labour practices.

The combination of these three proposals would require modest legislation which would, incidentally, simplify in a major way the present tangle of labour law, returning it to the framework of the original common law. The proposals for withdrawal of legal protection currently given explicitly or implicitly – a negative act which alone might not be sufficient to curb union power because of custom, practice and intimidation – combine with the invention of a weapon for positively changing labour practices regardless of employers', employees', and unions' own narrow interests, which may alone be insufficient to prosecute the public interest and may even interfere with it. This combination of negative and positive changes should be sufficient to introduce a very substantial degree of competition into the UK labour market over the next decade.

Legal details of these proposals with drafting suggestions etc. are now appended in some depth.

AN ALTERNATIVE SYSTEM OF INDUSTRIAL RELATIONS

Since the beginning of this century, trade unions have held unique privileges in law, and occupied an unrivalled position in the courts with the sole exception of the Crown itself. The immunities from legal process are considered in Appendix A and need not be reiterated here. The general impression is that these immunities are unnecessarily wide, and have been used by unions to acquire and secure inequitably powerful advantages over others with whom they deal. We therefore call for the restitution of the rule of law and equality of treatment before the courts, so as to provide a more balanced position for those who are parties to collective agreements, and to permit unions to represent their membership interests in a more efficient and responsible way. It is our opinion that the only way in which the necessary changes can be effected, is by the abolition of all legal privileges conferred upon trade unions and by the restoration of the common law to situations in which unions are a party. By abrogating the unique privileges presently conferred by statute, such bodies would still be powerful enough to represent their members' interest effectively, but not irresponsibly. The acceptance of common law principles represents the acceptance of common sense in an area which seems so sadly neglected by such considerations. Given this constitutional claim, we shall now consider the likely impact of such a change upon the face of industrial relations and then detail its likely effects.

The Common Law Basis

It should be made clear at the outset that our proposed adoption of a common law basis in no way affects the existing legal provisions as between employer and employee as detailed in Appendix A. Its only effect is upon the position of trade unions, their officials and related persons.

The main effect of adopting the common law basis would be to make the union and its officials liable to common law actions such as attempted or actual inducement to breach of contract of employment. Clearly the proposals would expose unions to an extensive range of legal liabilities, and it is our view that one way in which the union may seek to restrict this exposure is by entering into legally binding collective agreements with employers and their associations. The idea of collective contracts is not particularly radical, since it has been widely adopted in a number of overseas countries (for example, France, West Germany and the United States) and indeed it was an assumed situation under the Industrial Relations Act 1971.

The coupling of a contractual basis with the abrogation of immunities, which is our preferred framework, can be seen as conferring a number of advantages over the existing scheme of industrial relations. First, it provides a fairer and more responsible basis for industrial bargaining, by removing the rights of unions unilaterally to break agreements with impunity. It would be more equitable also for employers who formerly encountered difficulties in bringing actions against individual workers, rather than the more powerful and wealthy unions who frequently inspired or induced such breaches. Second, whilst some would argue that the alternative basis of industrial relations would be met by the same vituperative actions and malignant reactions as those encountered by the former Conservative administration, we would point out that our proposals are in no way coercive or paternalistic. For if unions do not wish to enter into a contract, they are in no way required to do so. They are simply open to the common law remedies if, for example, they attempt to induce a breach in the contract of employment between the employer and the employees. Viewed in this light, unions may recognize the advantages of a contractual basis, since it affords rights as well as responsibilities.

Assuming such a basis were adopted, the significance of the proposals can best be seen by considering their likely effect upon strikes and other forms of industrial conflict. Clearly unions would be liable for any breach of the collective contract and could be sued by the employer, or any other third party not too remote from damage. Strikes, including political strikes and other forms of industrial action, would be taken, subject to *de minimis* rule, to represent a fundamental breach of the contract giving the employer the normal common law remedies. It may be argued that this adds little to existing, proposed and contemplated legislation, but this misses the point that, whereas successive governments have adhered to the central theme of immunity, attempts have been made to whittle away a number of specific immunities. By adopting such a course, there have been a succession of harmful confrontations between the protagonists, which we feel is best resolved by a once and for all change in the legal environment pervading the industrial relations scene. Moreover by adopting the new comprehensive legal regime, all union nominated officers, as well as unofficial or even disruptive representatives, are put on the same liability basis, since legal actions may now be instituted against these 'third parties'. By contrast, the existing and contemplated legislation fails adequately to get to grips with these fundamentals and will produce piecemeal and partial legislative solutions as confusing as they are confused.

However, by far the most important advantage of our proposals over any form of legislative provision (whether providing extended or restricted immunities) is that, by removing externally imposed restraints and privileges, the parties to collective bargaining are more able freely to negotiate their own terms as to the price and conditions of labour supply, without the distortionary impact of one party having a statutorily indemnified unilateral right of repudiation. Lest it be argued that the ending of legal protectionism will result in all trade union and other industrial action becoming unlawful, it is to be noted that the ending of legislative immunities does not necessarily preclude the possibility of collusive *de facto* immunities being established between employers and trades unions. Nor does it prevent the negotiation of contracted immunities, which we would regard as providing flexibility in the new scheme, as well as forming central issues in the negotiations as to the price and conditions of labour supply.

The negotiation of contractual immunities can be viewed in both positive and negative terms – indeed, at the present time, it is possible for employers to negotiate 'non strike' clauses, and for this employers invariably make compensatory finance available. However, under the new scheme, strikes and other forms of industrial action will *prima facie* give rise to contractual and/or tortious liability, unless the contracting parties permit such actions as part of the collective contract. A period of more active negotiation and contract drafting is therefore envisaged, in which such issues as defining the permitted rights, for exercise in the defined circumstances, after exhausting prescribed procedures (e.g. 30 days' notice of strike, or cooling-off period, or balloting of plant membership, arbitration etc.) become part of the wage determination process itself. The central difference between the proposed legal framework and the existing one is that, by removing the unfair privileges currently enjoyed by unions, and making them responsible for their agreements, the commitments which are made will be more likely to reflect the true economic value of labour services, undistorted by legislative regulation.

On a more practical level, we envisage the provision of such a framework as reducing the need for industrial conflict rather than permitting it. As indicated earlier, not every employer will bring an action for every breach. Forbearances on the right to bring actions will lead to *de facto* immunities being established, and the development of these and similar understandings will lubricate the workings of the new system as they do at present in relation to most breaches of contract by individual employees. Indeed we expect most employers to be at least as reluctant to bring legal actions against the unions under the new scheme, as they have been in the past to bring actions against individual employees in breach of their contract of employment. The main reason for this reticence is that good employers want good industrial relations, and this cannot be brought about by suing unions for every single breach, indeed to attempt to do so would be prohibitively expensive. However, by adopting the alternative legal framework, unions would be bound so that actions *could* be brought for breach, thereby providing employers with a back-up position which is not available to them under the existing scheme. Moreover, such agreements will provide an agreed objective guideline having a restraining influence upon trades unions in exercising their *de facto* power, and at the same time providing them with a shield against irresponsible and unrepresentative elements within the union who may otherwise have sought to break the undertakings with employers.

The contractual unprivileged basis would also require reasonableness by the latter, as well as the former, for if contracts were enforced with undue rigidity then either employers or unions would be forced into financial difficulties. Taking the extreme example of a firm which, after a number of breach actions against the union, was able to bankrupt it, the union would have little to lose by subsequent actions and may reciprocate by encouraging disruptive action eventually leading to the firm's liquidation. By this somewhat extreme example we can clearly see how our framework actually deters legal involvement, yet provides a useful shield behind which both the parties can extract compliance with the terms of their agreement. The removal of immunities and restoration of a fairer basis to collective bargaining will ensure the necesary background for the development of good industrial relations with the minimum reliance on the law and its current immunities.

To ensure the successful implementation of our proposals, a number of potentially difficult areas must be isolated and dealt with. Clearly, if employees do not wish to accept the terms of employment offered them by a specific employer, they may leave that firm and seek employment elsewhere. However, in the case of a monopoly employer, attempts may be made to force workers to accept 'unfair' wages. In such a situation we see the union and employees bringing this matter to the attention of the LMC which will investigate and report on the contract and determine whether or not its terms are such that only a monopolist employer could have imposed them. An affirmative declaration by the Commission would then require the parties to renegotiate the relevant terms by reference to comparable market conditions. Conversely, if a collusive agreement were entered into by the parties, one or both of whom had monopolistic powers, then the terms of the agreement could also be examined by the Commission, to determine whether that agreement was contrary to the public interest. Similarly, if the terms of any collective agreement were to attempt to override the rights granted by employers in individual contracts of employment with their workers, the LMC would have powers to intervene. Before considering the role of the Commission in detail, let us consider the likely impact of the substantive reforms on actions pursuant to strikes, such as picketing.

The new legal framework would not permit such action during the currency of any existing contract. Even under the existing law this may constitute breach of contract and this, as we have noted, would not be affected by our proposals. As for trade unions or other persons engaged in picketing, this would now give rise in all cases to actions for inducing a breach or conspiracy or intimidation. Picketing or other forms of industrial pressure could be brought after the expiration of the current contract, and before renegotiation of the new contract. Such picketing would of course be subject to the criminal law of intimidation, breach of the peace, obstruction, etc. But if individual workers, whether or not members of the union, were to accept management's offer by being prepared to work, the pickets would be liable for inducement to breach of contract, or collectively for conspiracy, if they attempted to prevent those persons from working. In the case of a union concerting such action, it too would be liable. It is remarkable that, whilst our proposals appear radical, many of the law reforms in this and other countries are simply retractions of earlier immunities which are now realized as unnecessary incumbrances upon the freedom of collective bargaining.

The Closed Shop and Status Provisions

In addition to the effects upon strikes and other industrial disputes, the proposed framework may also have significant implications for the closed shop. Under the new framework, employees and trade unions would contract with employers, and although unions could impose closed-shop conditions on employers, and they in turn impose it as a pre- or post-entry qualification for workers, it should be legislatively provided that the personal contract between employer and employee is not subject to any 'status' qualifications (other than that presently required by statute, e.g. race or sex legislation). As such, the employer will not be empowered to ask any questions which directly or indirectly touch upon trade union status (this works for the benefit of unionists as well as non-unionists) and any terms in a collective agreement which provide otherwise shall be null and void. In the case of breach of this provision, the prospective employee may bring an action for loss of prospective earnings which he may otherwise have enjoyed had the contract been offered to him. The mechanisms of obtaining a *declaration of prevention of free entry* will be considered shortly, as will the case where an existing employee has been dismissed as a result of non-union membership. Where such a person can show that the employing firm has (either of its own accord or as a result of union pressure) dismissed him as a result of a *de facto* status provision, then he may obtain a *declaration of enforced dismissal.*

A LABOUR MONOPOLIES COMMISSION

The second major reform which we see as complementing our first proposal involves the establishment of a Labour Monopolies Commission which would be an independent statutory body with administrative functions and quasi-legal powers to investigate, report and direct upon monopoly powers which appear to exist within labour markets. Its primary administrative function would be similar to that exercised by the Monopolies and Mergers Commission (MMC) under the various competition legislations, but confined solely to matters relating to labour monopolies. The position, powers and effects of trade unions on labour markets would certainly be one of the main areas of concern, but as indicated in our earlier reform proposals, monopolistic employer and union forms of 'unfair labour practices' (e.g. pre-entry closed shops and enforced dismissals) would also be within its purview. Indeed the Commission would be actively engaged in investigating and reporting on any situation or practice which could be considered as uncompetitive or restricting market responsiveness. Whilst the general tenor of the proposal is to carry over the product monopolies legislation into labour market situations, there are a number of important differences between the two markets and this leads us to advocate the need for an independent commission separate from the MMC with quite different procedures and enforcement powers.

The first difference concerns what criteria should be used in determining whether or not a labour monopoly exists. Clearly the definition of monopoly for product markets (e.g. the 25 per cent rate) would be too restrictive. Indeed it is our opinion that any per cent rate will be similarly unsatisfactory, although such a basis may be a useful back-up if expressed in terms of occupation and/or industry. Our own preference is for an activity definition of the labour market expressed in terms of the 'public interest', where the latter term is defined so as to embrace all potential situations. A consolidating definition embracing the Fair Trading Act 1973 (s.84) and the Restrictive Trade Practices Act 1976 (ss.10 and 19) as suitably amended, could be employed as an 'initial' basis for jurisdiction, although drafting along the lines of the Competition Act 1980 (s.2) and the Fair Trading Act 1973 (s.79(5)), would be more appropriate for giving the Commission powers to investigate the unfair labour practices discussed earlier. In any event, these are drafting details which need not detain us here. What is important to note is that the scope of the Restrictive Trade Practices legislation and the anti-monopolies and competition legislation are too narrow and isolated to have any real impact on labour market monopolies.

Whilst we feel that this central economic objective in itself establishes the need for an independent Commission, there are a number of procedural difficulties which would be encountered if the MMC were given extended jurisdiction to carry out the terms of our second reform proposal. For example, under existing provisions the method of referrals to the Monopolies and Mergers Commission seems particularly passive and ineffective, and its procedure for enforcement appears singularly inappropriate. The investigative function is initiated not by the body itself but by the Director of Fair Trading (a government appointment) or the Secretary of State for Industry, and this basis of referrals seems unsatisfactory for the purposes we have in mind.

Similarly, the MMC has no effective enforcing powers itself. If a monopoly which is contrary to the public interest is found to exist, then the report is enforced by the Secretary of State, after Parliamentary approval, in the Courts. For example, it has recently been held by the High Court that the Secretary of State for Trade was not bound by conclusions reached by a majority of the MMC that a proposed merger was against the public interest – the Trade Secretary had 'a complete discretion whether to make any order or whether to make or order at all' [*Regina* v. *Secretary of State and Another*, 1983 TLR 4/2/83]. In such a sensitive area' as trade union restrictive and monopoly practices, we would prefer to see the institution of an autonomous LMC and its reports being implemented by the common law courts, where the adjudication could also be challenged or reviewed.

If this procedure were adopted, it would then be incumbent upon the monopolist defendant to consider whether or not to challenge the evidence, and whilst this may lead to a certain degree of duplication of the earlier investigation, it does afford a certain 'safeguard' to defendants, whilst the sanction of heavy legal costs will at least inhibit spurious and 'political' defences becoming the established practice. Alternative enforcement procedures are of course available, such as the LMC having its own powers of enforcement. Indeed this may very well be the best method of dealing with at least some of the unfair industrial practices referred to earlier. After an extensive examination of those alternatives we feel that the above procedure is not only the most acceptable, but also the least controversial, and if the first proposal considered earlier were adopted, an integrated scheme of competitive industrial relations would be established, and collectively they would be enforced by the ordinary courts of the land.

Although our preference is for an independent Labour Monopolies Commission, quite distinct in function, procedure and enforcement from the MMC, we do see it as having similar powers of information and requirement of witnesses, as well as means of enforcing those procedures by way of contempt, just as currently enjoyed by the latter. Moreover, transfers of information and possibly joint enquiries are envisaged, so as to remove the monopoly powers and practices which have plagued our industrial and commercial competitiveness and caused significant and unnecessary increases in unemployment. The programme of reducing monopolies and increasing flexibility and competitiveness, which has expanded during the present administration, should now be put into full effect.

5

Wages Councils and Labour 'Protection' Laws

Unions and the labour movement generally have recognized that political activity can be useful in achieving their aims. If a law can be passed which forces employers to undertake certain costly activities to the benefit of union members, this *pro tanto* reduces the organizational and other effort the unions must put in to achieve their objectives. In this chapter we consider two main results of their political activity: Wages Councils and laws on factory conditions, dismissal, and conditions of employment, or so-called labour protection laws.

MINIMUM WAGES AND WAGES COUNCILS

Effective minimum wages – that is those that succeed, by inspection and enforcement, in raising wages above market-clearing levels – have an effect like that of union power. They reduce jobs where wages have been raised and displace workers into other sectors not so regulated, where wages fall until supply equals demand. In essence, the government is acting as a union for the workers whose wages are then raised. In some cases, the government actually does this in response to requests from unions unable to exert enough power themselves.

It follows clearly enough that a government which wishes to create jobs by curbing union power should also act in its own 'backyard' by putting an end to minimum wages. This is the least it can do.

The present minimum wage and related regulations in force are documented in what follows.

In 1909 Wages Councils were established with the intention of protecting workers from sweat-shop conditions and low rates of pay, particularly in fragmented industries in which it was hard to

Table 5.1 List of Wages Councils* (Wages Councils Act 1979)

Aerated Waters Wages Council (England and Wales)
Aerated Waters Wages Council (Scotland)
Boot and Shoe Repairing Wages Council
Button Manufacturing Wages Council
Clothing Manufacturing Wages Council
Coffin Furniture and Cerement Making Wages Council
Cotton Waste Reclamation Wages Council
Flax and Hemp Wages Council
Fur Wages Council
General Waste Material Reclamation Wages Council
Hairdressing Undertakings Wages Council
Hat, Cap and Millinery Wages Council
Lace Finishing Wages Council
Laundry Wages Council
Licensed Non-residential Establishment Wages Council
Licensed Residential Establishment and Licensed Restaurant Wages Council
Linen and Cotton Handkerchief and Household Goods and Linen Piece Goods Wages Council
Made-up Textiles Wages Council
Ostrich and Fancy Feather and Artificial Flower Wages Council
Perambulator and Invalid Carriage Wages Council
Retail Bespoke Tailoring Wages Council
Retail Food and Allied Trades Wages Council
Retail Trades (Non-Food) Wages Council
Rope, Twine and Net Wages Council
Sack and Bag Wages Council
Toy Manufacturing Wages Council
Unlicensed Place of Refreshment Wages Council

Notes: *Unless their title indicates otherwise, all Councils cover the whole of Great Britain.
Address of Secretary of all the Councils:
Office of Wages Councils
12 St James's Square
London SW1Y 4LL.

organize collective bargaining. As such they were a substitute for trade unions in these areas. The number of Wages Councils grew rapidly after the First World War, but since the Second World War there has been a moderate decline. There are now 26 Wages Councils (see table 5.1) covering about 2¾ million industrial workers and about 400,000 establishments in the UK. Parallel to Wages Councils is the Agricultural Wages Board which is separate, but has a similar role and powers covering only agriculture.

At present under the Wages Councils Act 1979, supported by the Employment Protection Act 1975, councils, independently of government have the legal power to fix minimum wage rates and other conditions of employment such as holiday entitlement, hours of work, etc. in certain specified industries. These awards have the power of law and employers can be subject to substantial fines for failure to comply with such awards. The Councils' members are appointed by the Employment Secretary, though independent of government. Usually they consist of nominees of employers' associations and trade unions, with some form of independent chairman. They are backed up by the Wages Inspectorate, an arm of the Department of Employment.

The British system of minimum wage legislation has enabled the UK to ratify the International Labour Office (ILO) Convention No. 26 of 1928. It will be possible to renew or renounce such ratification again in 1985. Other industrial countries, e.g. USA, France, West Germany, etc, have similar minimum wage laws. In the USA, the Fair Labour Standards Acts of 1945 and 1960 have established the principle there, but there are now moves afoot to dismantle certain aspects of these Acts.

The two largest Councils in the UK, the Retail Food and Retail Non-Food, cover around 1.75 million of the total 2.7 million workers, and over 230,000 establishments (58 per cent of total) whilst, at the other end of the scale, the Flax and Hemp Council covers some 2,300 workers in 12 factories and the Ostrich Feather Council embraces 28 individual plants and 1500 workers. The coverage is generally of the older types of industry and trade with a large component of small firms.

Once established, however, it has proved historically somewhat difficult to abolish any Wages Council. For instance 19 years occurred between the last meeting of both the Drift Net and Fustian Cutting Councils before they were finally formally abolished. Eleven Councils were abolished in the period 1974–8 and only one – the Pin, Hook and Eye Council – has been abolished since 1979. Others, however, have been merged, but continue to function as before in their new clothing. The abolition of a Council in reality entails a reference under the two relevant Acts (Employment Protection Act 1975 and Wages Councils Act 1979) to the independent Advisory Conciliation and Arbitration Service (ACAS) with no scope for a time limit for reporting, thus making it very difficult indeed to achieve any early or prompt abolition despite any economic damage a Wages Council may be causing. There have consequently been no references to ACAS since 1979 for any abolition. This compares somewhat unfavourably with an equally important area of employment policy, namely industrial training, where a joint Department/Manpower Services Commission (MSC) review of Industrial Training Boards (ITBs) led to a rationalization of ITBs so as to align with other employment policy initiatives. No such action has been possible over Wages Councils, although their retention is inconsistent with present employment policy.

In terms of direct public expenditure cost, Wages Councils and their associate Inspectorate cost around £3 million annually. The staff numbers involved have recently been reduced as part of the policy to reduce civil service numbers, but around 25,000 units are still visited annually by wages inspectors.

Indirectly, as a result of jobs destroyed by Council awards, there will be a further revenue cost, but we have no estimate of this. Qualitative evidence, however, suggests that many Council awards have not reflected the individual financial or geographic aspects of the firms and industry in question. There have been cases where firms, especially small ones, have been forced to close or abandon an extension as a result. There has been little concern over the ability to pay. Often awards have been retrospective and difficult to interpret, making budgeting and future development planning extremely difficult, particularly for the small businessman. Some recent awards (for example, that in 1982 by the Retail Food Council of about 9 per cent plus a shorter working week and increased London weighting) were clearly unwarranted by market pressures.

The contribution of Wages Councils to the relief of poverty and to assisting the socially disadvantaged has been generally adjudged negative both in the UK and USA. The record shows that Councils have not improved the relative position of the low-paid, nor alleviated poverty. Consequently the only argument here for retaining the Councils is that the relative position of the low-paid would be worse if the Councils were to be abolished, but no evidence can be found to support this. Similar arguments can be applied to youths, women and ethnic minorities – many awards have resulted in pricing these people out of jobs. The disadvantaged groups in a normal labour market situation naturally warrant a lower rate of pay and any attempt to increase it by a Council over the market rate only serves to limit their employment opportunities; this has been particularly true for young workers. Recent American research backs up British experience on this aspect (see for example Linneman, 1982; and Forrest and Dennison, 1984 provide a useful survey of the literature).

In any case, financial aid to those in work on low earnings is now met nationally through FIS and various associated social security schemes and locally via rebate schemes, e.g. housing benefit. Proposals in this book will maintain this system, but in a manner that avoids the poverty trap. Council awards are therefore unnecessary in this aspect, besides causing unemployment among the very groups where help is aimed.

Wages Council awards are also inconsistent with other aspects of current employment policy, e.g. the Young Workers Scheme (YWS), whereby lower wages for youth are encouraged and subsidized so as to stimulate employment, or the Youth Training Scheme where low allowances are paid with the objective of keeping apprentice rates of pay well down.

Abolition of the Wages Council system would, it can be confidently postulated, serve to expand employment, offer competitive wages for the socially disadvantaged, create an incentive for youth training, remove inconsistencies with other parts of present employment policy and alleviate rather than promote poverty. In short, if a Wages Council comes to be regarded as effective, it is therefore harmful; if it is looked upon as ineffective, it is therefore otiose and useless. Both counts add up to a positive case for steps towards the removal of minimum wage legislation, namely through the eventual abolition of Wages Councils. The declaratory effects, as well as the economic ones, would be a firm signal to all concerned.

LABOUR PROTECTION LAWS

The term 'conditions' is potentially as important as 'pay' in the well-worn phrase 'pay and conditions'. By getting Parliament to legislate for better conditions, the unions can concentrate their efforts on pay, and merely 'police' industry's delivery of the legislated changes.

Those who espouse the unions' cause often attempt to vilify opponents of such protective legislation by arguing that 'decent conditions' satisfy minimum standards in a 'civilized society'. They point to child labour, industrial diseases, and such like as examples of abuses that have been 'put right' by these laws.

What they conceal, or forget perhaps, is the pressure on competitive firms competing for labour to offer – within what they can afford to pay – the most attractive mix of 'pay' and 'conditions'. In a competitive market, where there was also strong pressure on workers to take available jobs (because out-of-work benefits were low relative to wages), workers themselves would effectively choose the mix. Their *total* pay would be fixed by their (marginal) productivity, this being the amount at which it is just worthwhile to employ them at all.

Assuming that the workers had as full information about their work situation as anyone else, no one could argue that their choice could be 'wrong'. *They* made it. If one argues that they do not have full information, then government has a role in *publishing* any additional information it has and they do not. There is no case at all here for legislation.

It is sometimes said that firms are not competitive but monopoly buyers of labour, enabling them to 'exploit' workers, both on pay and conditions. In certain historical episodes, there may have been some truth in this. Any monopoly buying power would, however, have had to be protected by governmental restrictions if it were to survive for long, since otherwise rival firms could always enter the market, bid the exploited labour away at better rates, and make a super-normal profit. This process would continue until competitive pay and conditions were once more stabilized. Be history as it may, there is no evidence of any such monopoly buying power in the private sector. It exists solely in the nationalized sectors where to allege 'exploitation' would be a bad joke – the main problem in these sectors being the collusion of unions with management to maximize joint rewards from the taxpayer. Were someone to uncover such monopoly-buying power in the private sector, it would come within the purview of the Monopolies and Mergers Commission and the regulative powers of the Department of Trade and Industry. There is thus no need for legislation on conditions for this reason.

Let us now suppose that civilized society is nevertheless shocked by the pay and conditions of its least productive members in the competitive market we have described. Should it not then legislate for better conditions and for better pay – labour protection and minimum wage laws?

No, it should not. We have already discussed this argument in the context of minimum wages. By forcing employers to pay additional costs, government reduces employment. (Alternatively, if it legislates better conditions only, the employees will now be forced to take lower wages to pay for them, and the mix will now be worse from their viewpoint.)

The correct way to help the lower-paid is through direct cash transfers to them in work, financed by general taxation. By subsidizing the incomes of the low-paid, government will also improve their conditions, for the low-paid themselves will now insist on a mix of pay and conditions that veers more towards better conditions now that their take-home pay is higher. With a properly worked out system of negative income tax, such as we have already discussed, there would be simply no need for any labour protection laws whatsoever. Even now, with the imperfect in-work benefits system we have (FIS, child benefits, housing benefits and so on), there is no need. Employers that did not provide 'decent' conditions – as seen by their workers in receipt of these state allowances – would simply not attract workers.

What the state must concentrate on in their decision is the *total* living standard of its low-paid subjects, think how large a subsidy to them is justified weighing up their interests and those of the taxpayer, and leave to these subjects themselves the decision on *mix* of pay and conditions. For what state can tell whether its subject is better off working in a dirty, untidy factory for £10 per week more than in a beautifully clean and well decorated factory?

Let us now consider one last argument: that workers might decide to put up with *unsafe* conditions in return for more pay, and that this must be stopped *in their own interests*. This is the ubiquitous paternalist argument which we faced up to in our discussion of health, pension and education spending.

In the case of health insurance and pensions, we argued – on the paternalists' side – that citizens should be forced to pay the cost, since were they not to do so and either to fall seriously ill or to live to a ripe old age unexpectedly, society would not stand idly by and let them be unattended or starve. Thus there is here a form of moral hazard: *given* this attitude of society, the citizen knows he *need* not take out health insurance or a pension in order to avoid these appalling risks. Some citizens may therefore capitalize on this weakness of society and become 'free riders'. Hence there is a public good argument for paternalism in this case.

In the case of education spending, the argument is different, though again on the paternalists' side: it is a matter of the rights of *children*. Parents must respect their children's right to be educated, and sacrifice their own consumption to that end.

Now consider factory legislation. Workers, let us assume, have health insurance, and this permits them to exercise their tastes within certain bounds, which include working in factories with an element of 'lack of safety'. Remember that safety and risk are necessarily relative. You cannot have 'absolute safety' (there are roads to be crossed, dangerous boilers to be fed with fuel, machines to be tended which may be faulty, etc.). Can these workers not judge their own tastes?

The best we can do for the paternalist here is to suppose that the worker is running a 'high' risk not insured by the 'normal' policy. Suppose he is working on oil rig maintenance in the North Sea. If he falls and is badly injured, his health insurance will not cover him without an additional premium. Yet again suppose he does not pay it and is injured, society will insist that he is tended back to health. He should surely, on the same principle as before, be forced to pay the additional premium.

But of course these are the exceptions. They do not justify factory legislation, but merely the buying of additional insurance premiums so that the costs of these activities that *society* bears should be paid for by the individual.

Armed with this mode of analysis let us now confront some of the 'horror stories' that well-meaning 'liberals' bring forth to shame 'reactionaries' such as ourselves.

Child labour: this has strictly nothing to do with factory legislation today. Nevertheless, it was very emotive and linked to it historically. To a family with low-paid mother and father the temptation to send children out to work instead of to school is intense. This is a violation of children's rights. The answer to it is to make education compulsory and to subsidize low pay.

Industrial disease (such as pneumoconiosis or asbestosis): if the risks of contracting such diseases are *known*, no sane worker will run them. Legislation is otiose. The problems arise when the risks are *unknown*. Then the workers will not know them and nor will anyone else. What help can legislation be here? We may as well prohibit everything, for unknown risks by definition may attach to everything. Ordinary workers will judge which activities they wish to undertake according to their own tastes in these uncertain situations – i.e. those of everyday life. There is a last case: where the risks are *known to some* but not to the workers. If those who know be the management or the employer then, by not divulging them, they would be liable at law for massive damage suits. The common law of third party damages (negligence) applies with rigour. Should government know, then it is only necessary for it to divulge the information to workers to avoid the consequences. Finally, should others – private citizens not within industry – know, there is no case obviously for factory legislation. There is a question, however, as to whether liability should be extended to them should they not pass their knowledge on, if necessary at a price, to those potentially affected. This question is too complex to pursue here. Thus again in this general case of knowledge not fully distributed, factory law is otiose.

Racial discrimination: this is somewhat analogous to the pay and conditions of the least productive whom society wishes to help just as they wish to help those who are discriminated against because of racial prejudice. The difference is that the former are objectively least productive, whereas the latter are just as productive and the victims of subjective prejudice or dislike, the tastes of their fellow citizens, or so it is alleged. Notice now that if this is so, those who exercise racial discrimination will be penalized by the market, if the state does nothing. For they will have to pay higher wages for whites or yellows or whatever they prefer, than for their black or white or whatever alternatives who are just as productive. Their competitors who are racially indifferent will eventually force them, under competitive pressure, to hire more of the racial group to survive and so force equality of wages. Should the prejudiced firms insist on not hiring in this way, they will be driven out of business and the other firms will equalize wages for them. Hence, discrimination based on racial prejudice would be eradicated by the free market.

Nevertheless, society will no doubt be disturbed by the transitional travails of the group discriminated against and wish to help it. Then it should do so by direct cash transfer paid for out of general taxation. This will not reduce employment among this group but will compensate them for discrimination. By contrast, insisting on 'equal pay for equal work' will reduce jobs for them, just as minimum wages do for the low-paid.

In short, then, the argument of this section is that, first, employment protection raises employers' costs just as do minimum wages, causing a reduction in employment; second, with some exceptions people are best able to judge what pay and conditions they will accept; third, any intervention to improve the lot of some group should be done via direct transfers and not by burdening the employer.

THE LAWS THEMSELVES

Appendix B contains a brief account of the complex mass of legislation for employment protection. The basic thrust of it, considered here, is, however, simple enough and well known. Essentially, it consists of (a) protection against 'unfair dismissal', compensation for redundancy, and various rights to time off and expenses, (b) health and safety rules for places of work, (c) sex and race discrimination provisions, including especially 'equal pay' for women. In the main these laws are enforced by special industrial tribunals.

The provisions of (a) on unfair dismissal and other rights were forged by the Employment Protection Act, 1975. Unfair dismissal protection has, since the 1980 Employment Act, been restricted to those who have been in their job for at least a year and for at least two years if they work for small businesses. Nevertheless, labour protection laws are still cited by small businesses as a major problem limiting recruitment. They fear not only the legal costs and possible damages, but also the loss of management time in fighting the cases brought against them. The problem is that even workers who have given no trouble for the minimum qualifying period cannot be guaranteed not to avail themselves of these rights once they have qualified for them, and the employer is then caught with large potential expenses. Many of the statutory rights are expensive, even without litigation, for example guaranteed payments for days when the employer cannot provide work (e.g. when a strike elsewhere deprives him of inputs), paid maternity leave and sick leave, and the right to information on the business.

Health and safety rules emanating from the 1974 Health and Safety at Work Act, and other enactments, are also extremely burdensome for small businesses. They flew in the face of the advice of the Robens Committee (1972) that there should be more self-regulation on these matters. A firm, for example, in the North West found that to comply with these rules it would have had to produce very costly documentation and procedures into what was a highly flexible and variable production operation (Kirby, 1985). Large businesses may be better able to absorb these costs in their overheads, though even for them there will be additional costs. One industry that has been heavily affected is the hotel industry. If one compares the costs and availability of hotel space in France and the UK, for example, it is striking how much better off the French are, with hotels which no doubt would be closed down here by the inspectors and yet are most welcome for travellers (who are of course quite free not to use them).

Equal pay for women (based on the Equal Pay Act 1970 and Sex Discrimination Act of 1975) was first introduced in 1975. In the most extensive study of it available, Snell *et al.* (1981) found that over the period 1974–7 it had resulted in a fall in numbers of women employed in most organizations studied and in two of them 'to little more than half the numbers employed at the start of the research in 1974'.

PROPOSED REFORMS OF THIS LEGISLATION

Our preferred solution is to abolish these laws, lock, stock and barrel, and let the worker protect himself against poor conditions by voting with his feet, given that we have in place a system of in-work benefits (whether negative income tax or the current system) to help the low paid.

This solution is out of tune with the 'step-by-step' philosophy that has been adopted by this Conservative Government, on grounds of political caution. Essentially, the worry is that one or two abuses could occur at a critical moment and cause a political storm if substantial control is not retained over a transitional period. There are also difficulties raised by external relations (e.g. below, the Equal Pay Act). A number of steps can be suggested in this case.

With employment protection, first, we suggest extending the qualifying period for all businesses to five years, and exempting small businesses altogether. Small businesses involve an essentially personal relationship between employer and employee, so the risk of 'abuse' is small in any case. It is further reduced by the maintenance of their rights for employees in other businesses, with whom small businesses must compete in their recruitment.

Second, we suggest that an employee be permitted to 'contract out' of these rights (an option denied him at present). Thus he may freely sign an alternative contract – possibly with more pay or other benefits than he would otherwise enjoy – in which he forgoes these statutory rights. Most large firms will not worry unduly about the matter. Those who find the Acts onerous may, however, well like to offer this contracting out procedure, to the benefit of all (their employees, if they prefer the alternative benefits, will be better off too).

In the case of health and safety legislation, we suggest a return to the Robens Committee's concept of self-regulation. At present, breach of the regulations constitutes a criminal offence – this should cease to be so. Instead, the regulations should have the status of an advisory code, and each industry's trade association or equivalent body should have the responsibility for seeing that the code is adhered to in a reasonable manner, allowing for the circumstances of the industry. Small businesses in particular would be given considerable latitude, merely having to satisfy those responsible that sensible precautions, appropriate to the firm's size and financial strength, have been taken. Ultimate responsibility for overseeing this process can be vested in a government ministry, and a report should be published annually on the state of health and safety measures. This solution would reassure the public that matters were being kept under surveillance, while removing the severe inflexibility of current arrangements.

The Equal Pay and Sex Discrimination Acts, finally, pose a problem for female employment. This, however, has been the most buoyant sector of the labour market, partly because women generally do not use the legislation and so mitigate its damage. Unfortunately, the European Court of Justice has declared 'equal pay for work of equal value' now as a matter of human right. As members of the EEC, the Government was forced to implement this in an amendment to the Equal Pay Act with effect from 1 January 1984. It is offensive to have a foreign court thus able to influence British law. However, it is one of the consequences of EEC membership. What the court cannot do is regulate how UK officials go about implementing the law. We suggest that the Equal Opportunities Commission be wound up and other executive branches of government told not to enforce this law. This would then leave it to individuals or unions to enforce these rights through the industrial tribunals. These cases are, however, difficult to prove because 'equal value' is hard to demonstrate and the law provides for a variety of exceptions. Therefore while this is not a satisfactory situation, it would no doubt significantly reduce the limited damage caused by the legislation.

A similar philosophy of permitting contracting-out, exemptions for small business, as well as non-implementation or benign neglect can be followed over other 'miscellaneous' pieces of employment protection (noted in Appendix B). There is much of this, but it is of much less importance than those we have examined and we do not go into details.

6

Housing, Mobility and the Regions

So far we have ignored the effects of regional differences arising from immobility of labour. Yet these differences are in themselves a major part of the unemployment problem. A combination of very high and below average unemployment in different regions will not only be less efficient and cause more social problems than evenly-spaced unemployment, but also implies higher national average unemployment.

Consider two regions – North and South – one of which, the North, has experienced a decline of demand (a deterioration in its terms of trade) relative to the other. The market for labour is depicted in figure 6.1.

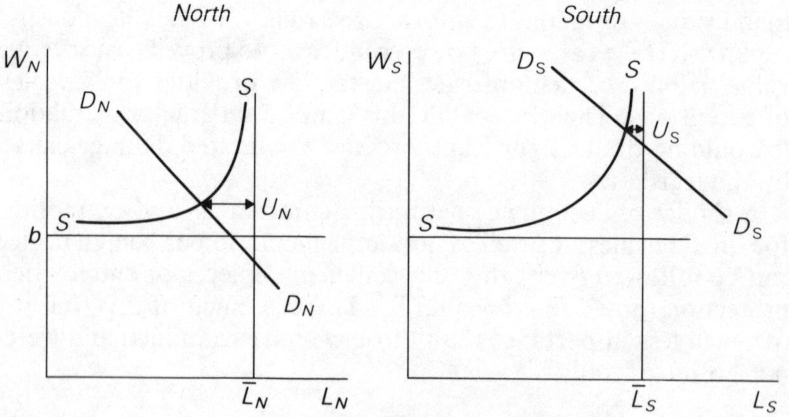

Figure 6.1 The regional problem

L = Labour quantity (N = North, S = South). SS = supply curve. DD = demand curve. w = real wages. b = real benefits. $\bar{L}$ = labour force available. U = unemployment.

As discussed earlier, the benefit rate sets a wage floor beneath the supply of relatively unskilled labour and tilts the supply curve as shown, so that it neither reaches the 'floor' nor the full labour force capacity, but becomes highly elastic (or flat) as it gets closer to the floor and highly inelastic (or vertical) as it gets closer to labour force capacity. The benefit is *nationally* set uniformly across the country at a level dictated by political pressures. Now demand varies between North and South and since real wages cannot fall far enough in the North, unemployment results, while in the South real wages rise sharply since labour supplies cannot be easily increased at these low levels of unemployment. One part of the inefficiency can easily be seen by considering the effect of moving one *employed* man from North to South. His extra product in the South will clearly be greater than the loss of his product in the North. The other part is the increased unemployment nationally.

The situation would be alleviated if people moved from North to South until real wages were equated – see figure 6.2.

This both eliminates significant differences in unemployment and reduces national unemployment. The reduction in national unemployment follows from the difference in the slope of the supply curve (provided the demand elasticities in the two regions are not extremely dissimilar). As ten men move South (and shift $\bar{L}_S$ out, $\bar{L}_N$ in), wages will fall substantially in the South while they will rise little in the North. Consequently job gains in the South will exceed job reduction in the North.

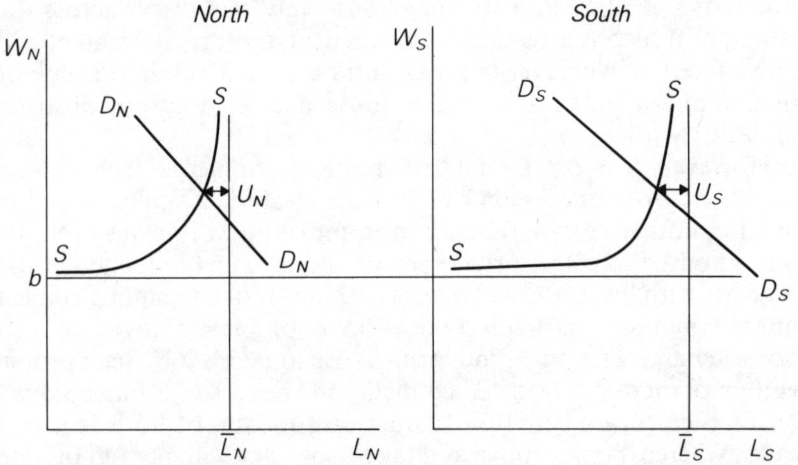

Figure 6.2 The regional labour markets with full mobility (symbols as in figure 6.1)

There is one further factor which must be mentioned. If union power is higher in the North, this will aggravate the problem of unemployment – both the differences between regions and nationally. As union power increases in the North, demand for labour in the union sector is reduced. The men made unemployed there seek work in the non-union sector but since wages there are already low, they are prevented from falling much by the benefit floor and few additional jobs are correspondingly created to absorb them. In terms of figure 6.1, we can think of union power as shifting the total demand curve for labour, $D_N D_N$, to the left, treating W_N as the non-union wage. The reason is that at a given non-union real wage, *union* wages are higher with higher union power, so demand for union labour is lower, so total labour demand (union and non-union) is also lower. Hence, union power in the North will further worsen Northern unemployment, for a given immobile labour force there.

HOUSING AND MOBILITY – THE INTERACTION BETWEEN THE HOUSING AND LABOUR MARKETS

The UK market for housing is, in the unregulated private sector, a unified market. Home owners may move from one region to another, selling and buying houses at the free market rate. Private renters may do the same, exchanging one rent for another in the (limited) free market. This links house and land prices across the country. It also means that home owners and private renters will move freely to wherever in the country they can obtain the highest (hedonic) real wage and so the house market does not obstruct mobility.

However, it is not the end of the story. Someone who rents a council house in one region will have the greatest difficulty in renting one in another region. Therefore to move he will have to rent or buy a house in the free private sector and give up his council house together with his subsidized rent. This limits mobility among council house tenants. It particularly does so among unemployed council house tenants who might move otherwise to take a job. Such people enjoy not merely subsidized council rents but also (as unemployed on supplementary benefits) 100 per cent rebates of both rent and rates, whereas if they move and take a job they will pay full private rents (or mortgages) and lose their rebates (or much of them depending on their eligibility for housing benefit). Similar arguments apply to people in the protected rental sectors scheduled by the Rent Acts – once they lose their 'sitting' tenant protection they will have to go into the free market.

This feature of the housing market – the limit on mobility of protected tenants, employed and unemployed – is what creates the problem of immobility in the labour market. A gap opens up for these people (mainly non-skilled and semi-skilled workers on lower than average pay), between non-union real wages in the South and non-union real wages in the North. Corresponding to this gap there is, as illustrated, a difference in unemployment. The lower non-union real wages in the North imply that more people are in the 'unemployment trap', with wage opportunities too close to the benefits they receive on the dole. (Remember that, though strong Northern unions will close the gap between *union* wages North and South, this will *increase* the gap between *non-union* wages in the two areas, as explained in chapter 2. For example, as they drive up Northern union wages, more people will be pushed into the non-union sector where they will drive wages down and increase unemployment.)

This approach to regional unemployment is supported by UK empirical evidence. The evidence also makes it possible for us to estimate the size of the welfare loss caused to the national economy by the immobility resulting from these housing problems. The welfare loss arises from the effect of the housing institutions on labour mobility. Because council tenants cannot move, they produce less for the nation than they would do in a different region. A simple measure would be the effect on *national* unemployment of this reduced mobility times the wages for an unskilled worker. The measure is overstated by assuming that 'unemployed' men do no significant work, which may not be strictly correct owing to the shadow economy (Matthews, 1982). Against this the measure omits the loss due to regional disparity in men's marginal product. So on balance it may suffice as an approximation.

We may *test* the theory as follows. It predicts that regional unemployment will rise, after adjusting for national factors, for three main reasons:

(1) reduced regional demand;
(2) higher regional union power;
(3) higher regional council house subsidies (and Rent Act protection).

This prediction is amply borne out by the UK evidence. We constructed indices corresponding to (1)–(3) above for each region by year from 1963 to 1979 – details are available in Minford, Peel and Ashton (1985). We then had 187 observations on regional unemployment and these indices, and we related regional unemployment to these and to national unemployment (to allow for the effect of common national determinants of unemployment). Table 6.1 shows the results.

We can use these results to obtain an approximate estimate of the *national* welfare loss from housing-induced immobility. Let us assume that any unemployment *reduction* in a high unemployment region as a result of emigration to a low unemployment region does not raise unemployment in the host region. The model suggests that this will be close to the truth because it will be *wages* in the host region that mainly adjust, being on the vertical part of its supply curve, well above the benefit 'floor'.

Our housing mobility index measures the extent to which a region's actual rents have been held below free market rents by housing market restrictions – especially by the Rent Acts and

Table 6.1 Dependent variable: regional unemployment percentage

	Constant	*IPSTAR*	*UNR*	*MI*	*UHAT*	*SEE*	R^2
Total effect of variations across regions and over time							
	−9.05	−7.6	21.8	0.04	0.69	1.66	0.51
	(1.7)	(1.4)	(4.3)	(4.7)	(3.0)		
Division of effects over region and over time							
Effect of variation over time only[a]							
	−6.3	−5.2	18.8	0.013	0.66	0.72	0.91
	(1.4)	(1.9)	(4.1)	(1.5)	(4.6)		
Effect of variation across regions only[b]							
	−4.19	−9.4	15.3	0.062	—	1.58	0.60
	(0.7)	(1.3)	(2.5)	(6.1)			

Notes: t-values in parenthesis.
IPSTAR = regional index of production relative to national index
UNR = unionization rate (fraction of labour force) for region
MI = mobility index for region
UHAT = national unemployment rate predicted by Liverpool model
SEE = standard error of estimate; R^2 = fraction of variation explained.
[a]This is achieved by including a dummy variable for each region.
[b]Achieved by including a dummy variable for each year and dropping *UHAT* which is then redundant.

subsidies to council house rents. A value of 100 implies no obstruction to mobility, while the average value in 1979 at 175.5 implied that free market rents were 75.5 per cent above what average renters were paying, so that these renters were correspondingly deterred from moving (for to move they would have to pay free market rents in a new area, as against their subsidized local arrangement). The average value in the eight regions other than the South East, East Anglia and the East Midlands (regions where unemployment was relatively low and which would therefore tend to be host regions) was 177.3.

The effect of this index on a region's unemployment rate is estimated at 0.04 (i.e. 10 points on the index raise the unemployment rate by 0.4 percentage points). On our assumption that the host region's unemployment rate is unaffected by an influx of surplus labour from elsewhere, a fall in the eight regions' index to the *lowest* regional value prevailing (that of the South West at 161) would have reduced national unemployment by $16.3 \times 0.04 \times$ share of 8 regions in total unemployment (0.685 in 1981) $= 0.45$ per cent. Thus the national unemployment rate could fall about half a percentage point if all problem regions were to adopt 'best practice' in application of existing Rent Act and Council subsidy regulations.

A more dramatic result would occur if all rent restrictions were abolished. That is, the Rent Acts would be made null and void in effect and council house rents raised to free market levels, thus bringing the Mobility Index to 100 in all regions (for such a big change, the host regions would need to abolish restrictions also, so that the housing market could produce an adequate supply of new rented accommodation for the resulting influx). According to our equation this would have an effect on national unemployment of $77.3 \times 0.04 \times 0.685 = 2.1$ per cent. Clearly, this estimate is subject to greater uncertainty than the previous one, since our equations were estimated over a period when severe restrictions were always in effect, so we are extrapolating well beyond our direct experience. Nevertheless, the effects of total liberalization are as likely to be greater than estimated as they are lesser, so in our ignorance a figure of around 2 percentage points for the effects of housing-induced immobility can still reasonably be taken as a 'central' guide.

How much is this unemployment effect worth in terms of money product? Clearly some will be satisfied with the seriousness of the unemployment effect itself. But to get it in money terms we may multiply the unemployment in millions, about 0.5 million, by an average 'unskilled' wage. Average male manual earnings in 1984 prices are about £160 per week (£8300 per year) so it seems reasonable to suppose that the unemployed workers would be willingly employed by private firms at £100 per week or about £5000 per year. On this basis the loss of money value to the nation is $£5000 \times 0.5 = £2500$ million, or around £2.5 billion, just under 1 per cent of GDP.

IS THERE A SOLUTION TO THE PROBLEM?

The problem we have described has been the subject of two sorts of proposed solution: first, regional subsidies, and second, measures to increase mobility.

Regional Subsidies

It is argued by some that movements of population should be limited for various – mainly social – reasons. One is that communities in the North should be kept alive and prosperous if possible. This would preserve part of British culture and the warmth and quality of life in these communities, which would be destroyed by their dispersion. Another such reason is overcrowding in the South. Yet another – economic – reason is that extra infrastructure would need to be provided in the South, already available in the North.

These reasons can readily be questioned. Scottish communities for example have had massive emigration, yet the community links between emigrés and their home villages and towns are strong. With modern communications, links are easier to preserve than ever before.

Southern 'overcrowding' is patchy and controlled by relative prices, which could be allowed still greater play if Rent Act effects were eliminated. Areas of Central London are emptying, for example, while expensive suburbs are growing, yet migration of low-paid workers from the North would naturally go to those areas of Central London where rentals should be plentiful and cheap.

As for infrastructure, the cost of its infilling in the South is often trivial or zero, for the area is so well provided. If relative prices are allowed to induce people to go to these areas which Southern people are leaving, this will most particularly apply.

If, nevertheless, it is wished to give *some* support to regions from a balance of such arguments, what is the right way to do it? The objective could then most naturally be expressed as: to keep people and *employment for them* in these regions – i.e. a regional jobs objective.

The cheapest way to achieve this objective is to give a regional employment subsidy. A subsidy to capital – as has been the practice with regional grants and loans to projects – is perverse in its effect. Even if great care is taken to use the number of jobs per £ as the criterion for distributing these grants and loans, this only converts them into a selective employment subsidy. The problems with such selectivity are, first, that the 'dead weight' element is considerable and will grow over time towards 100 per cent. By this is meant that some of the jobs 'created' would have occurred anyway. Furthermore, as time goes by, the government money will be entirely captured by those who least need it because competition for the funds through the lobbying process will drive the price of lobbying up until it equals the value of the money. At this point only those companies will use it who would have made a profit of this amount from the operation anyway, and marginal job creation will not be induced.

A classic example of this process is the 'enterprise zone'. A place in such a zone is valuable because it is exempt from certain taxes and regulations. But since there is an excess demand for these places, the 'price' (in lobbying and other activities) of getting one is driven up eventually, so that nothing happens.

The second problem with selectivity is that it is arbitrary and a violation of equality under the law. Absurd and unjust anomalies can occur with firm *X* attracting subsidies and firm *Y* (just like it in all essential respects) not.

Thus a regional employment subsidy should be a straightforward per man subsidy restricted only to the given regions (varying perhaps with the unemployment of each region).

While a regional employment subsidy is the logical way to proceed, we are not in favour of it because we are not impressed by the arguments for any regional subsidy. It should in any case be recalled that the measures already proposed on taxes, benefits and union power will have a substantial equating effect on regional unemployment and very probably also on regional non-union wage differentials. They will therefore on their own very likely create a reduction in pressure to migrate, via revival in the regional economies. At the very least we would wish to see how well the regions could cope without subsidy through their own efforts. This is reinforced by the problem of moral hazard in the regions. The presence or prospect of subsidy dilutes pressures to improve local performance – as is only too obvious from the behaviour of politicians and local groups in an area like Merseyside.

Improving Mobility

Various government schemes exist to subsidize moving between regions. But they are little counterweight to the disincentive created by the housing market. For the latter reduces the net rewards from moving for a long period, possibly even permanently, while the former generally give a modest subsidy only to the cost of moving itself. Their effect has accordingly been found to be small, see Minford, Peel and Ashton (1985).

We briefly described earlier in this chapter how Rent Acts, the council house system, and benefit entitlements interacted to reduce the incentives to move, especially for the unemployed. A full account of the Rent Acts and council house system is beyond the scope of this book, but see Minford, Peel and Ashton (1985) on these too. The provisions of the Rent Acts particularly are extraordinarily complex, involving layer upon layer of regulation, control, and occasional derestriction. Essentially, and notwithstanding some (limited) deregulation measures in the Conservatives' 1980 Housing Act, substantial regulation of rents and of tenure exists for both furnished and unfurnished tenancies. It is still extremely hard to evict a tenant as the law generally requires either 'tenant misconduct' or the provision of suitable alternative accommodation. With rentable accommodation limited by the Acts, this is rarely possible. Our most recent estimates suggest that regulated rents are about 54 per cent below market-clearing levels on average across the country. A recent GLC survey (1985) of the private rented sector in London suggests that 'protected rents' were about 67 per cent below 'unprotected rents' in 1984 (para. 40).

Let us consider an idealized solution to the problem of housing reform. Suppose all tenancies were at free market rents under free market conditions of tenure (i.e. some contractual basis agreed freely and solely between landlord and tenant). Then for the employed man in the North, housing will not obstruct his decision to move. He will pay market rents wherever he is (minus whatever state rebate he may get via housing benefits).

But what about the unemployed man? Under our present system his rents will be 100 per cent rebated if he stays in the North, whereas he will only get a partial rebate if he takes work in the South. His incentive to move is even less! Furthermore, the comparison between his out-of-work income and his in-work income – even if he takes work in the North – will now be much more favourable to remaining unemployed, because his rents have gone up, with 100 per cent subsidy if unemployed, but only a partial one if employed. Hence ironically, on its own, letting rents rise to free market levels reduces mobility among the unemployed. It may well also increase unemployment in the North and will do so if the number of employed induced to leave (or not take) employment at low wages exceeds those induced to migrate to the South.

Since 1979 the Conservative Government has been following this policy on council house rents and, to the small extent it has loosened Rent Act restriction in protected tenancies. *It may well have worsened the problem.*

Such are the complexities forced on us by a system as heavily intervened-in as is ours. But we need not give up. There is an answer, which is perfectly reasonable and politically acceptable. This is to introduce the 70 per cent ceiling on benefits as a percentage of previous net income in work which was suggested earlier in this book. Such a gap between in and out of work income is a form of pressure on people to take a new job at rather lower rates of pay than their last one if they cannot find one at the old rate. If they do so, the state will, nevertheless, under our existing system (one whose principle we would retain but whose practice we must improve) support their in-work net income above a decent minimum living standard.

With this ceiling in place, the unemployed man will now find that his unemployment benefits do not go up. His incentive to find work in the North will be unchanged because he will still be 30 per cent worse off out of work. But his incentive to move to the South will now be considerably greater because he now has to pay a larger proportion of the economic rent if he stays in the North.

A simple arithmetical example may be helpful. Suppose in his previous job he was paid £100 (per week), with net pay of £80. His benefits under the ceiling are 70 per cent of £80 = £56 per week. Suppose that in the South he could earn £120, net pay of £95; but his rent would be £15 higher, and we suppose that he is not therefore interested in moving South (or in taking another job in the North at £100). Now his Northern rent goes up, because of deregulation, by £15.

His out-of-work benefit will not change, remaining at 70 per cent of his work income if he stays North. But it will now be only 58.9 per cent of his work income if he goes South (previously it was 70 per cent if you allowed for the rent factor). His incentive to move will have increased significantly.

The ceiling we have proposed is not the only way to create pressures on the unemployed to take available jobs at lower wages than before. Others exist from 'moral' pressure through 'workfare' schemes all the way to straight compulsion via cutting off benefits for job refusal. Let us leave it at that and assume that some such mechanism is functioning.

Then we can pursue our main purpose which is to reduce the obstacles to mobility posed by housing regulations as such. Clearly, our argument implies that the rental sector should be freed from regulation entirely.

But in practice some timetable is necessary. The easiest course would be, first, to announce that over the next five years the ceiling on regulated rents would be raised to free market levels in five equal percentage instalments, with all regulation of rents to cease in 1990. As for security of tenure provisions enjoined by the courts, a two-year transitional period could be announced in which *existing* security would prevail. At the end of this period, landlords and tenants would be expected to have freely negotiated contracts and the courts would no longer be involved in enforcing statutory 'security'.

Secondly, council tenants. Here we need only follow existing policy to raise council rents to market levels, but over a similar period to that for regulated tenancies, so that by 1990 these rents too are at market levels. That this implicit policy does not violate council tenants' rights might be considered clear from its failure to be contested to date. Those tenants who choose to buy their own houses are able to do so on most favourable terms, which might partially reflect their rights accumulated by years of tenure and partially the state's desire for them to become home-owners with a 'stake in society'; but should those who choose *not* to buy have their rights of tenure reflected in some way? The problem for them appears to be the same as that for regulated tenants: 'what the state giveth (at least relatively recently, via the 1980 Housing Act) the state may take away'. Their *rights* are comparatively weak. The *good fortune* of those who can buy is undeniable.

What of security of tenure for council tenants? Here there are statutory grounds (non-payment of rent, etc.) on which councils may evict tenants. But, in some cases, suitable alternative accommodation must be provided, and a council's power to evict for even 'gross under-occupation' is almost totally fettered. Council housing has now largely developed a status of 'renter of last resort' for the poor, the old, the handicapped and the unfortunate. There would seem to be every reason to move people out of this last resort housing as soon as they are capable of renting normally. Many of these will buy their own house within the next five years. Those that then remain will largely be the difficult cases, unlikely to move in any event. But we wish to ensure that those capable of moving are not deterred from doing so to their advantage by the existence of security of tenure (albeit at an economic rent) in their existing accommodation. All this then points to an additional statutory ground for moving tenants *who do not* fall into the 'renter of last resort' category, into suitable alternative accommodation outside the council sector.

Our proposals are 'step-by-step' in one sense, that they embody transitional periods and recognize existing rights. Even so, the announcement of such a programme for regulated and protected tenancies (not for council tenants where we advocate merely an extension of existing policies) could create a storm of protest from housing lobbies and so on. The storm could be weathered, but it might be risky.

Are there other measures that would reach the same conclusion, if by a more roundabout course?

One obvious variation would be to introduce a new criterion into the setting of 'fair rents' – that of scarcity. This single amendment would allow tribunals to raise rents towards market levels. Scarcity could be made a binding criterion (i.e. rents must not be below market levels) by a certain time, e.g. 1990.

A second series of variants could build on the innovations in the 1980 Housing Act (the assured tenancy and the shorthold) as well as on the licence agreement which has always been outside 'full' Rent Act protection. These measures should now be extended so as to deregulate all new tenancies, and relets. This one measure would instill confidence into existing and potential landlords – who are at present trapped in a legal minefield involving licences (unprotected) and tenancies (fully protected) – and stimulate the supply of new (unrestricted) lets.

A third variant would allow the landlord to draw up new (contractual) tenancies with a clause denying the tenant the right to go to the Rent Officer for assessment of a 'fair rent'. Since no landlord would be willing to let without such a clause, this would effectively place all new tenancies outside the Rent Acts' rent provisions.

This would still leave the problem of repossessing existing regulated tenancies. If rents were at market levels, it would be easy (a mere matter of telephoning market agencies) for landlords to offer tenants 'comparable' accommodation at comparable prices where at present it is often impossible. A general mandatory ground for eviction, after the tenancy agreement (contract) has expired, could be made such an offer by the landlord. (At present a landlord may only – at the court's discretion – obtain possession by providing 'suitable alternative accommodation' which must consist of either council accommodation or a (similar) regulated residence, and the court must be satisfied that it is 'reasonable' to order possession.) This would be our fourth variant.

Thus by these four variants, existing rents would be raised where there was scarcity (i.e. market rents exceeded regulated rents), existing tenants could be evicted (though, of course, there is no reason to suppose a landlord would evict a 'good tenant' paying a market rent – it is the fact that he can which is important) after their contract is up once market rents were reached, and new tenancies would be unrestricted.

The proposals made here will reduce the living standards of those who use protected rental accommodation, whether council or private. These people are for the most part poor. The distributional consequences of the proposals are therefore regressive.

As they stand, they also have no revenue cost because the higher rents will be paid by the renters themselves, under the assumption that out-of-work benefits are subject to a 70 per cent ceiling and that housing benefits are fixed (being related to income).

In principle it is possible for the distributive consequences to be offset by higher housing benefits (the 70 per cent ceiling would imply that only 70 per cent of this addition would accrue to the unemployed). However, this must be seen against a background of our proposals in chapter 2 for large tax cuts and a negative income tax. These would automatically ensure that no one would be pushed below 'subsistence' income while most poor people would be generally better off from being extracted from the tax net.

CONCLUSION

The British housing market is in a mess because it is over-regulated and this has serious effects on mobility, so on unemployment. It *is* politically feasible to reform the regulative system, particularly against the background of our proposals for tax/benefit reforms. We have suggested ways in which it could be done without sweeping aside existing institutions, by building on the 1980 Housing Act, the first 'step' in housing law reform put in place by this Government. The step-by-step approach that has proved so successful in union law reform could be used here too. Let us now have the second step. For this is one major way, in conjunction with our other proposals, to solve the regional problem.

7

Comparative Analysis of Four Major European Countries

THE NATURE OF TAX/BENEFIT SYSTEMS ON THE CONTINENT

We studied four Continental systems, those of Belgium, France, West Germany and Italy.* Before we get down to detailed analysis of each country, we can make a number of general points which are highly relevant to the UK.

There is effectively no 'poverty trap' in these countries. The major reason is that 'family assistance' is not means tested. There is no equivalent of the means-tested FIS and passported benefits. Instead, family benefits are paid, on the same basis as child benefits here, on the basis of number of dependents, regardless of income.

This is subject to qualification for the very lowest income groups who may receive social assistance. It has proved impossible to obtain absolutely precise information about this, which is discretionary ('according to need') in all four countries. The impression given by our contacts is that this assistance is not important, except for a very small minority of workers, i.e. it is a safety net from the most extreme poverty. We have assumed in what follows that this impression is correct.

A second reason for the absence of the poverty trap is the 'tapered' tax rates on low incomes employed in all four countries. Instead of the standard rate applying to these low incomes, each country has a set of 'tax tables' which embodies MRTs rising slowly towards the standard rate.

This means that, just as there is no poverty trap, so net incomes in work are permitted to fall quite steeply as gross income falls.

*The material in this chapter has not been updated. It therefore applies to the position as seen in mid-1982.

MRTs do not appear to exceed 40 per cent on low incomes (above the social assistance level).

As is well known, VAT is used to raise a higher proportion of taxes in these countries. Especially with higher rates on luxuries, this does not alter the picture of relatively low MRTs on low incomes. Even including VAT, MRTs do not exceed 50 per cent on low incomes, and are generally quite a lot lower than this.

Turning to unemployment compensation, the countries can be divided into two that have benefit/income *ratio* systems, where there is no 'unemployment trap' (France and Italy); one that has a system very like the UK with flat rate minimum entitlements where the unemployment trap is as serious as here (Belgium); and finally one that has a 'mixed' system intermediate between these (Germany) where there is evidence of a trap though only at the very lowest income levels. This difference has proved interesting, enabling us to compare experiences. It is certainly no coincidence that Belgium shares with the UK unemployment rates substantially higher than the other three.

We now briefly describe each country's system, our primary concern being with its impact on unemployment.

BELGIUM

There is no standard rate of income tax in Belgium. Tax is levied on the basis of graduated tax tables up to 80 per cent above average earnings, and tax allowances are given for dependents. Marginal tax rates start at around 30 per cent at one half of average earnings, and rise continuously up to 47.5 per cent at this point. From here, the MRT rises to 72 per cent at 10 times average earnings. These figures include social security contributions by employees at 10.1 per cent (average and marginal at all incomes). Table 7.1 illustrates this.

VAT is levied at 17 per cent in Belgium (but exceptionally 6 per cent on basic necessities and a further tax of 8 per cent is added making 25 per cent for 'luxuries'). Hence total MRT's for employees rise from around 42 per cent at one half of average earnings, reaching a top rate of around 80 per cent at 10 times average. These rates are much lower than in the UK at low incomes, similar at average earnings and about 10 percentage points higher for higher incomes.

Table 7.1 Marginal and average rates of (direct) tax[a] in Belgium (1981) (average earnings = 100)

	Single		*m + 2 – wife not working*	
Earnings	*MRT*	*ART*	*MRT*	*ART*
150	47	32.8	47	29.7
100	44.5	26.7	39.4	22.8
70	36	20.8	36	15.2
50	30	17.4	30	11.8

Note: [a]Employee social security contributions included: the rate is 10.1 per cent (average and marginal) at all income levels.

Social security contributions by employers are at the rate of 38.85 per cent of gross wages. This is very high compared with the UK's 12 per cent, and turns out to be an important element in Belgian performance.

'Family welfare' is dealt with via child benefits only. These are, however, somewhat higher than rates in the UK. For example, for two children aged 7 and 11, child benefit in 1980 was around £13.50 per week (against £11.70 in 1982 in the UK); for four children (aged 7, 11, 14, 16) it was around £40 per week (against £23.40 here). These benefits do not vary with income.

There is no family income supplement otherwise, apart from 'public assistance', administered by local authorities on a rigorous and discretionary basis. There are no benefits (such as housing cost subsidies, free school meals), related to income levels. (This statement does not apply to benefits for the old or invalids or other special groups which are excluded from our analysis.) Public assistance is reported as being used sparingly for cases of real hardship and descends from the medieval poor laws. It appears therefore that this is of minor significance.

Unemployment compensation which is not taxable is at the rate of 60 per cent of gross earnings for all employees in their first year of unemployment. Thereafter heads of households only (with minor exceptions) receive this rate indefinitely, while others drop to a rate of 40 per cent of gross earnings indefinitely. However, these ratios to gross earnings are qualified by minimum and maximum flat rate payments (which in 1980 were BF 4910 (about £60) per week maximum for all employees and BF 3740 (£47) minimum for heads of households, BF 2900 (£36) for others).

Table 7.2 Belgian replacement ratios[a] (1981) (average earnings = 100)

Earnings	*m + 2 – wife not working*	*Single*
For heads of households (ratios are for year 1 and all successive years)		
150	65	66
100	89	92
70	96	101
50	124	143
	Year 1	*All subsequent years*
For others (assume have taxable status as single)		
150	66	66
100	92	61
70	101	78
50	143	110

Note: [a]Assumes work expenses of BF 660 per week.

It is these qualifications which give the system its close similarity to that of the UK's now completely flat rate system.

The effect is illustrated in table 7.2. Replacement ratios for heads of household rise from around 90 per cent of *net* income (after work expenses) at average earnings levels, up to 124 per cent at one half of average earnings if they have a typical family, and 143 per cent if they are single (worse because tax hits them harder at work). These are indefinite in duration. For others, after a year, at these levels the ratios drop respectively to around 60 per cent rising to 110 per cent. This 'unemployment trap' is in fact more vicious than that in the UK. For the lowest income groups, income in work is not subsidized and therefore replacement ratios rise well over 100 per cent, whereas in the UK they hover around 100 per cent for these families. For single persons, ratios are much higher in Belgium than in the UK at all income levels because Belgian compensation as a fraction of gross earnings does not vary with family size.

According to estimates from Eurostat, trade union membership in Belgium has risen from 62 per cent of registered workers in 1960 to 76 per cent in 1978. The great majority of unions are organized into three large confederations. The degree of power exercised by unions is likely to be considerable. The unionization rate is

20 percentage points higher than that in the UK, and centralization appears to be greater. The rise in unionization over the last two decades is of the same order as in the UK. Nevertheless, it has been commented that these estimates are unreliable, with conflicting estimates from other sources.

Table 7.3 Estimates for Belgium on UK-style model of real wages and unemployment

(Quarterly data: 1962.1–1980.1, t-values bracketed)

Dependent variable	*log* w_t		U_t *(millions)* *(Non-linear least squares)*
Constant	−5.36	Constant	−2.1
	(1.91)		(2.9)
$D1$	−0.019	$D1$	−0.008
	(4.0)		(3.9)
$D2$	−0.006	$D2$	−0.023
	(1.4)		(9.3)
$D3$	−0.024	$D3$	−0.025
	(5.2)		(9.5)
T_{Lt}	0.83	$\log \hat{O}_t$	−0.116
	(1.6)		(7.0)
$\log b_t$	0.19	$(\log \hat{w}_t) + T_{Ft}$	0.08
	(3.8)		(7.6)
$\log N_t$	0.3	t	−0.0002
	(1.0)		(.9)
UNR_t	0.51	$\log U_{t-1}$	0.92
	(2.1)		(53.8)
$\hat{U}_t$ (millions)	−0.28	$\log N_t$	0.26
	(3.7)		(2.9)
t	0.004		
	(4.8)		
$\log w_{t-1}$	0.34		
	(3.5)		
$\bar{R}^2$	0.998		
DW	2.25	ϱ_2	−0.36
			(2.9)
χ_4^2	8.4	χ_4^2	2.1
		DW	1.72

Notes: $D1$, $D2$, $D3$ are seasonal dummy variables; $T_L =$ direct tax rate; $b =$ real benefits; $N =$ labour force; $UNR =$ unionization rate; $w =$ real wages; $U =$ unemployment; $O =$ real GDP; $T_F =$ employers' tax rate on labour; $t =$ time; $\varrho i = i_{th}$ order autocorrelation coefficient; $DW =$ Durbin–Watson statistic; $\chi_4^2 = \chi^2$ statistic for 4th order autocorrelation (Godfrey, 1978); variables with circumflex (ˆ) have been replaced with instrumental variable predictors.

Table 7.4

	Real wage equation				Unemployment equation	
L/R coefficient on	*Real benefits*	*Tax rates*	*Unemployment*	*Unionization*	*Real labour costs*	*Output*
Belgium	0.29	1.2	0.055[b]	0.77	7.7[b]	–11.2[b]
UK[a]	0.48	0.48	0.10	1.96	4.1	–8.5

Note: [a]Quarterly equation, 64.2 – 79.2, original *UNR* data.
[b]Belgian effect converted to UK basis by calculating at mean unemployment in sample period, 0.13 million.

This brief description suggests that the appropriate labour market model for Belgium is the one used for the UK. The total labour supply curve (i.e. that responding to non-union real wages) will resemble that for the UK. Unions will fix a mark-up over non-union real wages heavily influenced by real benefits grossed up for direct taxes on workers. Taxes on employers will shift the demand curve for labour to the left in both union and non-union sectors.

Estimates of this model are shown in table 7.3. In the real wage equation the coefficients on benefits and unemployment are very well determined. That for *UNR* is just significant at the 5 per cent level, while the significance of T_L just falls short of this. Data problems may account for these less robust estimates. *UNR* was noted earlier as being somewhat unreliable. The T_L series is accurate only from 1970; the data prior to this was constructed from the social security contribution rate, assuming the income tax rates were constant at 1970 levels. There is no evidence of autocorrelation in the equation. The unemployment equation is estimated by non-linear least squares because of evidence of autocorrelation. The key coefficients in the equation are well determined; in particular real labour costs have a strong positive effect on unemployment.

With the necessary *caveats* at this stage, it is quite striking how similar the coefficients are to those for the UK. The long-run values compare as is shown in table 7.4.

Though we have not been able to research Belgium to the same depth as the UK, we must regard the Belgian model as striking corroboration of our UK thesis, even to the extent of orders of magnitude. This is, however, not surprising in view of the close parallels in their unemployment compensation systems. The parallelism is mirrored in the unemployment trends of the two countries. Unemployment rates stand at 14 per cent now in Belgium, against 13 per cent in the UK; in 1964 they stood at 1–2 per cent in both countries.

Though we have not yet completed work on a full model of Belgium, we would guess that simulated total effects from introducing benefit ratio ceilings in Belgium would be of similar order to those simulated earlier for the UK.

FRANCE

As in Belgium, there is no standard rate and tax is levied in a graduated way. Allowances for family size are given by a quotient system. Marginal tax rates rise continuously from about 10 per cent on the lowest incomes to a maximum of 75 per cent. These rates include social security contribution rates of 11.9 per cent on gross wages up to FF6590 per month (1.5 times average earnings) with 5.5 per cent as the *marginal* rate above this (see table 7.5).

Table 7.5 Marginal and average tax rates in France (1981) (average earnings = 100)

Earnings	*Single*		*m + 2*	
	MRT	*ART*	*MRT*	*ART*
140	39	26.1	22	15.1
100	33	21.9	18	12.7
70	28	18.3	12	12
60	33	15.8	12	12

VAT is generally levied at 17.6 per cent; the exceptions are 33.33 per cent on 'luxuries' and 7 per cent on food, transport, books, and other 'necessities'. Total MRTs for employees hence rise from about 25 per cent to 80 per cent; these rates are lower than in the UK for low incomes.

Social security contributions by employers are 30.75 per cent of gross wages up to FF6590 per month, with a marginal rate of 8 per cent above this.

Family welfare is again dealt with solely by child benefits. There is no benefit on the first child, but benefit rises sharply with family size. For the second, the benefit in 1980 was FF70 per week (about £7), the total amount therefore for a typical family (against £11.70 in the UK in 1982). For a family with four children (aged 7, 11, 14 and 16) total benefits were FF296 per week (about £30), against £23.40 in 1982 in the UK. As compared with the UK larger families get more benefit, small families get somewhat less.

The system of emergency poor relief ('social aid') resembles that of Belgium as far as can be ascertained. There are here too no tied subsidies related to income levels. Social aid is dispensed at the local level on a discretionary basis, and appears to be of negligible importance.

The tax and family welfare system therefore implies reasonable incentives and low MRTs for those in work, while setting an income 'safety net' at very low 'subsistence' levels.

The similarity with Belgium however ends, as we turn to the unemployment compensation system. Virtually all employees are eligible for benefit ('special benefit') averaging about 68 per cent of gross earnings in their first year of unemployment. The exact formula is a small flat amount plus 65 per cent in the first quarter of unemployment, falling to 50 per cent in the fourth quarter. For the second year of unemployment, the percentage drops to around 50 per cent ('basic benefit', consisting of the same flat amount plus 42 per cent of gross earnings). For older workers only does this rate of benefit continue for up to the fourth year of unemployment, but for workers under 50 it ceases at the end of the second year. Once this basic benefit has ceased, the worker receives 'end of entitlement benefit' which in 1980 was a very small flat rate amount of FF154 per week (around £15).

Though the percentages given relate to gross earnings, they are less distorted than in Belgium as a guide to true replacement ratios, because in France alone of these four Continental countries benefits are taxable.

Furthermore, there are no minimum flat rate benefits in France. There is only a maximum flat rate which occurs at incomes 4.5 times average earnings or above. The result is that replacement ratios do not rise substantially as income levels fall, except the very lowest covered by social aid; at the same time they only start to drop

Table 7.6 French replacement ratios (1981) (average earnings = 100)

	Unemployed for				
Earnings	*3 Months*	*6 Months*	*1 Year*	*2 Years*	*After 2 Years*
m + 2[a] – wife not working					
50	n.a.	n.a.	127.8	108.8	57.2
66	100	101.4	108.9	90.3	39.9
100	98.9	96.6	96.2	77.8	27.8
200	96.6	91.7	n.a.	n.a.	n.a.
Single					
50	n.a.	n.a.	132.4	110.2	50.2
66	100.7	101.4	120	97.5	36.5
100	98.9	96.6	108.5	86.1	25.4
200	96.6	92.1	n.a.	n.a.	n.a.

Source: for 3 months and 6 months figures only: OECD (1982) *Unemployment Compensation Replacement Rates*. These ratios do not allow for work expenses; for other ratios: our estimates, including work expenses.

Note: [a]Aged less than 50, dismissed for 'economic reasons'.

significantly at very high income levels. Table 7.6 illustrates this. Hence the French employment system is close to a pure ratio system, that is, one where the ratio is constant across the income scale. The ratio itself is high for the first year but then drops steeply over time. For most employees after two years, the system becomes flat rate but at such a low level that for only the very poorest would it afford a replacement ratio of any interest.

Because of the difference in systems, our model could not be applied to France in the same form as to the UK. Figure 7.1 illustrates the nature of the French labour market. The supply curve

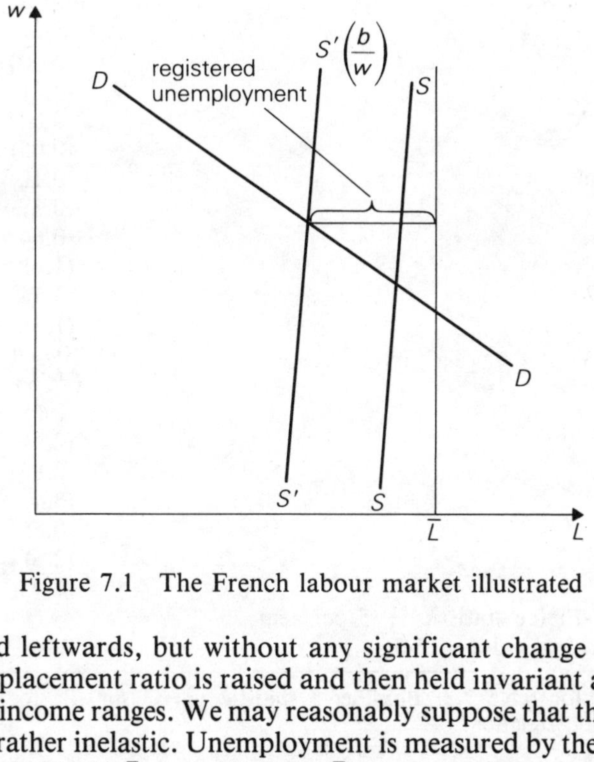

Figure 7.1 The French labour market illustrated

is shifted leftwards, but without any significant change in slope, as the replacement ratio is raised and then held invariant across all relevant income ranges. We may reasonably suppose that this supply curve is rather inelastic. Unemployment is measured by the distance between $S'S'$ and $\bar{L}$, provided that $\bar{L}$ corresponds to those eligible for benefits.

Now our model determines unemployment as a function of the (exogenous) benefit ratio and (exogenous) demographic factors, with little if any impact from real wages. Real wages are then mainly determined by the interaction of the total supply of labour (i.e. $S'S'$ minus unemployment, already determined) with the demand for

Table 7.7 Unemployment equation in France (quarterly data: 1963.1–1980.4, non-linear least squares, *t*-ratio bracketed)

Dependent variable	U_t *(millions)*
Constant	−0.35 (0.04)
$D1$	−0.08 (2.1)
$D2$	−0.15 (3.1)
$D3$	−0.08 (2.3)
$\left(\frac{b}{w}\right)_t$	0.007 (2.8)
$\log N_t$	0.044 (0.05)
$\log \hat{w}_t$	0.12 (0.5)
T_{Lt}	0.64 (1.4)
UNR_t	3.3 (1.3)
U_{t-1}	0.74 (4.6)
ϱ_1	0.65 (2.9)
ϱ_2	0.82 (8.4)
ϱ_3	0.55 (2.6)
DW	1.93
Box-Pierce statistic χ^2_8 (5 per cent critical value = 15.5)	10.4

Notes: As for table 7.3; Box-Pierce statistic $\chi^2_8 = \chi^2$ statistic for 8th order autocorrelation.

labour. From our point of view, the real wage equation is of little interest, since real wages do not affect unemployment. The result of this set-up is that variables which affected unemployment in the UK and Belgium – such as employer taxes, union power, personal direct taxes, and world trade – barely do so here, rather they affect essentially the level and/or structure of real wages. For example, increased union power will raise real wages in the union sector, but because the total labour supply is unchanged, it will lower real wages in the non-union sector in such a way that the total demand for labour is unchanged. Its effect is to raise the union/non-union wage differential, but to leave average real wages broadly unchanged (this being incidentally the 'classical' effect of unions in an otherwise undistorted labour market).

We estimated an unemployment equation for France along these lines (table 7.7). To construct the benefit/wage ratio we used the real value of benefits paid to a married man with two children in the first three months of unemployment, and divided it by our real wage series. It is a somewhat crude measure however.

The equation, apart from seasonality, has as its main arguments this ratio and total labour force to proxy demographic factors; to maintain generality and to test our theory, we also included real wages, the tax rate and unionization. The equation is estimated by non-linear least squares because of autocorrelation. It has substantial explanatory power and no residual autocorrelation appears to remain. In particular the benefit ratio is well determined, though the possibility of measurement error requires caution at this stage. In confirmation of our theory, the other variables are in no case significant, though some small effects cannot be ruled out for *UNR* and T_L.

The elasticity of unemployment to the benefit ratio (in the units here this is 17) at its mean is 0.9. This is lower than both in the UK and in Belgium, but this is what one would expect, because no individuals would decide under the French system to remain unemployed for long periods, let alone indefinitely. The effect of this system will be to encourage workers to take higher duration spells but to continue to participate in employment on a regular basis.

GERMANY

The tax and welfare system is similar to that of France and Belgium. Graduated tax tables produce MRTs which rise from about 35 per cent to a top rate of 65 per cent inclusive of 11 per cent social security contributions by employees (see table 7.8). VAT at 13 per cent (with a reduced rate of 6.5 per cent on 'necessities') raises these MRTs to a range from 43 per cent to 70 per cent. Employers' social security contributions are at a rate of 20.9 per cent of gross wages.

Table 7.8 Marginal and average tax rates in Germany, 1981 (average earnings = 100)

	Single		*m + 2*	
Earnings	*MRT*	*ART*	*MRT*	*ART*
133	53.9	32.5	35.4	24.3
100	45.8[a]	26.7	35.4[a]	20.7
60	37.7	23.3	35.4 (100)[b]	13.5 (11.1)[b]

Notes: [a]Interpolated.
[b]figures in brackets assume 'social aid'; illustrative levels in text.

Family welfare again consists only of child benefits which are not means tested. The rates in 1980 were 11.5 DM per week (first child), 23 DM (second child), 46 DM for each subsequent child – respectively about £2.75, £5.50 and £10.75. These are lower than UK rates for average family size, but higher for the largest families.

There is also 'social aid'. As in France and Belgium it is administered by the local authorities. Income has to be supplemented up to 'levels of need', but there seems to be substantial discretion. Also '*Wohngeld*' is provided on a means-tested basis, i.e. housing costs are paid in full for those who fall below the statutory poverty levels. It has been possible to extract 'illustrative' details of these levels from German officials. These are of considerable interest since they are the closest approximation to the British supplementary benefit system to be found on the Continent.

The illustrative figures are 78 DM per week for a man, 62 DM for his wife, 59 DM for children over 11, 51 DM for children aged 8–11, 35 DM for younger children, 115 DM for rent (*Wohngeld*).

Replacement ratios and MRTs using these figures are placed in brackets in tables 7.8 and 7.9. It can be seen that, if local government officials were to stick to them closely, and the criteria became widely known, there would be both a poverty trap and an unemployment trap in Germany as in the UK. At this stage it is probably wrong to make this assumption.* It appears that local discretion is considerable, that some secrecy surrounds possible practices in each locality, and that quite possibly there are in many localities stringent tests of 'willingness to work' etc. Nevertheless, social aid payments have become significant since the mid-seventies: in 1978, they

*On the basis of very recent work (Minford, 1985b) this judgement seems mistaken. The German system has become rather close to the UK system, with *Sozialhilfe* and *Wohngeld* operating much like UK supplementary benefit.

Table 7.9 Replacement ratios – Germany, (1981)[a] (average earnings = 100)

		Unemployment duration		
Earnings	*3 months**	*6 months**	*1 year*	*Thereafter*
m + 2 – wife not working				
66	94.2	88.8	79 (114)	69 (114)
100	94.0	88.3	75	65 (75)
200	92.2	81.2	n.a.	n.a.
Single				
66	93.0	86.7	77	65 (74)
100	96.3	88.5	74	63
200	92.7	84.0	n.a.	n.a.

**Source:* 3 months and 6 months (1978) OECD, 1982. These ratios do not allow for work expenses.
Note: [a]Figures in brackets assume 'social aid' illustrative levels set out in text.

were DM 10.45 billion, and in addition DM 2.1 billion was paid in *Wohngeld*.

Unemployment compensation in principle follows a ratio system. For the first year, the worker receives 68 per cent of his net income, thereafter 58 per cent indefinitely. While there are no explicit minimum rates, social aid may have introduced them implicitly; a maximum rate also occurs at 1.7 times average earnings. Table 7.9 shows the resulting replacement ratios net of 33 DM per week assumed work expenses.

The German labour market is therefore rather closer to the UK flat rate benefit regime than to a ratio regime such as Italy or France. Unlike France, too, benefit support is indefinite in duration. It can be pictured as in figure 7.1, showing a regime with a benefit ratio, only there will also be some tendency towards flattening at the lower end of the supply curve owing to social aid. The implication is that unemployment will depend not only on the statutory benefit ratio but also on real wages (negatively) and on union power (positively). Such an equation is shown in table 7.10 (without tax rate, since no time-series for this was available).

Non-linear least squares was used because of autocorrelation in the residuals; no significant autocorrelation beyond that allowed for here appears to remain. The statutory benefit ratio (now 68 per cent) in the first year was used for the replacement ratio series, *B*. This in fact only changed once in the period, in 1975 first quarter, when it rose from 62 per cent where it had been since 1960, to the

Table 7.10 Unemployment and real wage equation for Germany (quarterly data, non-linear least squares, *t*-values bracketed)

Dependent variable	U_t *(millions)* *1961.4–1980.1*		$\log w_t$ *1961.4–1980.4*
Constant	29.7 (1.0)	Constant	−0.01 (0.8)
*D*1	0.15 (11.6)	*D*1	−0.0014 (0.3)
*D*2	−0.04 (1.0)	*D*2	−0.011 (2.1)
*D*3	−0.05 (3.7)	*D*3	−0.036 (6.5)
		t	−0.0003 (1.1)
B^*_t	2.5 (2.3)	T_{Ft}	−0.11 (1.6)
$\log N_t$	−3.7 (1.2)	$\log \hat{O}_t$	0.24 (7.9)
UNR_t	17.9 (2.4)		
$\log \hat{w}_t$	−0.18 (0.5)	$\hat{U}_t$	0.03 (5.2)
U_{t-1}	0.23 (1.1)	$\log w_{t-1}$	0.77 (22.9)
ϱ_1	0.92 (6.6)	ϱ_1	−0.32 (2.6)
		ϱ_2	−0.58 (4.6)
ϱ_3	−0.09 (1.1)	ϱ_3	−0.28 (2.2)
		ϱ_4	−0.24 (2.0)
DW	2.08	*DW*	1.93
Box-Pierce statistic (χ^2_8)	7.1	χ^2_8	13.7

*statutory replacement ratio for 1st year: (i.e. 68 per cent in 1982)
Notes: As for tables 7.3 and 7.7.

current 68 per cent level. Hence B_t moves like a dummy variable. The coefficient on it is nevertheless well determined, in spite of its limited variation. The long-run elasticity of unemployment to the benefit ratio at the mean is 4.2. This is consistent with a sizeable impact on German unemployment (around 0.2 million) arising from the rise in rates enacted in 1975. A further large increase appears to have arisen from the rise in unionization by about 4 percentage points since the mid-seventies (the long-run impact of a one percentage point change in *UNR* is 0.23 million, about the same as in the UK at current unemployment). Since then in fact German unemployment has risen by one million.

A contributory factor may also have been the increasing use of social aid, which we have not incorporated in this analysis. It should also be stressed that, unlike French benefit ratios, German ratios stay indefinitely at over 60 per cent.

Given the 'mixed' nature of the German model, we also estimated an equation for real wages (regarded as a 'demand price'). This equation is also shown in table 7.10 and is of some interest. Rises in output (rise in demand) and unemployment (fall in supply) raise real wages as expected, also rises in employer taxes (leftward shift of demand) lower them, though the coefficient falls just below the 5 per cent significance level.

ITALY

The Italian tax and welfare system follows the lines of the previous three. MRTs (table 7.11) rise from 8 per cent to a top rate of 82 per cent reached at 60 times average earnings. These rates include employee social security contributions of 7.8 per cent. Standard VAT at 15 per cent (with four other rates, 2 per cent, 8 per cent, 18 per cent and 35 per cent), implies that VAT-inclusive MRTs rise from 22 per cent to a top rate of 84 per cent. Employers' social security contributions are at the rate of 40.25 per cent, one of the highest in Europe.

Table 7.11 Marginal and average tax rates – Italy (1981) (average earnings = 100)

Earnings	*Single*		*m + 2*	
	MRT	*ART*	*MRT*	*ART*[a]
150	26	16.3	26	16.3
100	23	12.6	23	12.6
70	16	8.4	16	8.4
50	8	8	8	8

Note: [a]excluding child benefit.

Italy has a history of massive tax evasion, culminating in the tax reforms of 1974, which brought about the current system. This has reduced evasion; nevertheless, employers are believed still to evade the very high rates of social security contribution and there is certainly general evasion. Total tax evaded was recently estimated by a former Italian Finance Minister at 30,000 billion lire (about 7 per cent of GDP and 25 per cent of current tax revenue). The black economy in Italy has been variously estimated at 15–40 per cent of GDP. Hence the tax rates must be used carefully – and largely discounted – in any analysis.

Family welfare is dealt with by family allowances. These are flat benefits paid to each dependent provided their independent income does not exceed certain thresholds, but they do not vary with income otherwise. They are also extremely small. In 1980, a married man with two children and non-working wife would have received 6840 lire per week (under £4).

Social aid operates in Italy at the local authority level as in the other three Continental countries. It is a discretionary payment of the poor law type. Little information could be obtained about the level of these payments, but the impression gained is that they are of little importance.

Unemployment compensation is on a pure ratio basis. There is a short-time scheme where workers laid off for a part of the week receive 80 per cent of their lost pay (net); this is in practice renewable

Table 7.12 Replacement ratios – Italy (1981) (average earnings = 100)

Earnings	*3 months**	*6 months**	*1 year and all subsequent years*
m + 2 – wife not working			
50	n.a.	n.a.	90
66	77.2	59.4	83
100	85.0	61.8	79
200	79.2	57.1	76
Single			
50	n.a.	n.a.	88
66	77.8	55.2	81
100	77.9	54.7	76
200	78.4	55.4	73

**Source:* OECD (1982) for 3 months and 6 months 1978; these ratios do not allow for work expenses.

indefinitely. Such workers are not of course recorded as unemployed but as on short time, though the distinction with such indefinite support is a fine one. For those wholly unemployed, compensation is paid at the rate of two-thirds of previous net pay; it is renewable in practice indefinitely.

This 'special' benefit was started in 1968 and restricted to those made redundant. For those ineligible, 'normal' compensation is an exiguous 800 lire per day (less than 40p). This is paid indefinitely but can be ignored. There are no maximum or minimum rates set in respect of special benefit. Hence it is a pure ratio system (apart from the 'normal' compensation).

We treated the Italian case as the French one, estimating an unemployment equation with the benefit ratio (the 'special' one) and labour force as arguments, see table 7.13. Though the coefficient on the benefit ratio is significant, significant autocorrelation of 4th order is present, indicating that our seasonal adjustment procedure is deficient; allowance for the 4th order process reduces the benefit ratio effect to insignificance.

Table 7.13 Unemployment equation – Italy (quarterly data: 1962.1–1980.4, *t*-values bracketed)

Dependent variable	U_t *(millions)*
Constant	−11.1
	(1.5)
$D1$	0.083
	(1.8)
$D2$	−0.173
	(3.8)
$D3$	0.088
	(1.9)
B^*_t	0.13
	(2.0)
$\log N_t$	1.15
	(1.6)
U_{t-1}	0.75
	(8.6)
$\bar{R}^2$	0.78
DW	2.00
X^2_4	25.4

*the special benefit/income ratio: 0 to 1968; 0.68 thereafter.
Notes: As for table 7.3.

It would appear that in Italy the problems of data, perhaps more importantly of the rival lay-off subsidy scheme, and of the informal economy, make it hard to identify any clear effect of the formal benefit system; deeper research into Italian data and institutions is desirable, but likely to be difficult, at the least.

CONCLUSIONS

While our work on these four Continental countries is far from complete, there are a number of interim conclusions that emerge with relevance to UK unemployment.

First, the nature of the benefit system is crucial. Specifically, it matters much whether it is a *ratio* system, preventing the ratio of benefits to earnings from rising to high levels, or a flat rate system where the unemployment trap is likely to become progressively serious as incomes fall. Flat rate systems, as in the UK, are likely to induce high unemployment. This is illustrated by Belgium which alone of the four countries studied had such a system, very similar to that of the UK. Belgium has a very high unemployment level, rather higher than that of the UK and substantially higher than in the other three countries.

Second, the formal statistical tests have shown that the ratio of benefits to wages plays an important role in the determination of unemployment in at least three out of the four countries as in the UK.

Third, union power has a statistically important effect on unemployment. Both in the one country with a flat rate benefit system (Belgium) and in a second country (Germany) with a system intermediate between ratio and flat rate, union power has a powerful effect on unemployment. In the other two as expected, union power does not affect unemployment significantly. Rather – though this was not investigated – it is likely to affect only the relative wages of union and non-union workers.

Fourth, there is no poverty trap of real importance in these countries (with the possible exception at very low incomes of Germany), because income assistance is given at the local level under stringent conditions descended from poor laws, while family allowances and child benefits are not in general means tested.

Finally, the evidence of these countries confirms that a *ratio* system of unemployment benefit (such as is implied by the cap proposal discussed earlier in the book) can be socially acceptable, as it is indeed accepted in France, Italy and (with some modification) Germany. In similar vein, less generous and more discretionary income assistance to the poor in work is socially accepted in all four countries. The proposals made earlier for improving the poverty trap rank as substantially more generous relative to average income levels than these Continental systems, and should accordingly be easily capable of social acceptability.

In all, we regard this examination of Continental experience as yielding substantial corroborative evidence and support for our policy proposals.

DATA SOURCES

Belgium

1. Consumer price index – all items 1960:1–1981:4
2. Industrial production index – total 1960:1–1981:3
3. Unemployment – insured unemployed 1960:1–1981:4
4. Index of hourly wage rates – mining, manufacturing, transport 1960:1–1981:4
5. Money supply – MI 1960:1–1981:3

1.–5. From OECD main economic indicators and DRI data bank

6. Trade unionization rate (linearly interpolated) Annual, 1960–1980

From *Chiffres Significatifs de l'Evolution Sociale dans la Communauté Européenne de 1960 à 1980 (1981) Brussels, September*

7. Civilian labour force (linearly interpolated) Annual, 1960–1980

From Eurostat 'Chronos' Computer, SOEC Luxembourg

8. Benefits (linearly interpolated) Annual, 1971–1980

From *Office National de l'Emploi Rapport Annuel 1980* 1971 figure benefits = 0.6 gross wages used as a base to determine benefits from 1960 to 1970 from a wage index

9. Employer social security contributions 1960–1980

From *Office National de Securité Sociale* (ONSS)

10. Employee social security contributions and average tax loss by married man plus two children constructed from series from ONSS.

France

1. Consumer price index – total	1960:1–1981:4
2. Industrial production index – total	1960:1–1981:3
3. Unemployment – total	1960:1–1981:4
4. Index of hourly earnings – manufacturing	1960:1–1981:4
5. Money supply – MI	1960:1–1981:3
1.–5. *Source:* as for Belgium.	
6. Trade unionization rate (linearly interpolated) same source as Belgium	Annual, 1960–1980
7. Civilian labour force (linearly interpolated) same source as Belgium	Annual, 1960–1980
8. Benefits (used to construct ratio) From INSEE	1960–1982
9. Employers' social security contributions	1960–1981

From *Conseil National du Patronat Français*

10. Employee's social security contributions and average tax loss by married man plus two children constructed from series from *Ministère du Travail*

Germany

1. Consumer price index – total	1960:1–1981:4
2. Industrial production index – total	1960:1–1981:4
3. Unemployment – total	1960:1–1981:4
4. Index of hourly earnings – manufacturing	1960:1–1981:4
5. Money supply – MI	1960:1–1981:4
1.–5. *Source:* as for Belgium.	
6. Trade unionization rate (linearly interpolated) same source as Belgium	Annual, 1960–1980
7. Civilian labour force (linearly interpolated) same source as Belgium	Annual, 1960–1980
8. Benefits – ratio used as in main text	
9. Employer social security contributions	1960–1980

From German Economic Institute

Italy

1. Consumer price index – all items	1960:1–1981:4
2. Industrial production index – total	1960:1–1981:4

3. Unemployment – total 1960:1–1981:4
4. Index of hourly wage rates – manufacturing 1960:1–1981:4
5. Money supply – MI 1960:1–1981:4

1.–5. *Source:* as for Belgium.

6. Trade unionization rate (linearly interpolated) same source as Belgium Annual, 1960–1980
7. Civilian labour force (linearly interpolated) Annual, 1960–1980
8. Benefits – ratio used as in main text
9. Employer social security contribution 1960–1980

From *Istituto Nationale Della Previdenza Sociale, Roma* (INPS)

10. Employee social security contributions and average tax loss by married man and two children
    From *Ministro per le Finanze* and INPS, Rome.

Appendix A

Trade Union Immunities and the Closed Shop

This appendix provides a summary of the material which appeared in the 1983 edition of this book (Appendix D), together with an outline of recent developments relating to trade union immunities and the closed shop.

TRADE UNION IMMUNITIES

The immunities of trade unions, officials and individuals, against actions in tort were enshrined in the Trade Disputes Act 1906. These immunities were cut back by the Industrial Relations Act 1971, but subsequently re-emerged and were re-enacted in a more extended form in the Trade Union and Labour Relations Act, 1974. The Employment Act 1980 took the first major step to reduce these immunities by removing immunity in tort from pickets, unless they (peacefully) picket at their own place of work; and from the organizers of secondary industrial action unless it is directly targeted against the immediate suppliers or customers of the employer in dispute, to prevent or disrupt the supply of goods or services under a contract subsisting between them.

The provisions in the Employment Act 1982 took another major step to curb these immunities. The blanket immunity previously enjoyed by trade unions in tort was removed. Unions may be sued on the same terms as any other individual, save for certain limits on the amount of damages recoverable. In addition a trade union is liable in tort and its funds put in jeopardy (up to a maximum of £250,000 in damages in any one action, depending on the size of the union) where it (through a responsible person) has authorized or endorsed the unprotected industrial tortious acts of its officials (s.15). A 'trade dispute' is restricted to cover only disputes 'between workers and their employer'. Trade unions and their officials will lose tortious immunity when a dispute is confined solely to a union and an employer. The limited immunity to take secondary industrial action is further curbed in that a union, its officials or individuals who organize (induce) secondary action against an employer, not in dispute with his own employees, cannot 'create' a 'dispute' with that employer. As a consequence they have no immunity for secondary action otherwise 'permitted' by s.17 of the 1980 Act. Nor is immunity conferred on tortious acts where secondary action is taken on the grounds of non-union (or union) membership and 'union exclusion'. Disputes between workers and workers (e.g. a demarcation dispute) are also excluded from the ambit of tortious immunity, as are those with specified workers who have ceased to be employed by an employer and certain disputes occurring outside the UK. Wide immunity is still furnished in torts for organizers of workers taking primary industrial action against their own employer, e.g. strikes, blackings, work to rule, or a go slow. The Act does, however, curb immunity in tort for organizers of primary action where a dispute is not taken to relate wholly or mainly to the prescribed industrial matters in s.29 of the 1974 Act. Thus personal and political disputes or any other disputes not relating wholly or mainly to the matters prescribed, do not attract immunity. In addition, those who organize primary action on the grounds of non-union (or union) membership and 'union exclusion', subject to certain exceptions, also lose immunity for tortious acts. Finally an employer is able to dismiss employees who are striking, at his particular 'establishment', without facing unfair dismissal claims for 'victimization', where some employees have returned to work and have been retained in employment prior to such dismissals.

The Trade Union Act 1984

The Act seeks to democratize trade unions' internal procedures with a view to making them more responsive to their members' views and wishes (HMSO, Cmnd. 8778). The complex provisions in the Act hinge on the mandatory requirement that unions must secretly ballot their members to elect a voting member of a principal executive committee (the governing body of the union); to retain any existing immunity conferred on a union when it sanctions industrial action; and periodically to review members' wishes regarding the use and continuation of political funds. The provisions relating to political funds and the election of voting members are outside the scope of this Appendix.

Secret Ballots Before Industrial Action

The Trade Union Act 1984 marks the Government's third major legislative step in its continuing programme of trade union reform. Part II of the Act is concerned solely with immunities conferred on unions where they authorize or endorse industrial action as outlined in s.15 of the 1982 Act. A union will lose all industrial immunity where it has authorized any form of industrial action (whether or not strike action) which breaches or interferes with a worker's contract of employment, unless it has the *prior* support of a secret ballot with a majority of its members voting in favour of the proposed action. A favourable ballot will also be required, to preserve immunity, prior to a union endorsing unofficial industrial action. In addition a union will lose all industrial immunity, with an otherwise valid ballot, if the unions' endorsement or authorization of strike action occurs more than four weeks *after* the date of the ballot.

The Act's balloting provisions impose stringent requirements on unions. These requirements include: granting to all members, who at the time of the ballot the union reasonably believes will be called upon to take industrial action, entitlement to vote in that ballot. No other person must be allowed to vote. These requirements extend to other members of the union who *might* be called upon to take industrial action (e.g. in other areas, or against other employers) whether or not such action is primary or secondary. If only one member of a union is denied his entitlement to vote, and is subsequently induced by the union to break or interfere with his contract of employment, then an otherwise favourable ballot is nullified. Failure to meet any of the above balloting requirements results in a union losing immunity for any sanctioned industrial action which is dependent on an otherwise favourable ballot.

Where a union escalates any form of industrial action, which has the previous support of a favourable ballot, then in the vast majority of cases, the prior support of a fresh ballot will be required to retain immunity for the escalated action. Furthermore, unions authorizing or endorsing 'permitted' secondary or 'sympathetic' industrial action will be required to ballot their members in accordance with the Act to retain any (restricted) existing immunity. Where a union *does* have the requisite support of a valid ballot, then it will *still* remain liable in tort, for any industrial action it has sanctioned, where such action falls outside the parameters of industrial immunity conferred by the 1974 Act (as subsequently restricted by the 1980 and 1982 Acts).

If a union fails to comply with the balloting requirements, then any person who has suffered damage (e.g. arising from breach of commercial contracts) which emanates from the industrial action, may sue the union for damages and/or an injunction. However, the Act does not require a ballot to review a decision to take industrial action (e.g. in a long strike) once such action has the favourable support of an initial ballot. Ballots will not be required where the union has not authorized or endorsed industrial action (unofficial action) under s.15 of the 1982 Act.

The balloting provisions came into force on 26 September 1984 for industrial action sanctioned by a union which commenced on or after that date. Within one month of the provisions coming into effect, two successful applications (to prevent unions authorizing industrial action prior to holding a ballot) had been made to the High Court. In the first case, the photographic company Ilford was granted an injunction restraining the General, Municipal and Boilermakers' Union from calling an overtime ban until a ballot had been held. In the second case, Austin Rover obtained an injunction instructing six unions to withdraw their call for strike action, because a ballot had not been held (see The *Guardian* 7 November 1984 'Car plant unions meet on court ruling').

The balloting provisions in the 1984 Act add another complex layer of legislation to the 1980 and 1982 Acts. An example may serve to illustrate the interlocking nature of the various Acts and the possible stages a judge might have to follow to determine *union* immunity. A plus (+) means a union has industrial immunity and a minus (−) means the union has no immunity. Stages 1–3 apply equally to individuals.

Stage 1 has an industrial tort been committed? (s.13 of the 1974 Act as amended by 1982 Act). If it has not, the union is not liable and does not require immunity. If it has, see Stage 2.

Stage 2 was the action, which resulted in the commission of an industrial tort, within s.13, taken in contemplation or furtherance of a trade dispute? (s.29 1974 Act as amended 1982 Act). If it was not, −, if it was, +.

Stage 3 If + under s.13 and s.29, did the action constitute secondary action under s.17 of the 1980 Act? If it did, was it permitted secondary action under s.17? If it was not, −, if it was, +. If the action constituted picketing, was it carried out peacefully at or near the place of work of those picketing? (s.16 1980 Act). If it was not, −, if it was, +. If the picketing constituted 'secondary picketing', was it permitted by s.17? If it was, +, if it was not, −. Was the action taken on the grounds of non-union (or union) membership or 'union exclusion' in breach of s.14 of the 1982 Act? If it was, −, if it was not, +.

Stage 4 (which could equally be decided prior to stage 2). Did a 'responsible person' from the union authorize or endorse the action in accordance with s.15 of the 1982 Act? If he did, then the union is liable for any industrial action which does not attract immunity at stages 2 and 3.

Stage 5 Has the union held a valid majority ballot prior to endorsing or authorizing primary or secondary industrial action (under s.15 of the 1982 Act) in accordance with ss.10 and 11 of the 1984 Act? If it has not, then it loses any immunity attracted at an earlier stage.

An argument could certainly be made out for simplifying the present legislation by codifying and consolidating it into one coherent Act. Two recent cases, concerned with the Acts of 1980 and 1982, have criticized their clarity and referred to the 'wearisome and tortuous journey' which had to be negotiated to determine union industrial immunity. (See *Merker Island Shipping Corp.* v. *Laughton* 1983, ICR 490 HL; *Dimbleby & Sons* v. *National Union of Journalists* 1984, 1 All ER 117 CA; 1984, 1 All ER 751 HL.)

However, the Government appears committed at the present time to legislate to remove union immunities in certain essential services where strikes are called prior to the exhaustion of 'agreed procedures' between unions and employers (see The *Guardian* 5 September 1984, 'Union Law').

The last decade has witnessed a fundamental shift in the industrial immunities conferred on trade unions. From a position in 1974 when unions had total immunity against industrial tortious actions, they will now be stripped of all industrial immunities unless, prior to sanctioning industrial action, they obtain the support of a majority of their members in a secret ballot.

As with other civil remedies, employers may, in certain disputes, choose not to pursue actions in the interests of 'good industrial relations'. It remains to be seen whether the legal changes which seek to diminish union power (by curbing immunities) are translated into a diminution of their *de facto* power in industrial disputes. However, the recent flow of cases emanating from the 1980 and 1982 Acts, suggest that private employers are more willing at present to pursue legal actions than they were in the recent past. For example the first award of damages against a union under the 1982 Act, as opposed to injunctions and fines for contempt of court, occurred recently. It involved unlawful picketing and secondary action under the 1980 Act, and unlawful action to compel acceptance of closed shop membership (under ss.12 and 14 of the 1982 Act). Damages of £125,051 were awarded to the Messenger Newspapers Group, with costs expected to total £150,000, against the NGA (see *The Times* 31/7/84 'Judge attacks "mobocracy"'; see also: *Marina Shipping Ltd.* v. *Laughton 1982*, ICR 215, CA; *Universal Tankships* v. *International Transport Workers Federation* 1982, TLR 8/4/82 HL; *BAA* v. *Ashton* 1983, LSG 1601; *Express Newspapers* v. *Mitchell* 1982, TLR 14/8/82; *Mercury Communications* v. *Scott Garner* 1984, 1 All ER 117 HL; *Messenger Newspapers Group* v. *NGA* (1982) 1984, IRLR, 397; 1984, ICR 345, CA).

THE CLOSED SHOP AND RELATED PRACTICES

A closed shop is generally understood to mean an agreement or some form of arrangement, whereby employees can obtain or continue in employment, only if they become or remain members of specified trade unions. Closed shops may for practical purposes be divided into two categories. In 'pre-entry closed shops', a union controls the supply of labour to employers by restricting entry to those who hold the 'appropriate union card' prior to their application. In 1979 16 per cent of those covered by closed shop arrangements fell into this category. The remaining 84 per cent fell into the second category of 'post-entry' closed shops (see Gennard *et al.*, 1980). Here the union does not control the supply of labour by making membership a precondition of entry into employment, rather the employee must agree to join a particular trade union at some specified time thereafter.

The formation and implementation of closed shops is a purely private agreement or arrangement between employers and unions in which statutory law does not directly intervene. Rather, the law pertaining to closed shops is, in the main, concerned with an individual's statutory rights not to be unfairly dismissed, or to have action short of dismissal taken against him, for refusing to join, or remain a member of, a union.

The Extent of the Closed Shop in the British Economy

The first major survey of closed shop membership in Britain (McCarthy, 1964) revealed that in 1964 about 3.76 million workers (approximately 16 per cent of the workforce) were covered by closed shop agreements or arrangements. By 1979 closed shop coverage in Britain had grown significantly. A minimum of 5.25 million workers (representing about 23 per cent of all employees, and approximately 43 per cent of TUC affiliated union membership) were subject to closed shop agreements or arrangements. (See Gennard *et al.*, 1980 and Dunn, 1981). A recent survey (Dunn and Gennard, 1984) shows that closed shop membership declined significantly, from its peak level of 5.25 million in 1979, to an estimated 4.5 million in 1982. It is thought that the decline in membership is largely attributable to the contraction of industries, such as engineering and steel, which have traditionally had large closed shop populations. It is interesting to note that, although closed shop membership fell by about 14 per cent between 1979 and 1982, membership as a proportion of the workforce (about 22 per cent in 1982), and membership as a proportion of TUC affiliated union membership (about 43 per cent in 1982) remained essentially unchanged (see figure A1).

Summary of the Law on the Closed Shop and Related Practices

The law pertaining to closed shops (Union Membership Agreements, or UMAs) is concerned with providing employees with a right not to be unfairly dismissed, or to have action short of dismissal taken against them, for refusing to join or remain members of trade unions in relation to which UMAs operate. Where an industrial tribunal upholds a complaint of unfair dismissal it may redress the complainant with the following remedies: (a) a compensatory award; or (b) reinstatement (whereby the complainant is treated as if he had not been dismissed); or (c) re-engagement (whereby the complainant is re-employed but not necessarily in his former position).

The 1971 Act was the first statute to offer protection to employees who objected to being members of closed shops. The Act rendered pre-entry closed shops void, and an employee who was dismissed for refusing to join any form of closed shop could seek redress for unfair dismissal. However, the Act did permit 'agency shops' and 'approved' closed shops to operate, provided certain conditions were met. In these circumstances an employee who refused to join a closed shop could be fairly dismissed unless his objection was based upon grounds of conscience.

These rights were curtailed severely by the 1974 and 1976 Acts which limited protection against unfair dismissal, to an objection based upon religious belief only. The 1980 Act restored and extended protection to employees who objected to membership of trade unions covered by closed shop agreements. The provisions in the 1980 Act were re-enacted in the 1982 Act in a greatly extended form.

Dismissal for Non-membership of a Union in Accordance with a UMA

Section 3 of the 1982 Act extends and amplifies the protection, originally found in s.7 of the 1980 Act, to all closed shops. Dismissal of an employee by an employer for non-membership of a UMA will automatically be unfair, in relation to all *existing* closed shops, unless within five years before the dismissal a secret ballot has been held (in accordance with s.58A) in which not less than 80 per cent of those entitled to vote, *or* not less than 85 per cent of those who voted, were in favour of the UMA. These particular provisions (on balloting 'existing' closed shops) were postponed, as the Employment Secretary explained at the time, 'to give one or two years after Royal Assent for proper preparation for ballots'. The provisions finally came into force on 1 November 1984. However, in relation to the implementation of 'new' closed shops which came into operation after 14 August 1980 (since which date the following provisions have been in force), then not less than 80 per cent of those entitled to vote must vote in favour of the UMA. It is clear, therefore, that pre-1980 closed shops have a less rigorous first balloting requirement.

On a second or subsequent ballot, which logically will have to be held at maximum five-yearly periods, in what amounts to a periodic review, the balloting requirements (for both 'existing' and 'new' closed shops) become much more severe. Both a minimum 80 per cent of those entitled to vote *and* 85 per cent of those voting must be in favour of the UMA (s.58A(7)). It should be made clear that failure to comply with any of the above balloting requirements does not in any way render a UMA unlawful. Rather, where a ballot is not held, or does not attain the requisite majority, the dismissal of an employee, because he refuses to become or remain a member of a union, will be automatically unfair, thus entitling the employee to seek greatly enhanced levels of compensation (see ss.4 and 5).

Where the balloting requirements *are* met, then such a dismissal will be fair unless an employee can bring himself within one of the other protected categories, which were initially enacted in s.7 of the 1980 Act, as later amended in s.3 of the 1982 Act. These categories are where:

(1) The employee 'genuinely objects on grounds of conscience or other deeply-held personal conviction to being a member of any trade union whatsoever or of a particular trade union'. A recent important decision of the Employment Appeal Tribunal (EAT) (*Home Delivery Services Ltd.* v. *Shackcloth*, 1984, TLR 3/10/84) has widened the rights available to employees under this particular heading. It had been argued in this case that 'deeply held personal conviction' must, from previous case law, be based on moral considerations. However the EAT ruled that a potential reason for an employee wishing to leave a union 'would be a deeply held personal belief that it had failed to look after his interests; for to have his interests looked after was why he joined a union and paid his subscription'. This decision has obvious import for members of UMAs who are dissatisfied with the way their unions are being run.

(2) The UMA took effect after 14 August 1980 and the employee was entitled to vote in the ballot through which the agreement was approved (if it was not approved the dismissal would be unfair under the balloting provisions above) and the employee has not, at any time since the date of the ballot, been a member of a trade union in accordance with that agreement.

(3) An existing employee has not at any time been a member of a trade union to which the UMA relates, since its introduction.

(4) At the time of the dismissal for non-membership of a UMA, there was a declaration made under s.4 of the 1980 Act, of unreasonable exclusion or expulsion from a trade union, or proceedings on such a complaint were pending.

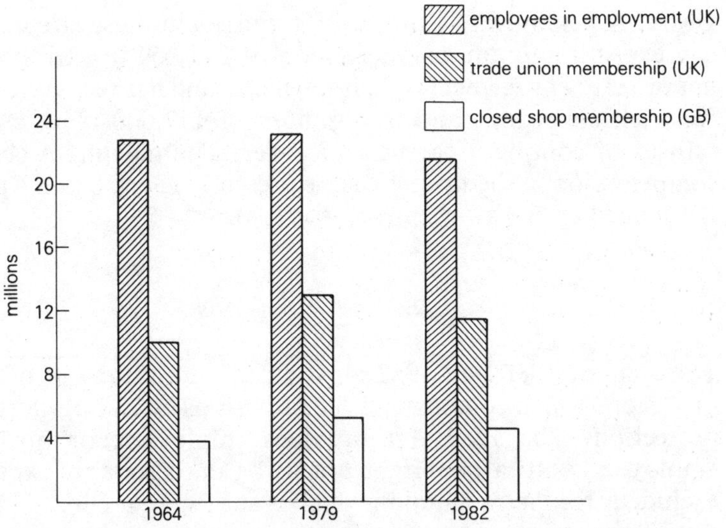

Figure A1

In a case where (1) or (4) above does *not* apply, then an employee may still have redress if: (a) he holds qualifications which are relevant to his employment; (b) he is subject to a written code which governs the conduct of those persons who hold those qualifications, and (c) he has: (i) been expelled from a trade union for refusing to take part in a strike or other industrial action; or (ii) refused to become or remain a member of a trade union. If the above requirements are met, then a person may still claim unfair dismissal if the principal reason for his refusal (in the case of (c)(i)) is that his taking part in the action would be in breach of the code; or (in the case of (c)(ii)) that if he became or remained a member he would be required to take part in a strike, or other industrial action, which would be in breach of that code.

Parallel protection to that outlined above is available to an employee who is dismissed where a UMA operates, for not complying with a requirement (whether or not imposed in his contract of employment) that he will make 'one or more payments' or his employer is entitled to deduct 'one or more sums from his remuneration', in the event of his failure to become, or on his ceasing to remain, a member of a trade union. An example might be where an employee has 'promised' to pay his union dues or pay the same to charity if he does not remain a member of the union.

The 1982 Act also provides greatly enhanced rates of compensation for employees dismissed by virtue of their non-membership of a

UMA. A person who is unfairly dismissed in these circumstances can expect minimum compensation of £12,000 if a tribunal does not order re-engagement or reinstatement (and has received a request for such an order), and a minimum of £17,000 if an employer refuses to comply with such an order. The maximum claim for compensation in the former case is presently £31,850 (see Appendix B for median unfair dismissal awards).

Related Provisions

The Acts of 1980 and 1982 also introduced a number of related provisions which complement the provisions extending closed shop protection. The 1980 Act provides employees, or prospective employees, with a new right not to be unreasonably expelled or excluded from a trade union which is subject to a UMA. The 1982 Act allows employees to claim compensation directly from trade union funds (by joining them in tribunal proceedings) in unfair (and action short of) dismissal cases where it is claimed that the union exerted pressure on the employer to take the action complained of. In addition enterprises employing non-union labour are afforded protection against commercial discrimination and industrial action on such grounds.

RESTRICTIVE LABOUR PRACTICES: THE FAIR TRADING ACT 1973

Section 79 of the 1973 Act introduced an innovatory, and little discussed, power whereby 'restrictive labour practices' may be referred to the Monopolies and Mergers Commission (MMC), who may then determine whether such practices are against the public interest, and if so, what adverse effects have occurred or may be expected to occur. In broad terms a reference may be made to the MMC where any restrictions or requirements operate in relation to the employment of workers in any UK commercial activities (but not where they relate exclusively to rates of remuneration) which are not necessary for, or are more stringent than is necessary for, the efficient conduct of those activities (s.79(5)). In considering a reference, the MMC must not examine anything done, or omitted to be done, in contemplation or furtherance of an 'industrial dispute' (sic). Apart from the restrictions on the scope of investigations, and unlike references concerning monopolies and mergers, the MMC's remedial powers are totally fettered in that, when a restrictive labour practice is identified, the MMC *cannot* make orders rectifying any effects which they consider are contrary to the public interest. Any report, however, must be laid before Parliament and subsequently published. It is then open to public scrutiny. In any event to date, and perhaps reflecting the impotency of s.79, not one reference has been made to the MMC.

CONCLUSION

It has been suggested that the decline in closed shop membership, from its peak level of 5.26 million in 1979 to 4.5 million in 1982, is partly due to union members ceasing to give the closed shop 'a high priority', and that 'there is evidence that employers are changing their attitudes towards giving unions the same degree of support as in the past . . . and . . . many employers are no longer as willing to negotiate union membership agreements . . .' (Roberts, 1984, p. 292). How far the new balloting requirements on existing closed shops will accelerate this trend (if at all) remains to be seen. A recent survey conducted shortly before the new provisions on balloting came into effect (Labour Research, August 1984, p. 199), found some evidence of employer pressure to enforce closed shop ballots, but that 'few employers had taken steps to introduce ballots or terminate existing agreements'.

Clearly, the joinder provisions in the 1982 Act will increase the pressure on some trade unions to reassess the efficacy of operating closed shop agreements (with unions liable to face compensation claims in excess of £30,000 in any one unfair dismissal case). In some instances the closed shop may prove to be inoperable.

However, the greatly extended protection now available to employees applies only where a person is dismissed or is subject to action short of dismissal. No protection is afforded to those seeking employment who object to closed shop membership. This is particularly pertinent where a pre-entry closed shop operates. All closed shops remain 'lawful' even if they do not obtain the requisite approval under the Act's balloting provisions. The Government does not appear to be planning any further legislative reform of the closed shop at the present time.

Appendix B

A Review of Employment Protection Legislation

The purpose of this appendix is to examine the vast array of statutory individual employment rights – as opposed to collective rights, e.g. the statutory immunities of trade unions – conferred on employees, and the concomitant duties and associated costs borne by employers. Due to the huge amount of complex statutory provisions, regulations and case law presently prevailing in this area, we are able only to attempt a brief sketch of the major statutes.

In part I of the appendix we outline how employment protection legislation has evolved into its present state. In part II we describe the statutory individual employment rights which are presently conferred on employees.

THE EVOLUTION OF EMPLOYMENT PROTECTION LEGISLATION

Prior to the introduction of statutory intervention, the employer–employee relationship was governed – and still is where statutory law does not intervene – by contractual law, underpinned by common law principles. Under contractual law an employee could be dismissed without explanation or reason, provided he was given due notice in accordance with the terms of his contract of employment. If due notice was not given, an employee could sue – and still can – for wrongful dismissal and claim the wages he would have been entitled to, had he been given proper notice. However, through collective agreements and informal arrangements *de facto* protection was – and still is – afforded to employees against arbitrary (unfair) dismissal and other 'wrongs'.

The first legislative enactment dealing with dismissals was the 1963 Contracts of Employment Act. The Act gave workers the right to minimum periods of notice, i.e. 1 week's notice after 26 weeks' continuous employment, rising to 4 weeks after 5 years' service, or payments in lieu of notice, prior to being dismissed.

Two years later the 1965 Redundancy Payments Act introduced a scheme of compensation – for workers who had been dismissed due to economic criteria or for 'no fault dismissals' – whereby redundant employees could claim lump sum payments up to a maximum of £800 after 20 years' service. Space does not permit us to analyse the considerable body of work which the Act and its underpinning policy has generated (see, e.g. Drake and Bercusson, 1981, pp. 22–7). But the rationale of the scheme appears to have been to facilitate increased labour mobility and to secure a greater acceptance by workers of the need for economic and social change (see, e.g. Grunfeld, 1980, ch. 1). The social objective has been to provide 'financial compensation for the social and economic cost incurred by the individual as a consequence of his involuntary redundancy' (Parker *et al.*, 1971, OPCS, p. 3).

Part of the drive towards statutory protection against unfair dismissal was fuelled by the lack of *de facto* protection afforded to non-unionized workers, to whom the 'voluntary system' did not extend. However, the joint union–employer representatives on the 1967 National Joint Advisory Committee on Dismissal Procedures, were not in favour of statutory intervention, but – endorsing the views expressed in an earlier TUC report on the subject in 1961 – preferred to see an extension of existing 'voluntary procedures' (see Dickens *et al.*, 1984, p. 4). However the Donovan Commission, reporting in June 1968, expressed concern about the inconsistency of voluntary procedures and about the number of unofficial strikes – an annual average of 276 between 1964 and 1966 – which emanated from disputes concerned with the employment of individuals, their suspension or dismissal. Furthermore, the Commission, who recommended that 'early' legislation should be passed to protect all workers against unfair dismissal, thought that statutory protection would encourage employers to improve their dismissal arrangements. '[It] may well spur employers and trade unions to establish joint procedures which can be exempted from the coverage of legislation' (Cmnd. 3623, p. 143, para. 1057).

In the wake of the Donovan Report, the incoming Conservative Government enacted the 1971 Industrial Relations Act – a major landmark in the evolution of individual employment rights – which conferred extensive new rights on workers, who had been in continuous employment for a minimum period of two years, not to be unfairly dismissed. The Act enabled industrial tribunals to award compensation up to a maximum of £4,160, or to recommend re-engagement, where a worker had been dismissed in circumstances which did not conform with the 'equity' and 'substantial merits' of the case. One commentator on the Act described the provisions as a 'striking new principle', the importance of which could be gauged from independent research carried out by the previous Labour Government – who planned to enact similar legislation – which indicated that about 200,000 claims of unfair dismissal would be lodged in the two years after the new rights came into force (Harvey, 1971, p. 195). But the actual number of claims registered with industrial tribunals over this period amounted to 14,547 (*Employment Gazette* 1974, pp. 503, 616). Nevertheless, six years later a survey of the impact of employment protection laws, as reflected in the views of the management of 301 manufacturing plants, revealed that 'the aspect of employment protection legislation to have had most impact upon employers was unfair dismissal' (Daniel and Stilgoe, 1978, p. 74).

The next major evolutionary development in employment protection law was the enactment of the 1974 Health and Safety at Work Act (HSWA). The Act imposed new and extensive duties on employers, and conferred new rights on employees to be represented and consulted, with regard to health and safety issues. The HSWA with its accompanying codes and regulations (which are *general* in nature and cover virtually *all* employers and employees) marked a fundamental shift in policy from previous health and safety enactments. Examples are the 1961 Factories Act and the 1963 Offices, Shops and Railway Premises Act, the provisions of which the HSWA is supposed gradually to replace, but which still survive largely intact. These are specific in nature and impose *precise* and *detailed* duties with regard to *particular* plants, processes and premises.

The first Factories Act of 1802 set limits on the number of hours which apprentices in cotton mills were permitted to work, and imposed specific duties on factory owners with regard to working conditions such as heating and light. There followed a surfeit of *ad hoc* statutory measures culminating in the 1961 Factories Act. However, in 1970 the Labour Government, in response to mounting concern about the increase in accidents at work during the 1960s, and the increasing disquiet expressed by employers over the burdens imposed by the mass of prevailing legislation, appointed the Robens Committee on Safety and Health at Work (1972), to assess whether any changes in the scope and nature of existing legislation were required. The Committee recommended that a more self-regulating system should be implemented, to replace the over-complex and ever-increasing statutory regulation, within a single unified framework and under the umbrella of a new national authority. The Committee thought that a new 'enabling' Act should replace existing statutory provisions, supported by regulations and non-statutory codes (Cmnd. 5034, paras. 452–5). These and other recommendations were, to a large extent, incorporated in the HSWA, although as two eminent commentators on the Act have stressed, 'what does seem to be doubtful is the realisation of the Robens hope for more self-regulation with regulations as a last resort, inasmuch as we are seeing a plethora of regulations which in time will produce a complex regime of law – more law, not less' (Drake and Wright, 1983, p. 37). It is not surprising, therefore, that Daniel and Stilgoe (1978, p. 41) discovered that, along with unfair dismissal provisions, the HSWA 'topped the list' of pieces of legislation which had had most impact on managers.

In 1975 three major enactments dealing with individual employment rights came into force. These were the 1970 Equal Pay Act, the 1975 Sex Discrimination Act and the 1975 Employment Protection Act.

The Equal Pay Act – under which employers must afford equal treatment, in terms and conditions of employment, to men and women performing 'like work' – was preceded by a lengthy campaign dating back to 1888 when the TUC passed a resolution in support of equal pay. It has been termed 'the longest standing wage claim in the history of the trade union movement' (Snell *et al.*, 1981). By the early 1960s, both the Labour and Conservative Parties had manifesto commitments to act on equal pay, but the main spur to statutory intervention emanated from TUC pressure to ratify the 1951 International Labour Organization Convention on equal pay, and the requirement to satisfy Article 119 of the Treaty of Rome on 'equal remuneration'. Implementation of the Act was postponed for a five year 'transitional period' – to enable employers and unions to prepare for the provisions and to incorporate them into existing work practices – and came into force on 25 December 1975, the same day as its sister Act dealing with sex discrimination.

Pressure to legislate against sex discrimination began to mount in the mid-1960s following the introduction of sex discrimination legislation in America. By 1970 the Conservative Party had a 'firm intent' to remove sex discrimination, and by 1972 the TUC also supported statutory intervention. Thereafter pressure to legislate, in the form of private members bills, select committee reports and consultative documents, increased, before the Sex Discrimination Act – which renders unlawful any employer discriminating on the grounds of sex or against married persons – reached the statute book.

Perhaps the most significant event in the evolution of employment protection laws occurred when the Labour Government enacted the 1975 Employment Protection Act (EPA). The EPA, which was the final plank in the so-called 'statutory floor' of individual employment rights, aimed 'to provide employees with a series of fundamental new rights and greater job security' (Drake and Bercusson, 1981, part II).

The Act, in the first place, reinforced and extended existing employment rights in several ways. For example it (a) increased the periods of notice an employer had to give under the 1963 Act (as consolidated in the Contracts of Employment Act 1972); (b) extended and strengthened the remedies available to employees who had been unfairly dismissed, as well as reducing the classes of employees excluded from protection; (c) eased the qualifying periods of 'continuous employment' with regard to nearly all individual statutory rights, and thus brought more workers into protection.

In the second place, the EPA introduced a number of new and substantive employment rights. These new rights included guaranteed payments for days on which an employer cannot provide work; protection against dismissal on the grounds of pregnancy; paid maternity leave and a right to return to work after confinement; wide-ranging rights to time off work, e.g. for trade union duties; payments for time off work during suspension on medical grounds; and new employee rights to information.

The proliferation of individual employment rights in the 1960s and 1970s has resulted in a mass of statutory enactments, regulations, codes and case law which are bewildering in volume and complexity. We can only attempt to give an outline of these comprehensive rights and duties. We do this by first dealing with the major statutory rights which pertain on the *termination* of a worker's employment, and follow this with a summary of the major individual rights which are conferred on employees *during* their employment. It should be noted that we only discuss the statutory (minimum) employment rights conferred on employees. Many workers receive greatly enhanced employment protection through collective agreements and other arrangements with employers, which may or may not be incorporated into an individual's contract of employment.

EMPLOYMENT PROTECTION: AN OUTLINE OF PREVAILING INDIVIDUAL EMPLOYMENT RIGHTS

Most of the statutory rights discussed in the previous section save for those dealing with health and safety, sex discrimination and equal pay, have now been consolidated in the 1978 Employment Protection (Consolidation) Act (EPCA) as amended by the Employment Acts of 1980 and 1982.

Statutory Rights on the Termination of Employment

Unfair dismissal. There can be little doubt that the rights conferred on employees not to be unfairly dismissed are widely perceived as the most important of all individual employment rights and, on the evidence of existing empirical studies, have had the most widespread impact on employers (see, e.g., Clifton and Tatton-Brown, 1979, p. 16; Daniel and Stilgoe, 1978, p. 74). The importance of these provisions is also reflected in the high proportion of unfair dismissal claims, relative to other employment protection rights, which are lodged with industrial tribunals. For example, in 1983 (see *Employment Gazette* 1984, p. 488) the proportion of claims received by industrial tribunals, under the various categories of individual employment rights, were as shown in table B.1.

Perhaps the best way of outlining these important rights is to begin by describing those workers who are excluded from protection. This area of unfair dismissal has proved to be one of the most volatile in terms of statutory change. For example, in order to qualify for protection in 1971 workers had to have completed a minimum of two years 'continuous service' with their employer. In 1974 the

Table B.1

	%		%
Unfair dismissal	73.4	Sex discrimination	0.8
Redundancy payments	9.4	Equal pay	3.2
Unfair dismissal / Redundancy payments	5.5	Race relations	1.3
		Other	0.9
Other employment protection rights	5.5		

minimum period was reduced to one year, and in 1975 it was further reduced to six months.

However, in 1979 the incoming Conservative Government acted in response to claims from small business groups, that the protection was too severe and deterred recruitment. For example, one business federation reported that 'the right not to be unfairly dismissed . . . has led to rigidity in employment; it has restricted mobility of labour; and it has discouraged expansion'; NFSS, 1979, p.8). The 'continuous service' qualification was raised to one year (S.I. 1979, No. 959). Then in 1980, in an attempt to boost small business recruitment, the Government increased the minimum qualifying period of continuous employment to two years for firms which employ 20 or fewer employees (s.8, 1980 Act). The increase in qualifying periods is thought to be the principal cause of a fall in the number of unfair dismissal cases disposed of by industrial tribunals, from 33,383 in 1979 to 28,624 in 1980 (see also Hepple, 1981, p. 66).

In specified cases – such as unfair dismissal due to sex discrimination, 'union activities' or non-membership of a closed shop (see Appendix A) – there is no service qualification at all.

Another important class of employees who are excluded from protection are those with fixed term contracts of *one year or more* (prior to 1980 the period was two years or more) who are dismissed after the expiry of the contract and who have agreed in writing, before expiry, to exclude their rights to claim for unfair dismissal.

Other classes of employees excluded from protection include employees who, prior to dismissal, have reached normal retiring age; employees who work outside Britain; registered dock workers, and members of the police and armed forces. In addition part-time employees who normally work less than 16 hours a week are excluded from protection, but an employee *will* qualify for this (unfair dismissal) protection and for *other* employment protection rights, if he has worked for a minimum of *8 hours* a week, and completed at least *five* years' continuous service.

Finally, although s.140 of the EPCA forbids employers and employees from contracting out of the Act's employment provisions, it does empower the Secretary of State (on an application from the parties concerned) to exclude from unfair dismissal protection those workers who are party to a 'dismissal procedures agreement' between an employer and a union (provided various stipulations in the Act are strictly adhered to). To date only one such agreement (involving the Electrical Contractors Association and the EEPTU) is in force.

Similar provisions in s.40 empower the Secretary of State to exclude employees from exercising their statutory rights to claim guaranteed and redundancy payments.

Having dealt with those workers who are excluded from protection, we can now outline the unfair dismissal rights which are still afforded to the vast majority of full-time employees. The dismissal (the term includes a dismissal with or without notice, or where an employee resigns due to the employer's 'conduct') of an employee will be unfair unless an employer can show that the *principal reason* for the dismissal falls into one of the following categories: (a) a reason related to the conduct of the employee; or (b) a reason related to the capability or qualifications of the employee to perform his work; or (c) the employee is redundant; or (d) where a statutory duty or restriction prevents the employment from being continued; or (e) some other 'substantial reason' justifying the dismissal (this last category is wide-ranging and it has, for example, been held to include reasons related to economic or business efficiency and organizational interests).

However, even where the employer proves that he has dismissed an employee for one of these reasons, an industrial tribunal will still find the dismissal unfair unless it is satisfied that the employer has acted *reasonably* in treating the reason as sufficient to justify the dismissal (s.57 EPCA). Prior to 1 October 1980 the burden of proving 'reasonableness' fell on the employer, but s.6 of the 1980 Act removed this burden of proof from employers, and also stipulates that in determining reasonableness the tribunal must now take into account 'the size and administrative resources of the employer's undertaking'.

In certain specified circumstances a tribunal must treat a dismissal as *automatically* unfair. For example (i) dismissal for refusing to join an 'unapproved' closed shop or on other specified closed shop grounds (see Appendix A); or (ii) dismissal for trade union membership or activities, i.e. where an employee is dismissed because he was a member of, or proposed to join, a union, or proposed to take part in union activities; or (iii) dismissal because an employee is not a member of a union or has refused to become or remain a member of a union (but see closed shop, Appendix A); and (iv) dismissals related to pregnancy.

If a tribunal finds that an employee has been unfairly dismissed, it may make one of three orders: reinstatement, re-engagement (not necessarily into the same job) or an award of compensation. Where no order for 're-employment' is made, the tribunal will make an award of compensation which usually consists of two elements – a basic award and a compensatory award. The basic award (current maximum, £4,350) is calculated in the same way as a redundancy payment (below), but by virtue of s.9 of the 1980 Act the previous minimum (mandatory) basic award of two weeks' pay now has been abolished. The compensatory award – current maximum £7,500, making a current maximum compensation award of £11,850 – is assessed by reference to the 'damages' flowing from the dismissal, e.g. loss and future loss of earnings, loss of pension rights and benefits and loss of future employment protection (i.e. loss of the continuous service qualification). In specified circumstances a special award, in addition to the basic and compensatory awards, of up to (and possibly above) £20,000, may be claimed. The special award is only payable where the dismissal is found to be unfair on the grounds of trade union activities or membership, or for non-membership of a closed shop (Appendix A).

Each party to a tribunal hearing must bear his own costs, unless a tribunal finds that a party has acted unreasonably, frivolously or vexatiously (in which case costs may be awarded against that party).

The latest figures relating to unfair dismissal applications in Britain (*Employment Gazette*, 1984, pp. 487–91), show that in 1983 industrial tribunals dealt with 30,076 unfair dismissal cases, with a further 9,546 applicants reaching agreement on compensation through the conciliation services of ACAS (which in most cases approaches one or both of the parties, when an application is lodged). Of those cases proceeding to a tribunal hearing, 43.2 per cent were held to be fair, and 31.8 per cent were held to be unfair (the remaining 25 per cent were dismissed for other reasons). The median amount of compensation awarded by tribunals in 1983 was £1,345, only 99 cases resulted in an employee being re-engaged or reinstated, and the median amount of compensation agreed at conciliation was £421.

Of course, these statistics reveal only part of the story relating to dismissals. Many workers receive non-statutory protection against dismissal through union negotiated collective agreements and other arrangements relating to disciplinary action, dismissal and grievance procedures. For example, Deaton (1984, p. 63) found, from a study of 953 plants in manufacturing industry in 1977/8, that *inter alia* 'greater union density seems to provide some protection against dismissal'. This observation appears to support the results of an earlier survey (Dickens *et al.*, 1984, p. 505) which found that of 1,063 unfair dismissal claimants examined in 1976/7, only 32 per cent were members of trade unions. The authors concluded that the under-representation of union claimants was greater than this figure suggests, since most applicants were manual labourers, with a unionization rate of 65 per cent (*ibid.*). More recently the NFSS (1979, p. 1) have reported that, as a result of media attention and the stigma attached to appearing before tribunals, 'many large firms have a policy that in no circumstances will they appear before an industrial tribunal . . . and are buying off would-be applicants'.

Redundancy payments. Under the EPCA (ss.81–127) an employer *must* make a lump sum payment to an employee, provided he has worked for at least 16 hours per week and completed a minimum of two years continuous service, who has been dismissed by reason of redundancy.

However, certain employees are excluded from the statutory scheme, e.g. a man or a woman whose employment is terminated after he or she has attained the age of 65 or 60, respectively; an employee under a fixed-term contract of two years or more who has agreed to exclude his right to payment; and where a redundant employee unreasonably refuses an offer of suitable alternative employment from his employer or an associated or 'successor' employer.

A dismissal will be by reason of redundancy if it is wholly or mainly attributable to: (a) the fact that the employer has ceased, or intends to cease, to carry on the business for the purpose of which the employee was employed, or has ceased, or intends to cease, to carry out the business in the place where the employee was employed; or (b) the requirements of a business for employees to carry out work of a particular kind (or of a particular kind in the place where the employee was employed) have ceased or diminished, or are expected to do so (s.81, EPCA).

A redundancy payment is calculated in accordance with a statutory formula based on length of service, age and weekly pay (broadly based on the employee's weekly pay on the termination of his employment, but subject to a statutory limit, which is presently £145 per week). That is, the employee is entitled to 1½ weeks' pay for every year of continuous service between the ages of 41 and 65 (60 for a woman), but the payment is reduced by 1/12 for each month of work completed after an employee has attained the age of 64 or 59 respectively, 1 week's pay for every year of service between the ages of 22 and 40; and half a week's pay for each year of service between the ages of 18 and 21. The maximum number of years of service which may be taken into account is 20, thus the maximum redundancy payment is presently: $145 \times 1.5 \times 20 = £4,350$.

An employee may be precluded from claiming a redundancy payment if his employer could have terminated his employment by reason of his misconduct. Similarly, the right to a payment may be lost in consequence of strike action (see ss.92 and 110, EPCA). However, an employee who is made redundant may have a claim for unfair dismissal if he was unfairly selected for redundancy in contravention of an agreed procedure or customary arrangement, or on the grounds of trade union membership, non-membership or for trade union activities (s.59, EPCA). In addition, under the 1975 Act, various duties are imposed on employers relating to procedures for handling redundancies, e.g. an employer is under a duty to consult with unions on proposed redundancies, and is also under a duty to notify the Secretary of State where it is proposed to make 10 or more employees redundant (both within prescribed time limits).

Any dispute relating to a redundancy payment may be referred to an industrial tribunal to determine the issue.

The importance of the statutory scheme is illustrated by the fact that by the end of 1978 a total of 3.382 million employees had received a total of £1,336 million under the statutory redundancy scheme, since its inception in 1965, and by the end of 1983 the total number of employees who had claimed payments under the scheme had almost doubled at 6.181 million employees (see Grunfeld, 1980, p. 8; *Employment Gazette*, 1984, p. 217). Some indication of the trends in redundancy payments under the scheme is illustrated by the following figures. In 1966, 138,895 employees received an average statutory redundancy payment of £192; in 1978 the figures were 255,484 and £721 respectively; and in 1983 608,000 employees received statutory payments, with 137,539 employees receiving an average statutory payment of £1,460 during the period 1 July. 1983. to 30 September 1983 (ibid., p. 35).

Although an employer has to meet the employee's redundancy payment in full, he may claim a fixed rebate from the Redundancy Fund. The Fund is administered by the Department of Employment and financed from employers' and employees' national insurance contributions. In 1969 an employer could claim a 50 per cent rebate; in 1979 the rebate was reduced to 41 per cent (its present level); but in 1985 (from a date to be announced) the rebate will be further reduced to 35 per cent, thus increasing the burden on employers.

Many employers make redundancy payments in excess of the statutory minima. For example, a 1974 British Institute of Management study suggested that 80 per cent of companies provided payments in excess of the statutory minimum scales (see Bowers, 1982, p. 225) and through collective agreements and other arrangements many employees, who would otherwise be excluded from the statutory scheme, are entitled to 'voluntary' redundancy payments under private schemes. But an employer may only claim a rebate in respect of payments made under the statutory scheme.

Parker *et al.* (1971) in their survey of the effects of the Redundancy Payments Act although concluding that the Act had led to some improvements in the mobility and flexibility of labour, found, *inter alia*, that at that time 84 per cent of paid (compared to 87 per cent of unpaid) redundant employees eventually found employment; that 4 per cent of paid (compared to 3 per cent of unpaid) redundant workers moved home for reasons connected with work; and that 'six per cent of paid and 13 per cent of unpaid redundant informants had, at the time of the interview, moved from the area in which they were living when they were made redundant'. The survey also found that 36 per cent of employers thought the Act overprotected employees; 10 per cent expressed qualified agreement; and 49 per cent did not agree that the Act overprotected employees (Parker *et al.*, 1971, pp. 12, 69, 89, 113–14).

Statutory notice. Under the EPCA (ss.49–50) employers must give employees the following minimum periods of statutory notice to terminate their contracts of employment: one week's notice to an employee who has completed at least one month's continuous employment, increasing to two weeks after two years' continuous employment. Thereafter the employer must give one extra week's notice for each extra year of completed service, rising to a maximum of 12 weeks' notice after 12 or more years' service. However, the contract of employment may stipulate longer notice than the statutory minima, and an employee may waive his right to notice or accept a payment in lieu of notice.

Reason for dismissal. An employer must, at the request of a dismissed employee who has completed at least six months' continuous employment, provide him within 14 days of the request with a written statement of the reasons for his dismissal. In the event of an employer failing to comply with this duty, an employee may complain to an industrial tribunal, who must award him two weeks' pay if they find the employer has defaulted (s.53 EPCA).

Statutory Rights During Employment

Maternity rights. A pregnant employee may be entitled to claim one or more of the following statutory rights under the EPCA (ss.31A–49).

(1) *Antenatal care:* A pregnant employee (irrespective of length of service or hours worked) has a right not to be unreasonably refused time off work for the purpose of receiving antenatal care, with a concomitant right to be paid by her employer for the time she takes off. To qualify for these rights an employee must have made the requisite health appointment and, except on the first appointment, must comply with a request from her employer to produce a certificate of pregnancy and evidence of her appointment. Failure to comply with these requirements may result in an industrial tribunal ordering the employer to pay his employee the amount she would have received, had he carried out his statutory duties.

(2) *Maternity pay:* provided a pregnant employee has completed a minimum of two years' service (during which she has worked for at least 16 hours per week) and has continued to be employed until at least the eleventh week before her expected week of confinement, then she is entitled to receive maternity pay from her employer (irrespective of whether she intends to return to work). A qualifying employee is entitled to receive nine tenths of her weekly pay, less an amount equal to the flat-rate national insurance maternity allowance, for each of her first six weeks of absence after the beginning of the eleventh week before her expected week of confinement. The employer is entitled to claim a 100 per cent rebate from the maternity pay fund, which is itself *financed* by employers' national insurance contributions.

If an employer infringes these provisions he may be ordered by an industrial tribunal to make the appropriate payments to his employee. In the 10-month period between 6 April 1977 and 31 January 1978, 46,287 women received statutory maternity pay (Bowers, 1982, p. 71).

(3) *Right to return to work:* broadly, a pregnant employee who meets the same qualification requirements pertaining to maternity pay has a statutory right to return to her original employment, provided she returns to work within 29 weeks following her confinement (the week she gave birth).

An employer's failure to comply with this duty will render him liable to face an unfair dismissal claim (s.56 EPCA). However, the right to make a claim for unfair dismissal (under s.56) will be excluded if: (i) the employee's original job is no longer available due to redundancy, but where an employer has suitable alternative employment he must offer this to his employee, otherwise the right to claim unfair dismissal is reinstated. If no suitable employment is available the employee may claim a redundancy payment (s.45 EPCA); or (ii) an employer finds it is not reasonably practicable (for a reason other than redundancy) to permit his employee to return to her original job; and he or an associated employer has offered her a suitable alternative job, which she has either accepted or refused; or (iii) immediately before her absence began the employer and any associated employer employed five or fewer workers; and it is *not* reasonably practicable for the employer to reinstate her into the original job, *or* to offer her suitable alternative employment. These latter two exclusions were introduced by s.8 of the 1980 Act in an attempt to alleviate the burdens imposed on employers (by s.56) and, like many other changes made by the present Government, to relieve the hardship imposed on small businesses.

(4) *Dismissal and pregnancy:* Where an employee has been dismissed because of pregnancy or a reason related to pregnancy, then, provided she meets the qualifying conditions for unfair dismissal (above), the dismissal will be *automatically* unfair and she will be entitled to seek the remedies explained above (s.60 EPCA). But a dismissal on the grounds of pregnancy will not necessarily be unfair where: (i) the employee, because of pregnancy, is incapable of adequately doing her work, or (ii) she cannot continue in work without breaking the law (e.g. under Factory Act regulations).

Guaranteed payments. Most employees are entitled to receive statutory minimum guaranteed payments (though their contracts of employment may stipulate larger payments and impose wider duties on employers) from their employer for a 'workless day', which is lost because of a shortage of work or through any other occurrence affecting the normal working of the employer's business (s.12 EPCA). To qualify, an employee must have completed at least one month's continuous employment, and must normally have worked for not less than 16 hours a week. The right to claim is forfeited if the short-time or lay-off results from a trade dispute involving any employee of the employer (or an associated employer), or if an employee unreasonably refuses alternative employment or fails to comply with his employer's reasonable requirements to ensure that his services are available (s.13 EPCA). An employee also forfeits his right to claim if he is employed for a fixed term of three months or less.

By virtue of s.14 of the 1980 Act an employee's entitlement to a guaranteed payment is limited to five days in any three-month period (rather than the previous fixed calendar quarter). This amendment relieves employers from having to make (as they previously did) 10 days' payments where a 'lay off' spanned two fixed calendar quarters. The amount of guaranteed pay is calculated by reference to a statutory formula and is subject to a (present) maximum of £10.00 for any one day, or a normal day's pay, whichever is less.

If an industrial tribunal finds that an employer has not complied with his duties it will order him to pay the employee the amount due.

Time off work. Under the EPCA (s.27–32) and health and safety regulations, employers are under a duty to permit employees to take time off work for various stipulated purposes. In all cases (except health and safety) to qualify for these rights, an employee must have worked for at least 16 hours per week and, in the case of a redundancy only, must have completed a minimum of two years' service. Industrial tribunals are empowered to award compensation to an employee in respect of an employer's default.

Trade union duties. An employee who is also an official of an independent trade union (recognized by the employer) must be given reasonable time off work (with pay) to carry out industrial relations duties or to undergo industrial relations training.

Trade union activities. Employees who are members of an independent trade union are entitled to reasonable time off work (without pay) to take part in trade union activities, other than activities involving industrial action.

Safety representation. A health and safety representative appointed under the 1977 Safety Representatives and Safety Committees Regulations, is entitled to reasonable time off work (with pay) to carry out functions and to undergo training.

Public duties. Specified employees, such as a justice of the peace, a member of a local authority, or a member of a statutory tribunal, are entitled to take reasonable unpaid time off work to carry out their duties.

Redundancy. Employees who are given notice of redundancy are entitled to reasonable time off work (with pay) in order to look for new employment or to make arrangements for training for future employment.

Terms of employment. Most employees are entitled to receive from their employer a written statement of the terms of their employment, not later than 13 weeks after they started work. The statement must include such details as pensions rights, length of notice, holiday entitlement, provisions relating to injury, sickness and sick pay, hours of work, remuneration and method of payment (s.1 EPCA). If a change occurs in the terms of employment of any employee, the employer must (within one month) inform the employee of the nature of the change by means of a written statement (s.4 EPCA). An aggrieved employee may seek redress from an industrial tribunal.

Itemized pay statement. Under the EPCA (ss.8–11) most employees are entitled to receive from their employer a written itemized pay statement at or before the time they are paid. The statement must include such items as the gross and net amount of salary or wages, and the amounts of any fixed deductions, e.g. trade union subscriptions. If an employer fails to provide such a statement an industrial tribunal may award (discretionary) compensation (if unnotified deductions have been made) or declare which particulars should have been included in the statement.

Transfer of business. Under the 1981 Transfer of Undertakings (Protection of Employment) Regulations, certain safeguards are extended to employees when a commercial business is transferred to a new employer. Broadly, all employees are entitled to continue in work under their original contracts, with the new employer 'stepping into the shoes' of the old employer. The new employers must continue to recognize any independent trade union, and any employee who is dismissed (by the new or the old employer) wholly or mainly because of the transfer, has a right to claim unfair dismissal (above). In addition, the old employer must inform a recognized trade union, long enough before the transfer to enable consultation to take place, of such matters as the date of the transfer, the legal, economic and social implications for affected employees, and any measures the new or old employer intend to take which will affect employees. Any aggrieved employee or trade union may seek redress from an industrial tribunal.

Suspension on medical grounds. Employees are entitled to claim payments from their employers (provided they have completed at least one month's service, and normally work for not less than 16 hours a week) if they are suspended from work on medical grounds (under the HSWA) i.e. because their health might be endangered if they continued to be exposed to specified substances (ss.19–22 EPCA). An employee suspended on these grounds is entitled to receive his normal week's pay for a maximum of 26 weeks. The right to a payment will be lost if, *inter alia*, the employee unreasonably refuses an offer of suitable alternative work, or is employed for a fixed term of three months or less. Failure to comply with this duty may result in an industrial tribunal ordering the employers to make the appropriate payment. Furthermore, if an employer dismisses an employee who should have been suspended with pay, the employee has a right to complain he was unfairly dismissed (above).

Trade union membership and activities. Employees have an automatic right to claim unfair dismissal if they are dismissed (or selected for redundancy) for joining, or proposing to join, a trade union. Furthermore, an employee may seek redress from an industrial tribunal where his employer takes 'action short of dismissal' against him on these grounds. Exactly the same rights apply to employees who have the above action taken against them because they have taken part, or propose to take part, in trade union activities (ss.23, 58–9).

Disclosure of information. Under the 1975 Employment Protection Act (ss.17–21) employers (subject to specified exceptions) are under a duty to disclose to recognized trade unions any information (a) without which trade union representatives would be impeded in carrying out collective bargaining; and (b) which would be in accordance with good industrial relations practice to disclose for the purpose of collective bargaining. To enforce these duties the union must follow a laborious process involving the Central Arbitration Committee and ACAS.

The 1982 Employment Act (via s.1) imposed a new duty on companies (employing, on average, in excess of 250 employees a year) to include 'employee involvement' matters in their company reports. Company reports must include the action which has been taken during the financial year to introduce, maintain or develop arrangements aimed at providing employees systematically with information on matters of concern to them; consulting employees to ascertain their views before a decision is made which will affect them; encouraging employee involvement in company performance, such as employees' share schemes; and achieving a common awareness on the part of employees of the financial and economic factors affecting company performance.

Sex discrimination. The 1975 Sex Discrimination Act (SDA) renders sexual discrimination unlawful in both full and part-time employment, as well as a number of other areas. The Act is very extensive and also outlaws sex discrimination in the fields of advertising, recruitment, training, trade union membership, education, the provision of goods and services and, in relation to the employment field only, to discrimination against married persons. This outline is limited to discrimination in the employment field.

The SDA (which applies equally to sex discrimination against men) outlaws two forms of sex discrimination: (a) where a woman is treated, on the grounds of sex, less favourably than a man is, or would be, treated (direct discrimination), or (b) where an unjustifiable detrimental requirement or condition is applied to a woman, which applies or would apply equally to men, but which is such that the proportion of women who can comply with it is considerably smaller than the proportion of men who can comply (indirect discrimination).

Under s.6 of the SDA it is unlawful for an employer to discriminate against a woman (i) in relation to offers of employment; or (ii) in relation to opportunities for promotion, transfer or training; or (iii) in relation to the provision of any other benefits, facilities or services; or (iv) by dismissing her or subjecting her to any other detriment. However, it is not unlawful to discriminate against a person on the grounds of sex, in relation to (i) and (ii) only, if a particular sex is a 'genuine occupational qualification', e.g. where the essential nature of the job requires a man for reasons of physiology (excluding strength or stamina) or authenticity.

An employee may complain of discrimination to an industrial tribunal who, if they find the complaint well founded, may order the employer to pay the employee compensation (including damages for injured feelings) up to a current maximum of £7,500. If the discrimination also entitles the employee to complain she was unfairly dismissed, a basic award (current maximum £4,350) may also be claimed. Furthermore, an employer may be ordered to pay an additional award (current maximum £7,340) where he has refused to comply with an order to 're-employ' the complainant.

Equal pay. The 1970 Equal Pay Act (EPA) confers on employees of both sexes the right to equal treatment with regard to pay and other terms and conditions of employment, and covers both full- and part-time workers. A recent Employment Appeal Tribunal (EAT) decision has reinforced the rights of part-time employees, by enabling them to claim pro rata equal pay. The EAT held, following a decision in the European Court of Justice, that where part-time female employees are doing the same work as full-time employees, then, subject to exceptions, they are entitled to the same pro rata rates of pay (*Jenkins* v. *Kingsgate Ltd.* (No. 2), 1981, IRLR 388).

The EPA stipulates that a woman employed at any establishment in Great Britain is deemed to have included in her contract of employment an 'equality clause'. This clause automatically modifies her contract of employment to include terms no less favourable than those of a man, who is employed in the same employment, engaged in 'like work' or 'work rated as equivalent' under a job evaluation study (s.1). More recently, in what has been termed the most important development in employment protection law in 1984, 'the much criticised equal pay for work of equal value law . . . came into force' (IRRR, 1985, p. 7). Following a decision of the European Court of Justice, the Government had to amend the EPA (with effect from 1 January 1984) to include provision for 'equal pay for work of equal value'. Broadly, a woman is now entitled to claim equal pay (irrespective of whether she is employed on 'like work', etc.) if her work, in terms of the demands made on her (e.g. effort, decision, skill) is of equal value to the work performed by a man in the same employment.

An employee may complain to an industrial tribunal that the equality clause is being contravened by an employer. If the claim is successful the tribunal may order the employer to pay the employee any arrears of pay or damages flowing from the breach. However, no payment may be ordered in respect of a contravention which occurred more than two years before the proceedings commenced (s.2). The Equal Opportunities Commission (which was instituted to administer the SDA and EPA) may, amongst other things, initiate inquiries (whether or not a complaint has been made) into discriminatory practices. If the Commission finds that either of the

Acts are being contravened, it may issue a 'non-discrimination notice' requiring an employer to terminate the offending practice. The enforcement of a discrimination notice is a complex procedure involving, *inter alia*, injunction proceedings in the county court.

The EPA (ss.3–5) also seeks to remove sex discrimination in wages regulation orders and agricultural wage orders (via Wages Councils), collective agreements and wage structures. The Central Arbitration Committee is empowered to amend collective agreements (and contracts of employment which depend on them) to remove discriminatory practices.

There are a number of exemptions where the EPA and SDA do not apply. The most important of these are: (a) in relation to equal pay, the equality clause does not operate where an employer can prove that the variation in pay, or other terms of employment, is genuinely due to a material difference other than sex, and (b) in relation to sex discrimination, the SDA does not apply to an employer who employs five or fewer workers.

The total number of complaints, concerned with equal pay (EP) and sex discrimination (SD), dealt with by industrial tribunals under the EPA and SDA for the years 1976–82 are shown in table B.2.

Table B.2.

	EP	*SD*		*EP*	*SD*
1976	1,742	243	1980	91	180
1977	751	229	1981	54	256
1978	343	171	1982	39	150
1979	263	178			

Source: Employment Gazette 1983, pp. 165–9.

The number of complaints dealt with under the SDA, since its inception, has remained relatively stable compared to the significant fall in complaints under the EPA since 1979. This may be in response to the pressure of rising unemployment, or alternatively may signal increased compliance by employers following an 'adjustment period' after the Act's introduction.

The most extensive study of the effects of the EPA and SDA, in 26 organizations, was carried out by Snell *et al.* (1981, Department of Employment) between August 1974 and December 1977. The authors found that most employers complied with the minimum requirements of the EPA, and that the implementation of the Act had resulted in a 'considerable and sometimes dramatic narrowing' of the differentials in basic rates of pay between men and women (pp. 39, 90). The authors also discovered that the implementation of the EPA had resulted in a fall in the numbers of women employed in most organizations; and in two organizations 'to little more than half the numbers employed at the start of the research in 1974' (p. 59). Although the authors found it 'extremely difficult' to gather information on the costs imposed on employers by the EPA, they did report that 'increased labour costs due to equal pay were the final blow which led to the closure of one division which employed a high percentage of women . . .' (p. 51). So far as the SDA was concerned, the authors found that most organizations appeared to meet its requirements but that the effects of the Act were very limited, with occupational distribution almost unchanged, and widespread continuing job segregation (chapter 4).

Health and safety at work. This topic is extremely complex and copious. In consequence we only attempt a brief outline of the major statutory provisions.

As we noted in part I, the 1974 Health and Safety at Work Act (HSWA) marked a fundamental departure from earlier safety enactments. Whereas in the early 1970s about two-thirds of the workforce were protected by a large number of *ad hoc* statutory enactments (comprising in excess of 30 statutes and 500 statutory instruments) which imposed specific duties on employers, the HSWA covers the whole workforce (save for domestic servants employed in private households), and brought within its purview an estimated 8 million 'new entrants' who had not received protection under earlier legislation (see Selwyn, 1982, p. 4).

The Act is essentially criminal in nature and imposes extremely wide and general duties on employers (see ss.2–9). For example s.2(1) states 'it shall be the duty of every employer to ensure, so far as is reasonably practicable, the health, safety and welfare at work of all his employees.' This duty extends to the provison of maintenance of plant and systems of work; to arrangements in connection with the use, handling, storage and transport of articles and substances; to the provision of information, instruction, training and supervision; to the maintenance of the place of work; and to the provision and maintenance of employees' working environment and arrangements for their welfare (s.2(2)). In addition s.3 imposes a general duty on employers to ensure that persons outside their employment are not exposed to risks to their health and safety.

These general duties are supplemented and supported by regulations, which are more specific in nature, and by approved codes of practice. The Secretary of State is empowered to make regulations either on his own initiative, or in response to proposals submitted by the Health and Safety Commission (a new agency instituted under the HSWA in order, *inter alia*, to assist and encourage people to comply with the Act's general purposes) who are also empowered to approve codes of practice. Regulations are enforced in the same way as the general duties (below). Failure to comply with a code of practice does not itself constitute a crime, but may be taken as conclusive proof of contravention of any requirement or prohibition in the Act, to which any provisions in a code are relevant (s.17).

The main burden of enforcing the Act falls on the Health and Safety Executive (appointed by the Commission) which operates via inspectors (many of whom operated under previous health and safety legislation). Inspectors, as well as having powers to enter premises, to examine them, and to carry out investigations, may also serve improvement and prohibition notices. An improvement notice requires the employer to remedy any perceived contravention of the statutory duties within prescribed time limits (s.21). A prohibition notice may be served on a person who is in control of activities which the inspector believes involves a risk of serious personal injury. Such a notice orders the activity to cease, until the notice is complied with, and may take immediate effect where an inspector believes there is an imminent risk of personal injury (s.22). Failure to comply with either type of notice may (subject to an appeals procedure) render a person liable to prosecution.

In addition to, or as an alternative to, issuing notices an inspector may initiate criminal proceedings when he is of the opinion that any of the statutory provisions are being contravened. The penalties which may be imposed on conviction range from fines (which are unlimited on indictment) to a term of imprisonment of up to two years when a case is prosecuted in the Crown Court (s.33). In 1981 the Health and Safety Executive employed about 4,200 employees, with net annual expenditure approaching £70 million (see Drake and Wright, 1983, p. 53).

Finally, one of the main objectives of the HSWA is to replace the previous health and safety enactments (which still survive largely intact) by means of issuing new regulations supported by approved codes of practice (i.e. to incorporate the existing mass of complex enactments within a single statute – the HSWA – of general application). To this end the HSWA schedules 31 existing enactments (including the 1961 Factories Act) which, by the issue of regulations, may be assimilated in this way (s.15). However, as we have noted in part I, the Robens Committee's desire for more self-regulation, with statutory regulation as a last resort, appears doomed. For example, by 1982, 227 different sets of regulations had been issued under the HSWA since its implementation (see Drake and Wright, pp. 256–63); and in a six-month period alone (ending in December 1984) five new sets of regulations and two codes of practice were issued under the Act (IRRR, 1985, p. 9). As one distinguished commentator on the HSWA has stated, 'despite the criticism levelled by the Robens Committee against the legalistic and unintelligible nature of the then existing law, the new Act is turgid, soporific, and, in parts, about as meaningful as medieval metaphysics.' (Selwyn, 1982, p. 5).

Miscellaneous. Just some of the statutory rights conferred on employees, which space does not permit us to examine, include employee rights under the 1976 Race Relations Act; statutory sick pay; disabled persons' rights; employee rights on the insolvency of their employer; industrial injury rights; employee rights under the 1973 Employment Agencies Act; and a complex array of rights and duties under health and safety enactments, and more particularly, the 1961 Factories Act.

CONCLUSIONS

Prior to 1963, employers were relatively unencumbered by statutory individual employment rights, but *de facto* protection was extended to many employees, especially in the unionized sector, through collective agreements and other 'voluntary' arrangements with employers. Following this period a dramatic expansion in employment rights was propagated, culminating in 1974–5 with the enactment of four major statutes – the HSWA, EPA, SDA and Employment Protection Act – which laid the foundation for the so-called 'statutory floor' of individual employment rights. The proliferation of these rights resulted in a trebling of the number of applications to industrial tribunals between 1972 and 1976, since which time applications, save for the years 1981 and 1982, have fallen steadily (see table B.3).

Table B.3 Applications to industrial tribunals 1972–83

1972	14,857	1975	35,897	1978	43,321	1981	44,852
1973	14,062	1976	47,804	1979	41,244	1982	43,660
1974	16,320	1977	46,961	1980	41,424	1983	39,959

Source: Employment Gazette, 1984, p. 488.

A number of studies (sample surveys) which have been carried out to assess the impact of employment protection laws, are, at best, inconclusive with regard to the exact effects that employment laws have had on recruitment. The consensus view which emerges from these studies appears to be that the majority of employers (or personnel managers) have not adjusted their recruitment policies in response to the massive increase in employment protection legislation (see Parker *et al.*, 1971; Daniel, 1978; Daniel and Stilgoe, 1978; Clifton and Tatton-Brown, 1979; Snell *et al.*, 1981).

However, the representatives of small businesses, amongst others, believe that the increase in employment protection laws has acted as a deterrent to recruitment (see, e.g. NFSS, 1979; Mendham, 1984). For example, the NFSS have reported that the expansion of employment rights has imposed considerable costs on employers and 'like much government legislation, the growth of employment legislation has had an equal and opposite effect to that which was intended. Protecting jobs has led to fewer jobs being available' (p. 2).

Partly in response to the pressure from small businesses, the Government, in 1979 and 1980, introduced a number of (partial) 'deprotection' measures which were almost exclusively aimed at relieving the burden of unfair dismissal protection on employers, and more especially, small employers. In 1979, as we have noted earlier, the 'continuous service' qualification for unfair dismissal was raised from six months to one year; and in 1980 the service qualification was raised to two years, but only in respect of firms employing 20 or fewer workers. However, it has recently been reported (see *The Sunday Times*, 14 October 1984) that the Government is presently reviewing the whole area of employment protection law, including the HSWA and the Equal Pay Act. It would appear that the Government is considering 'a radical jobs deregulation exercise', aimed at removing the statutory barriers to the recruitment of young people and other key groups. One of the options, which is apparently under consideration, is to exclude persons between the ages of 17 and 19 from the ambit of statutory protection against unfair dismissal. Our own suggestions for such an exercise are contained in Chapter 5.

References

Adam Smith Institute (1983) *Defence Policy*, Omega File.

Ashton, P. (1984) 'Replacement Ratios and Unemployment Decisions', *Quarterly Economic Bulletin,* Liverpool Research Group in Macroeconomics, **5**, No. 4, pp. 24–7.

Atkinson, A. B., Gomulka, S., Micklewright, A. and Rau, N. (1984) 'Unemployment Benefits, Duration and Incentives in Britain: How Robust Is the Evidence?', *Journal of Political Economy*, 23 February, pp. 3–26.

Bauer, P. T. (1982) *Equality, The Third World and Economic Delusion*, London, Methuen.

Baumol, W. (1982) 'Contestable Markets: An Uprising in the Theory of Industrial Structure', *American Economic Review*, 72, pp. 1–15.

Beenstock, M. C. and Billington, S. (1982) 'Rational Pricing for Unemployment Insurance', mimeo, City University Business School.

Beenstock, M. and Warburton, P. (1984) 'An Econometric Model of the UK Labour Market', mimeo, City University Business School.

Beesley, M. and Littlechild, S. C. (1983) 'Privatisation: Principles, Problems and Priorities', *Lloyds Bank Review*, July, pp. 1–20.

Benjamin, D. and Kochin, L. (1979) 'Searching for an Explanation of Unemployment in Inter-war Britain', *Journal of Political Economy*, **87**, 3, pp. 441–70.

Benjamin, D. and Kochin, L. and Critics (1982) 'Unemployment and Unemployment Benefits in Twentieth Century Britain: A Reply to our Critics' and Preceding Critics' Comments', *Journal of Political Economy*, **90**, *pp. 369–436.*

Bowers, J. (1982) A Practical Approach to Employment Law, Financial Training Publications Limited.

Clifton, R. and Tatton-Brown, C. (1979) *Impact of Employment Legislation on Small Firms*, Department of Employment, July, Research Paper No. 6.

Daniel, W. W. (1978) 'The effects of Employment Protection Laws in Manufacturing Industry', *Department of Employment Gazette*, June, **86**, pp. 658–61.

Daniel, W. W. and Stilgoe, E. (1978) *The Impact of Employment Protection Laws*, PSI, June, 577.

Davies, R., Hamill, L., Moglan, S. and Smee, C. H. (1982) 'Incomes in and out of work,' *Employment Gazette*, **90**, pp. 237–43.

Deaton, D. (1984) 'The Incidence of Dismissals in British Manufacturing Industries', *Industrial Relations Journal*, Summer, **15**, 2, pp. 61–5.

DHSS (1984) *Tax/Benefit Model Tables*, November.

Dickens, L., Hart, M., Jones, M. and Weekes, B. (1984) 'The British Experience under a Statute Prohibiting Unfair Dismissal', *Industrial and Labour Relations Review*, **37**, 4, pp. 497–514.

Drake, C. D. and Bercusson, B. (1981) *The Employment Acts 1974–1980 with Commentary*, London, Sweet and Maxwell.

Drake, C. D. and Wright, F. B. (1983) *Law of Health and Safety at Work: The New Approach*, London, Sweet and Maxwell.

Dunn, S. (1981) 'The Growth of the Post-Entry Closed Shop in Britain since the 1960s: Some Theoretical Considerations', *British Journal of Industrial Relations*, **19**, pp. 275–96.

Dunn, S. and Gennard, J. (1984) *The Closed Shop in British Industry*, London, Macmillan.

Forrest, D. and Dennison, S. R. (1984) *Low Pay or no Pay*, Hobart Paper No. 101, Institute of Economic Affairs, London.

Gennard, J., Dunn, S. and Wright, M. (1980) 'The Extent of Closed Shop Arrangements in British Industry', *Department of Employment Gazette*, January, **88**, 1, pp. 16–22.

Gilmour, Sir Ian (1983) *Britain Can Work*, Martin Robertson, Oxford.

GLC (1985) *Going . . . Going . . . Almost Gone: What Price the Private Rented Sector?*, Preliminary Report on a GLC Survey of Private Tenants in London, 1983–4.

Godfrey, L. G. (1978) 'Testing against General AR and MA Error Modes when the Regressions Include Lagged Dependent Variables', *Econometrica*, **46**, 6, pp. 1293–301.

Griffiths, R. (1983) *Report on the Management of the NHS,* available from DHSS.

Grunfeld, C. (1980) *The Law of Redundancy*, London, Sweet and Maxwell.

Harberger, A. C. (1964) 'The Measurement of Waste', *American Economic Review*, 54, pp. 58–76.

Harvey, R. J. (1971) *Industrial Relations: Butterworths Annotated Legislation Service*, 195, London, Butterworths.

Henry, S. G. B., Payne, J. M. and Trinder, C. (1985) 'Real Wages and Unemployment: The Role of Unemployment, Social Security Benefits and Unionization, *Oxford Economic Papers*, **37**, 2, pp. 330–38.

Hepple, B. H. (1981) 'A Right to Work?', *Industrial Law Journal*, **10**, pp. 65–83.

HMSO (1968) *Royal Commission on Trades Unions and Employers' Associations Report*, June, Cmnd. 3623.

HMSO (1972) *Safety and Health at Work* (Robens Committee), June, Cmnd. 5034.

HMSO (1981) *Trade Union Immunities*, January, Cmnd. 8128.

HMSO (1982) *Report of the Commissioners for Year Ended 31 March 1982*, Board of Inland Revenue, Cmnd. 8514.

HMSO (1983) *Democracy in Trade Unions*, January, Cmnd. 8778.

HM Treasury (1985) *The Relationship between Employment and Wages, Empirical Evidence for the United Kingdom*, a review by Treasury officials, HM Treasury, London.

Holden, K. and Peel, D. A. (1981) 'Unemployment and the Replacement Ratio – Some Reduced Form Estimates for the UK', *Economics Letters*, **8**, pp. 349–54.

Industrial Relations Review and Report (1985) pp. 7–9, January, Industrial Relations Services.

Junankar, P. N. (1981) 'An Econometric Analysis of Unemployment in Great Britain, 1952–75', *Oxford Economic Papers*, **33**, 3, pp. 387–400.

Kay, J. A., Morris, C. N. and Warren, N. A. (1980) 'Tax, Benefits and the Incentive to Seek Work', *Fiscal Studies*, pp. 387–400.

Kirby, J. (1985) Letters, *Daily Telegraph*, 7 January.

Labour Research (1984) 'Ballots and the Closed Shop', August, pp. 198–200.

Lancaster, T. (1979) 'Econometric Methods for the Duration of Unemployment', *Econometrica*, **47**, pp. 939–56.

Lancaster, T. and Chesher, A. (1982) *An Econometric Analysis of Reservation Wages*, Hull Economic Research Paper, No. 71 (revised), University of Hull, October.

Layard, R. (1984) 'Two Steps to More Jobs', *The Guardian*, 5 December.

Layard, R., Metcalf, D. and Nickell, S. (1978) 'The Effect of Collective Bargaining on Relative and Absolute Wages', *British Journal of Industrial Relations*, November, **16**, pp. 287–302.

Layard, R. and Nickell, S. (1985) 'The Causes of British Unemployment', *National Institute Economic Review*, **111**, February, pp. 62–85.

Lewis, H. G. (1963) *Unionism and Relative Wages in The United States*, University of Chicago Press.

Linneman, P. (1982) 'The Economic Impact of Minimum Wage Laws: A New Look at an Old Question', *Journal of Political Economy*, **90**, pp. 443–69.

Littlechild, S. C. (1981) 'Misleading Calculations of the Social Costs of Monopoly Power', *Economic Journal*, **91**, pp. 348–63.

Liverpool Research Group in Macroeconomics (1984) *Quarterly Economic Bulletin*, March, **5**, 1.

McCarthy, W. E. J. (1964) *The Closed Shop in Britain*, Oxford, Basil Blackwell.

Mackay, D. I. and Reid, G. L. (1972) 'Redundancy, Unemployment and Manpower Policy', *Economic Journal*, **82**, pp. 1256–72.

Maki, D. and Spindler, Z. A. (1975) 'The Effect of Unemployment Compensation on the Rate of Unemployment in Great Britain', *Oxford Economic Papers*, **27**, 3, pp. 440–54.

Matthews, K. G. P. (1982) 'Demand for Currency and the Black Economy in the UK', *Journal of Economic Studies*, **9**, pp. 3–22.

Meade, J. S. *et al.* (1978) *The Structure and Reform of Direct Taxation*, London, Allen and Unwin for the Institute of Fiscal Studies.

Mendham, S. A. (1984) 'Exploiting and Overcoming Government Regulations', *The Forum of Private Business*, October.

Minford, A. P. L. (1983) 'Labour Market Equilibrium in an Open Economy', *Oxford Economic Papers*, **35**, November Supplement, pp. 207–44.

Minford, A. P. L. (1984) 'Response to Nickell', *Economic Journal*, **94**, pp. 954–9.

Minford, A. P. L. (1985a) 'Reply to Henry, Payne and Trinder', *Oxford Economic Papers*, **37**, 2, pp. 339–43.

Minford, A. P. L. (1985b) 'Germany and the European Disease', paper delivered at a Conference in the University of Siegen, mimeo, University of Liverpool.

Minford, A. P. L., Davies, D. H., Peel, M. J. and Sprague, A. (1983) *Unemployment – Cause and Cure* (first edition), Oxford, Martin Robertson.

Minford, A. P. L., Marwaha, S., Matthews, K. G. P. and Sprague, A. (1984) 'The Liverpool Macroeconomic Model of the United Kingdom', *Economic Modelling*, **11**, pp. 24–62.

Minford, A. P. L., Peel, M. J. and Ashton, P. (1985) 'Housing, Mobility and Unemployment', mimeo, Department of Economic and Business Studies, University of Liverpool.

Morris, N. (1983) 'Examining the Possible Development of the EEC Budget', Memorandum to House of Lords Committee on the EEC, mimeo, Institute of Fiscal Studies.

Mulvey, C. (1976) 'Collective Agreements and Relative Earnings in UK Manufacturing in 1973', *Economica*, **43** (172), pp. 419–27, November.

Narendranathan, W., Nickell, S. and Stern, J. (1984) 'Unemployment Benefits Revisited', London School of Economics, Discussion Paper No. 153 (revised), *Economic Journal*, **95**, pp. 307–29.

NFSS (1979) *Report: Employment Protection Act 1975 and Employment Protection (Consolidation) Act 1978*, National Federation of Self-Employed and Small Businesses, June, Research Paper 22.

Nickell, S. J. (1979a) 'The Effects of Unemployment and Related Benefits on the Duration of Unemployment', *Economic Journal*, **89**, pp. 34–49.

Nickell, S. J. (1979b) 'Estimating the Probability of Leaving Unemployment', *Econometrica*, **47**, pp. 1249–66.

Nickell, S. J. (1984) 'A Review of *Unemployment: Cause and Cure* by Patrick Minford with David Davies, Michael Peel, and Alison Sprague', *Economic Journal*, **94**, pp. 946–53.

Nickell, S. J. and Andrews, M. (1983) 'Unions, Real Wages and Employment in Britain, 1951–79', *Oxford Economic Papers*, **35**, 4, pp. 183–206, reprinted in *The Causes of Unemployment* in C. A. Greenhalgh, P. R. G. Layard and A. J. Oswald (eds) Oxford, Oxford University Press.

Parker, H. (1982) *The Moral Hazard of Social Benefits*, Research Monograph 37, Institute of Economic Affairs.

Parker, S. R., Thomas, C. G., Ellis, N. D. and McCarthy, W. E. J. (1971) *Effects of the Redundancy Payments Act*, OPCS, HMSO.

Parsley, C. J. (1980) 'Labour Union Effects on Wage Gains: A Survey of Recent Literature', *Journal of Economic Literature*, **18**, pp. 1–31.

Roberts, B. C. (1984) 'Recent Trends in Collective Bargaining in the United Kingdom', *International Labour Review*, **123**, 3, pp. 287–306.

Seldon, A. (1977) *Charge*, London, Temple Smith.

Selwyn, N. (1982) *Selwyn's Law of Health and Safety at Work*, London, Butterworths.

Snell, M. W., Glucklich, P. and Povall, N. (1981) *Equal Pay and Opportunities: A Study of the Implementation and Effects of the Equal Pay and Sex Discrimination Acts in 26 Organisations*, Department of Employment, April, Research Paper No. 20.

Stern, R. M., Francis, J. and Schumacher, B. (1976) *Price Elasticities in International Trade*, London, Macmillan.

Stewart, M. B. (1983) 'Relative Earnings and Individual Union Membership in the United Kingdom', *Economica*, **50**, 111–25.

Sunday Times (1984) 'Government Urge Easier Sacking in Drive for New Jobs', 14 October.

Symons, J. (1985) 'Relative Prices and the Demand for Labour in British Manufacturing', *Economica*, **52**, 205, pp. 37–49.

Treble, J. G. (1984) 'Does the Union/Non-Union Wage Differential Exist?', *Manchester School*, **52**, June, pp. 160–70.

Index